SAP S/4 Implementation

Other books written by Dave Karpinsky

Artificial Intelligence & Information Technology
- Artificial Intelligence (AI) for Daily Life: A Practical Guide to Artificial Intelligence
- AI and Creativity: How Machines are Changing Art, Music & Literature
- AI-Powered PM: Leveraging Artificial Intelligence for Enhanced Efficiency and Success
- Artificial Intelligence Rise and Humanity Fall
- Data-Driven Future: Harnessing AI and Big Data for Tomorrow's Challenges
- Deepfake Technology: The Dark Side of AI, Manipulation and Digital Deception.
- Fixing Failed Projects: How to Master the Art of Project Turnaround
- From Data to Decisions: The Role of AI in Business Intelligence
- Jobs AI Will Replace: Re-tool or Be Left Behind
- Mastering Advanced Project Management: Strategies for Excellence
- Mastering Project Management: In complex, stressful & high-pressure environments
- SAP S/4 Implementation: A Comprehensive Guide for Practitioners
- SAP S/4 Implementation Methodologies
- SAP S/4 Implementation – Volume 1: Prep & Explore Phases
- SAP S/4 Implementation – Volume 2: Realize & Deploy Phases
- SAP S/4 Implementation – Volume 3: When Projects Fail
- The Five-Day Organizational Change Manager
- The Five--Day Project Manager
- The Project Management Masterclass: Advanced Techniques for Success
- The Rise of Real-Time Analytics: Speed, Precision, and Competitive Edge

Business & Finance
- Building Wealth in Developing Nations: A Comprehensive Step-by-Step Guide to Empower Emerging Markets
- Chief Executive's (CxO) Playbook: The First 90 Days Guide to Success
- Creating a Deployment Plan: Navigating Complexity to Deliver Success
- Creating a Strategic Roadmap: Crafting the Blueprint from Vision to Execution
- Investing Strategies of the Rich and Famous: Discover How to Diversify Your Portfolio for Maximum Returns
- Outsmart the Game: Winning When the Rules Are Rigged
- The Data Delusion: Exposing False Metrics That Shape Your World
- Trust is the New Currency: How Connection Wins in the Age of AI

Life Coach & Mentor Series
- Aspiring Entrepreneurs
- Bored Housewife
- Career Transition
- Couples and Relationships
- Mid-Life Crisis
- Mindful Healthy Living
- Project Managers
- Seeking Life's Purpose
- Surviving Holidays with In-laws

Science & Physics
- Game Over. Reset Earth
- Quantum Entanglement: The God Effect and the Secrets of Reality
- Multiverse Parallel Dimensions: The Theories and Possibilities of Parallel Universes

- Space-Time Continuum: Navigating the Quantum of the Fourth Dimension
- The Hubble Tension: The Universe's Expansion, Cosmology Crisis, and the Limits of the Big Bang Theory
- The Singularity Shift: Unveiling the Future of Humanity and Intelligence
- Twin Paradox: Solving the Puzzle of Special Relativity

Sociology & Politics
- America at War: Russia, China, Iran, S Korea
- Blue Zones Volume 1: Mystery and Science of Blue Zones
- Blue Zones Volume 2: Longevity Lessons of Blue Zones
- Decline of American Supremacy: Understanding the Erosion, Shaping the Future
- Future of Military Technology Powered by AI: How countries are transforming their warfare
- Herd Instinct: Understanding the Human Psychology of Collective Behavior
- Our Idiot Species: Evolution in Reverse
- Preventing Squatters: A Comprehensive Guide to Protecting Your Property
- Puppet Masters: The Hidden Hands of Political Power
- The Great War of China vs Russia: A Future Battlefield that Reshapes the World
- The Modern Stoic: 365 Ancient Practices for Wisdom, Peace, Purpose ad Strength
- The Next Battlefield: How AI, Robotics, and Biotechnology are Transforming Warfare
- The Savage Guide to Winning: The Brutal Truth About Success
- The Trump Effect: Return to the White House
- The Vatican Murder Cover-Up
- Unf*k Yourself: A No-Bullsh!t Guide to Taking Control
- Warfare Redefined: Military Technologies and Tactics of Tomorrow's Superpowers
- Zero F*cks Given: How to Stop Worrying and Live Your Life
- God & AI Series:

- o Is There God: According to Artificial Intelligence (AI)
- o What is God: According to Artificial Intelligence (AI)
- o What is God's Plan: According to Artificial Intelligence (AI)

" You don't implement SAP S/4 to replicate the past. You
implement it to reimagine what's possible."
— *Dave Karpinsky*

SAP S/4 Implementation

A Comprehensive Guide for Practitioners

THIRD EDITION

Dave Karpinsky, PhD, MBA, PMP, Prosci

Green Parrot Media

Contents

PART A - INTRODUCTION

Chapter 1: Introduction to SAP

Overview of SAP

SAP, short for Systems, Applications, and Products in Data Processing, is a multinational software corporation headquartered in Walldorf, Germany. It was founded in 1972 by five former IBM engineers: Dietmar Hopp, Hans-Werner Hector, Hasso Plattner, Klaus Tschira, and Claus Wellenreuther. SAP is best known for its enterprise resource planning (ERP) software, enabling organizations to manage business operations and customer relations comprehensively and holistically.

SAP's product portfolio spans various applications and services, including finance, logistics, human resources, etc. The company's flagship ERP product, SAP ERP, and its advanced suite, SAP S/4HANA, are utilized by businesses of all sizes across various industries to optimize processes, increase efficiency, and drive growth.

SAP has continually evolved to meet the changing needs of businesses in the digital era. Its solutions support real-time processing, advanced analytics, and integration with cutting-edge technologies like artificial intelligence (AI), the Internet of Things (IoT), and blockchain. SAP's commitment to innovation and customer success has cemented its position as a leader in enterprise software.

History and Evolution of SAP

The Genesis of SAP

SAP began in the early 1970s when its founders left IBM to start a company focused on developing real-time software solutions that could process data. The first product, SAP R/1, was a financial accounting system that laid the foundation for future integrated business applications.

SAP R/2 and the Mainframe Era

In 1979, SAP released SAP R/2, which expanded its capabilities beyond financial accounting to include materials management and production planning. Running on IBM mainframes, SAP R/2 became popular among large European enterprises, providing integrated business process management across various functions.

Transition to Client-Server Architecture: SAP R/3

The early 1990s marked a pivotal moment for SAP, with the introduction of SAP R/3 in 1992. Unlike its predecessors, SAP R/3 was built on a client-server architecture, which offered greater flexibility, scalability, and accessibility. This architecture allowed businesses to implement and integrate only the needed components seamlessly with existing systems.

SAP R/3 was developed using the ABAP (Advanced Business Application Programming) language, facilitating software customization and extension. Its modular design and robust functionality quickly made it the ERP system of choice for businesses worldwide.

Expansion and Diversification

During the 1990s and early 2000s, SAP continued to expand its product offerings and market reach. The company introduced industry-specific solutions to cater to the unique needs of various sectors, such as manufacturing, retail, healthcare, and finance. SAP ERP, launched in 2004, consolidated these solutions into a comprehensive suite that managed core business processes across functions like finance, controlling, materials management, sales and distribution, production planning, and human capital management.

The Advent of SAP HANA

2010 SAP revolutionized enterprise computing by introducing SAP HANA (High-Performance Analytic Appliance). This in-memory computing platform processes data at unprecedented speeds, enabling real-time analytics and applications. By storing data in RAM instead of traditional disk storage, SAP HANA significantly reduces data retrieval times and enhances the performance of complex queries and calculations.

SAP S/4HANA: A New Era

Building on the success of SAP HANA, SAP launched SAP S/4HANA in 2015. This next-generation business suite is designed to run exclusively on the SAP HANA database, offering a simplified data model, enhanced user experience through the SAP Fiori interface, and advanced analytics capabilities. SAP S/4HANA integrates core business processes in real-time, enabling companies to operate more agilely and efficiently.

Cloud and Digital Transformation

SAP has expanded its cloud offerings significantly in response to the growing demand for cloud-based solutions. SAP S/4HANA Cloud provides the benefits of the S/4HANA suite with added advantages such as lower total cost of ownership, scalability, and faster implementation times. SAP Business Technology Platform (BTP) supports data management, analytics, application development, and integration, enabling businesses to quickly adopt new technologies and business models.

Industry-Specific Innovations

SAP has continued to innovate with industry-specific solutions tailored to the unique needs of various sectors. In manufacturing, SAP's solutions for Industry 4.0 enable smart factories with interconnected systems, predictive maintenance, and real-time insights. SAP's omnichannel commerce solutions help businesses deliver seamless customer experiences across digital and physical retail channels. Healthcare benefits from SAP's solutions for patient management, clinical data integration, and regulatory compliance, supporting improved patient outcomes and operational efficiency.

Evolution of SAP Products

Over the years, SAP has continued to innovate and expand its product offerings. The transition from R/3 to the SAP ERP (Enterprise Resource Planning) suite began a new era. SAP ERP integrates core business functions, providing a unified view of operations and enabling data-driven decision-making. Critical modules within SAP ERP include:

- **SAP FI (Financial Accounting):** Manages financial transactions, accounting, and reporting.
- **SAP CO (Controlling):** Supports planning, reporting, and monitoring of business operations.
- **SAP MM (Materials Management):** Handles procurement and inventory management.
- **SAP SD (Sales and Distribution):** Manages sales processes, from order to delivery.
- **SAP PP (Production Planning):** Assists in production scheduling and manufacturing processes.
- **SAP HCM (Human Capital Management):** Manages employee data, payroll, and recruitment.

In response to the digital transformation, SAP introduced SAP S/4HANA (SAP Business Suite 4 SAP HANA) in 2015. S/4HANA leverages SAP HANA's in-memory computing capabilities, providing real-time analytics, simplified data models, and enhanced user experiences through the SAP Fiori interface. This new suite was designed to help businesses run live by offering more agility, insights, and efficiency.

SAP offers several key platforms besides S/4HANA, each designed to address different aspects of business operations. Here are some of the notable ones:

1. **SAP SuccessFactors:**
   - **Description:** A comprehensive human capital management (HCM) suite.
   - **Function:** It helps businesses manage their workforce through modules covering core HR, payroll, talent management, and analytics. SuccessFactors aims to improve employee engagement and streamline HR processes.
2. **SAP Ariba:**
   - **Description:** A cloud-based procurement and supply chain collaboration solution.
   - **Function:** It facilitates efficient procurement processes, supplier collaboration, and spend management. Ariba helps organizations manage supplier networks and procurement activities to ensure better compliance and cost savings.

3. **SAP Concur**:
   - **Description**: An integrated travel and expense management platform.
   - **Function**: It simplifies managing business travel, expenses, and invoices. Concur automates and streamlines expense reporting, travel booking, and invoice processing to enhance visibility and control over spending.

4. **SAP Customer Experience (formerly SAP C/4HANA)**:
   - **Description**: A suite of solutions for managing customer relationships.
   - **Function**: It includes marketing, sales, commerce, service, and customer data cloud solutions. This platform helps businesses deliver personalized customer experiences, enhancing engagement and loyalty.

5. **SAP Fieldglass**:
   - **Description**: A cloud-based vendor management system (VMS).
   - **Function**: It manages contingent workforce and services procurement. Fieldglass allows organizations to procure, manage, and optimize their external workforce, including freelancers, contractors, and service providers.

6. **SAP Analytics Cloud**:
   - **Description**: An all-in-one cloud platform for business intelligence (BI), planning, and predictive analytics.
   - **Function**: It provides tools for data visualization, forecasting, and decision-making. This platform helps businesses gain insights from their data to make informed strategic decisions.

7. **SAP Integrated Business Planning (IBP)**:
   - **Description**: A comprehensive supply chain planning solution.
   - **Function**: It enables businesses to synchronize supply chain processes, including sales and operations planning, demand planning, and inventory optimization. IBP helps improve forecast accuracy and optimize supply chain performance.

These platforms extend SAP's capabilities beyond core ERP functions, offering specialized tools for various business needs and enhancing overall operational efficiency.

Key Features and Capabilities of SAP

SAP's strength lies in its comprehensive and integrated approach to managing business processes. Here are some of the key features and capabilities that distinguish SAP from its competitors:

1. **Integration:** SAP systems are designed to integrate various business functions seamlessly, enabling smooth data flow across departments and providing a holistic view of the organization.
2. **Real-Time Processing:** With SAP HANA, data is processed in real-time, allowing businesses to make quicker and more informed decisions.
3. **Scalability:** SAP solutions can scale to accommodate the needs of small and large enterprises, making it a versatile choice for companies of all sizes.
4. **Customization:** SAP offers extensive customization options to tailor the software to specific business requirements. This flexibility ensures that organizations can adapt the system to their unique processes and workflows.
5. **Compliance and Security:** SAP provides robust compliance and security features, helping businesses adhere to regulatory requirements and protect sensitive data.
6. **Advanced Analytics:** SAP's advanced analytics capabilities, powered by SAP HANA, allow for sophisticated data analysis, predictive modeling, and business intelligence.

Industry Solutions and Innovations

SAP has developed industry-specific solutions to address various sectors' unique challenges and requirements. Some of the key industries served by SAP include:

- **Manufacturing:** Solutions for production planning, quality management, and supply chain optimization.
- **Retail:** Tools for inventory, customer relationship management (CRM), and point-of-sale (POS) integration.
- **Healthcare:** Systems for patient management, clinical data integration, and regulatory compliance.

- **Finance:** Financial planning, risk management, and regulatory reporting solutions.
- **Public Sector:** Tools for managing public services, citizen engagement, and government operations.

In addition to these industry solutions, SAP has been at the forefront of innovation with technologies such as artificial intelligence (AI), machine learning (ML), the Internet of Things (IoT), and blockchain. These technologies are integrated into SAP's portfolio to enhance automation, improve predictive capabilities, and enable new business models.

SAP Ecosystem and Community

The vast SAP ecosystem includes diverse stakeholders, such as customers, partners, developers, and consultants. SAP partners are critical in implementing, extending, and supporting SAP solutions. They provide value-added services such as consulting, customization, and training, ensuring businesses can maximize the benefits of their SAP investments. The SAP PartnerEdge program offers partners the tools and resources to develop, sell, and implement SAP solutions, fostering collaboration and innovation.

SAP also fosters a strong community through initiatives like the SAP Community Network (SCN), SAP User Groups, and various training and certification programs. These platforms enable users to share knowledge, collaborate on projects, and stay updated on the latest developments in the SAP world. SAP invests in education and training through initiatives like SAP University Alliances and SAP Learning Hub, helping individuals and organizations build the skills needed to succeed with SAP.

The Road Ahead

As SAP continues to evolve, its focus remains on helping businesses run better through innovation, integration, and digital transformation. The company's roadmap includes advancements in AI, machine learning, and analytics, along with a continued emphasis on cloud solutions and industry-specific innovations.

Key Benefits and Features of SAP

Integration Across Business Functions

One of SAP software's primary benefits is its ability to integrate various business functions into a single unified system. This integration ensures smooth data flow across departments, providing a holistic view of operations and enabling better coordination and decision-making. For example, an order processed in the sales module automatically updates inventory levels in the materials management module and financial records in the accounting module.

Real-Time Processing and Analytics

SAP systems, particularly those running on SAP HANA, offer real-time data processing and analytics capabilities. This allows businesses to access up-to-date information, perform complex analyses, and generate reports instantly. Real-time insights enable companies to respond swiftly to market changes, optimize operations, and improve efficiency.

Scalability and Flexibility

SAP solutions are designed to scale with an organization's growth. Whether a small business or a large multinational corporation, SAP software can accommodate the increasing complexity and volume of business processes. Additionally, SAP's modular architecture allows companies to implement and expand the system as needed, ensuring flexibility and adaptability to changing business requirements.

Customization and Extensibility

SAP provides extensive customization options to tailor the software to specific business needs. The ABAP programming language and SAP's development tools enable businesses to modify or develop new functionalities. This flexibility ensures SAP systems adapt to unique processes, workflows, and industry-specific requirements.

Compliance and Security

SAP software includes robust features for compliance and security, helping businesses adhere to regulatory requirements and protect sensitive data. SAP systems support various compliance standards and offer tools for managing audits, risk, and internal controls. SAP's security measures include data encryption, user authentication, and access control to safeguard against unauthorized access and data breaches.

Advanced Analytics and Business Intelligence

SAP's advanced analytics capabilities, powered by SAP HANA, allow businesses to perform sophisticated data analysis, predictive modeling, and business intelligence. Tools like SAP BusinessObjects and SAP Analytics Cloud provide comprehensive reporting, dashboarding, and data visualization features, enabling companies to derive actionable insights from their data.

User-Friendly Interface

The SAP Fiori user interface enhances the user experience by providing a simple, intuitive, and responsive design. SAP Fiori apps are role-based, ensuring users can access the specific functionalities they need. This user-centric approach improves productivity, reduces training time, and enhances overall user satisfaction.

Support for Digital Transformation

SAP's solutions are designed to support digital transformation initiatives by integrating advanced technologies such as AI, machine learning, IoT, and blockchain. These technologies enable businesses to automate processes, enhance decision-making, and create new business models. For example, AI and machine learning can be used for predictive maintenance in manufacturing, while IoT can enable real-time monitoring of supply chains.

Cloud Solutions and Services

SAP offers a range of cloud solutions and services that provide flexibility, scalability, and cost-efficiency. SAP S/4HANA Cloud combines the capabilities of SAP S/4HANA with the benefits of cloud deployment, such as reduced infrastructure costs and faster implementation times. SAP Cloud Platform provides application development, integration, and data management services, enabling businesses to innovate and adapt quickly.

Comprehensive Training and Support

SAP invests in education and training through programs like SAP Learning Hub, SAP University Alliances, and certification courses. These resources help users build the necessary skills to leverage SAP software effectively. Additionally, SAP provides extensive support services, including maintenance, updates, and technical assistance, ensuring that businesses can maximize the value of their SAP investments.

Strong Partner Ecosystem

SAP's partner ecosystem is crucial in implementing, customizing, and supporting SAP solutions. SAP partners offer a wide range of services, from consulting and integration to managed services and support. This ecosystem ensures businesses can access the expertise and resources to deploy and manage SAP software successfully.

Innovation and Future-Readiness

SAP's commitment to innovation ensures that its solutions are future-ready and capable of supporting businesses' evolving needs. The company invests heavily in research and development, continually enhancing its product offerings and integrating new technologies. This focus on innovation helps companies stay competitive and adapt to the rapidly changing digital landscape.

Global Reach and Industry Expertise

SAP serves customers worldwide and has developed deep industry expertise over the years. Its industry-specific solutions are tailored to meet various sectors' unique challenges and requirements, such as manufacturing, retail, healthcare, and finance. This industry expertise, combined with SAP's global presence, ensures businesses can rely on SAP for comprehensive and practical solutions.

In summary, SAP's history and evolution reflect a journey of continuous innovation and adaptation to the changing needs of businesses. From its origins as a financial accounting system to its current position as a global leader in enterprise software, SAP has consistently delivered solutions that empower organizations to achieve their goals and drive success in the digital age. With its comprehensive suite of products, advanced technologies, and robust partner ecosystem, SAP remains at the forefront of enterprise software, helping businesses navigate the complexities of the digital era and achieve sustainable growth.

Chapter 2: Understanding SAP Modules

SAP as an ERP Platform

SAP ERP (Enterprise Resource Planning) is a comprehensive suite of integrated business applications designed to help organizations manage their core business processes efficiently and effectively. It enables businesses to streamline operations, enhance productivity, and gain visibility for real-time activity. SAP ERP covers various aspects of an organization's operations, including finance, human resources, manufacturing, sales, procurement, and supply chain management.

SAP ERP is known for its modular architecture, which allows organizations to implement and customize the specific modules that meet their unique business needs. This flexibility ensures that businesses of all sizes across various industries can leverage SAP ERP to improve their operational efficiency and drive growth.

One of SAP ERP's key advantages is integrating different business functions into a single, unified system. This integration ensures seamless data flow across departments, facilitating better coordination, decision-making, and overall business performance. Additionally, SAP ERP supports real-time data processing and analytics, enabling businesses to access up-to-date information and make informed decisions quickly.

Key SAP Modules

SAP ERP comprises several vital modules, each focusing on specific business functions. Depending on the organization's requirements, these modules can be implemented individually or in combination. Some of the most commonly used SAP ERP modules include:

1. Financial Accounting (FI)

The Financial Accounting (FI) module is one of the core components of SAP ERP. It is designed to manage a company's financial transactions and reporting requirements. Key functionalities of the FI module include:

- **General Ledger Accounting:** Manages all financial transactions and provides a comprehensive view of the organization's financial position.

- **Accounts Payable:** Handles vendor transactions, including invoice processing, payments, and vendor management.

- **Accounts Receivable:** Manages customer transactions, including billing, collections, and management.

- **Asset Accounting:** Manages fixed assets, including acquisition, depreciation, and disposal.

- **Bank Accounting:** Manages bank transactions and bank account reconciliation.

- **Financial Reporting:** Generates financial statements and reports, such as balance sheets, profit and loss statements, and cash flow statements.

2. Controlling (CO)

The Controlling (CO) module complements the FI module by providing tools for planning, monitoring, and controlling business operations. Key functionalities of the CO module include:

- **Cost Element Accounting:** Manages cost and revenue elements, providing a detailed breakdown of costs and revenues.

- **Cost Center Accounting:** Tracks costs associated with specific cost centers, enabling detailed cost analysis and control.

- **Internal Orders:** Manages costs related to specific projects or internal orders.

- **Activity-Based Costing:** Allocates overhead costs based on activities, providing a more accurate cost allocation.

- **Profitability Analysis (PA):** Analyzes profitability by segment, such as product lines, customer groups, or geographical regions.

- **Profit Center Accounting:** Tracks and analyzes the profitability of individual profit centers within the organization.

3. Materials Management (MM)

The Materials Management (MM) module focuses on procurement and inventory management. Key functionalities of the MM module include:

- **Purchasing:** Manages the procurement process, including purchase requisitions, purchase orders, and supplier management.

- **Inventory Management:** Tracks inventory levels, movements, and valuations.

- **Invoice Verification:** Ensures that invoices received from suppliers match the goods received and purchase orders.

- **Material Requirement Planning (MRP):** Calculates material requirements and generates procurement proposals based on production schedules and inventory levels.

- **Warehouse Management:** Manages warehouse operations, including stock placements, transfers, and picking.

4. Sales and Distribution (SD)

The Sales and Distribution (SD) module manages the sales process from order to delivery. Key functionalities of the SD module include:

- **Sales Order Processing:** Manages creating, tracking, and fulfilling sales orders.

- **Pricing and Discounts:** Manages pricing conditions, discounts, and surcharges.

- **Shipping and Delivery:** Manages the shipping process, including packing, transportation, and delivery tracking.

- **Billing:** Generates invoices for delivered goods and services.

- **Customer Management:** Manages customer information, including contact details, credit limits, and sales history.

5. Production Planning (PP)

The Production Planning (PP) module focuses on production scheduling and manufacturing processes. Key functionalities of the PP module include:

- **Demand Planning:** Forecasts product demand based on historical data and market trends.

- **Material Requirement Planning (MRP):** Calculates material requirements for production based on demand forecasts and production schedules.

- **Production Scheduling:** Plans and schedules production orders, considering resource availability and capacity constraints.

- **Shop Floor Control:** Manages production execution on the shop floor, including order tracking and work-in-progress monitoring.

- **Capacity Planning:** Analyzes and plans production capacity to ensure optimal utilization of resources.

6. Human Capital Management (HCM)

The Human Capital Management (HCM) module manages employee data, payroll, and human resources processes. Key functionalities of the HCM module include:

- **Personnel Administration:** Manages employee records, including personal details, employment history, and organizational assignments.

- **Organizational Management:** Defines the organizational structure, including departments, positions, and reporting relationships.

- **Time Management:** Manages employee attendance, work schedules, and leave requests.

- **Payroll:** Calculates employee salaries, deductions, and benefits.

- **Talent Management:** Manages recruitment, performance appraisal, and employee development.

7. Quality Management (QM)

The Quality Management (QM) module focuses on ensuring product quality and compliance with standards. Key functionalities of the QM module include:

- **Quality Planning:** Defines quality inspection plans and criteria.

- **Quality Inspection:** Manages quality inspections during production and procurement.

- **Quality Control:** Monitors and controls quality issues, including non-conformances and corrective actions.

- **Quality Certificates:** Manages quality certificates and compliance documentation.

Integration Between Modules

One of the most powerful features of SAP ERP is its ability to integrate various business functions into a cohesive system. The integration between modules ensures seamless data flow and consistency across the organization. Here are some examples of how key SAP modules integrate:

1. FI and CO Integration

The FI and CO modules are closely integrated to provide a comprehensive view of financial performance. Transactions recorded in the FI module, such as invoices and payments, automatically update the corresponding cost and revenue elements in the CO module. This integration enables detailed cost analysis and profitability reporting.

2. MM and SD Integration

The MM and SD modules manage the entire procurement and sales cycle. When a sales order is created in the SD module, it triggers a requirement in the MM module to check inventory levels and generate purchase requisitions if necessary. Once the goods are received, the MM module updates the inventory levels, and the SD module handles the delivery and billing process.

3. PP and MM Integration

The PP and MM modules are integrated to ensure efficient production planning and material management. The PP module uses material requirement planning (MRP) to calculate the materials needed for production. The MM module generates purchase orders for the required materials based on the MRP results. Once the materials are received, the PP module schedules and executes the production orders.

4. HCM and FI Integration

The HCM and FI modules are integrated to manage payroll and employee-related expenses. Payroll calculations in the HCM module generate accounting entries posted to the FI module. This integration ensures accurate financial reporting of employee costs and facilitates payroll reconciliation.

5. QM and PP/MM Integration

The QM module integrates with the PP and MM modules to manage quality inspections and control. Quality inspection plans defined in the QM module are used during the production process in the PP module and the procurement process in the MM module. Inspection results and non-conformances are recorded in the QM module, and corrective actions are initiated if necessary.

6. SD and FI Integration

The SD and FI modules are integrated to manage the financial aspects of sales transactions. When a sales order is billed in the SD module, it generates an accounting document in the FI module, updating the accounts receivable and revenue accounts. This integration ensures accurate financial reporting of sales activities and facilitates customer account management.

7. Cross-Module Reporting and Analytics

SAP ERP's integration capabilities extend to reporting and analytics. The system provides real-time access to data across different modules, enabling comprehensive reporting and analysis. For example, financial reports can include data from FI, CO, and SD modules, while inventory reports can draw data from MM and PP modules. This integrated reporting capability provides a holistic view of business performance and supports informed decision-making.

Benefits of Integration

The integration between SAP ERP modules offers several key benefits:

- **Consistency and Accuracy:** Integrated modules ensure data consistency and accuracy across the organization. Information entered in one module is automatically updated in other relevant modules, reducing the risk of errors and data discrepancies.

- **Efficiency and Productivity:** Integration streamlines business processes by automating module data flow. This reduces manual data entry and eliminates redundant tasks, improving overall efficiency and productivity.

- **Real-Time Visibility:** Integrated modules provide real-time visibility into business operations. Managers can access up-to-date information across different functions, enabling timely and informed decision-making.

- **Improved Collaboration:** Integration fosters better collaboration between departments. For example, integrating sales and procurement ensures that sales orders are fulfilled promptly, enhancing customer satisfaction.

- **Enhanced Reporting:** Integrated modules enable comprehensive reporting and analysis. Businesses can generate reports that provide a complete view of their operations, facilitating performance monitoring and strategic planning.

SAP BTP

SAP Business Technology Platform (SAP BTP) is a comprehensive suite of tools and services designed to help businesses integrate, extend, and innovate their SAP and non-SAP applications. It provides a unified environment for developing and managing enterprise applications and data. Here are the key components and features of SAP BTP:

1. **Integration:**
   o **Seamless Connectivity:** SAP BTP provides integration capabilities to connect SAP and non-SAP systems, both on-premise and in the cloud. It includes tools like SAP Integration Suite, which supports various integration patterns and protocols.
   o **Pre-Built Integrations:** It offers pre-built integrations and APIs for standard applications and processes, reducing the effort and time required to connect different systems.
2. **Database and Data Management:**
   o **SAP HANA Cloud:** The platform includes SAP HANA Cloud, a robust in-memory database that offers advanced data processing and analytics capabilities. It supports real-time data access and processing for large volumes of data.
   o **Data Orchestration:** Tools like SAP Data Intelligence help orchestrate and manage data flows across diverse landscapes, ensuring data consistency and quality.
3. **Application Development and Extension:**
   o **SAP Extension Suite:** This suite provides development tools and environments for building custom applications and extending existing SAP applications. It supports various programming

languages and frameworks, including Java, Node.js, and Python.
- o **Low-Code/No-Code Tools**: SAP BTP includes low-code/no-code development environments like SAP Business Application Studio and SAP AppGyver, enabling business users and developers to create and deploy applications quickly.

4. **Analytics and Artificial Intelligence**:
   - o **Advanced Analytics**: SAP BTP offers analytics tools like SAP Analytics Cloud, which provides capabilities for data visualization, planning, and predictive analytics.
   - o **AI and Machine Learning**: The platform includes services integrating AI and machine learning into business processes, such as SAP AI Core and SAP AI Foundation. These services enable the creation and deployment of intelligent applications.

5. **Security and Compliance**:
   - o **Robust Security Features**: SAP BTP ensures enterprise-grade security with features like identity and access management, data encryption, and compliance with global standards and regulations.
   - o **Compliance and Governance**: The platform supports governance and compliance requirements, helping businesses adhere to industry-specific regulations and standards.

6. **Cloud-Native Capabilities**:
   - o **Scalability and Flexibility**: Being cloud-native, SAP BTP offers scalability and flexibility to meet changing business demands. It leverages cloud infrastructure to provide elastic scaling and high availability.
   - o **Multi-Cloud Support**: The platform supports deployment across multiple cloud environments, including SAP Cloud, AWS, Azure, and Google Cloud, allowing businesses to choose their preferred cloud providers.

SAP BTP empowers organizations to innovate, integrate, and optimize their business processes by providing a robust, scalable, and flexible technology foundation. It enables businesses to leverage the full potential of their data and applications, driving digital transformation and competitive advantage.

SAP ERP is a robust and comprehensive solution that helps organizations manage their core business processes effectively. Its modular architecture allows businesses to implement and customize the specific modules that meet their unique needs. Key modules such as FI, CO, MM, SD, PP, and HCM cover various business functions, providing a unified platform for managing finance, procurement, production, sales, and human resources.

One of the most significant advantages of SAP ERP is its integration capabilities. The seamless integration between modules ensures consistent and accurate data flow across the organization, improving efficiency, productivity, and real-time visibility. This integration also supports comprehensive reporting and analytics, enabling businesses to make informed decisions and drive growth.

As businesses evolve in the digital age, SAP ERP remains vital for organizations seeking to optimize operations, enhance collaboration, and achieve sustainable success. By leveraging the power of SAP ERP and its integrated modules, businesses can streamline processes, improve performance, and stay competitive in an ever-changing market.

PART B – IMPLEMENTATION PHASES

Chapter 3: Project Preparation

Prepare Phase

- **Objective**: Establish the project foundation and prepare for the detailed implementation activities.
- **Activities**: This phase focuses on setting up the project governance, assembling the project team, defining the detailed project plan, and conducting kick-off meetings. Key activities include establishing project standards, setting up the project infrastructure, and preparing for the subsequent phases.
- **Deliverables**: Detailed project plan, project charter, governance model, and team onboarding.

Defining Program Methodology

While diverse in their specific approaches, SAP implementation methodologies generally follow a common framework consisting of distinct phases: requirements gathering, design, build/configuration, testing, and deployment. This structured approach ensures the implementation is systematic, organized, and aligned with the organization's business objectives.

Despite variations in methodology names and specific activities, this overarching structure provides a consistent roadmap for successfully deploying SAP solutions.

Requirements Gathering: The initial phase in any SAP implementation methodology is the requirements gathering phase. This step involves engaging stakeholders to understand the business needs, processes, and objectives. Consultants and project teams work closely with end-users and managers to collect detailed information on what the system needs to achieve. This phase is crucial as it lays the foundation for the entire project, ensuring that the subsequent phases are aligned with the business's strategic goals and operational needs.

Design: Following the requirements gathering, the design phase takes center stage. During this phase, the project team translates the business requirements into a detailed system design, including creating process flows, system architecture, and data models. The design phase is also where the solution blueprint is made, ensuring that all business requirements are addressed. This phase often involves iterative discussions with stakeholders to refine the design and ensure it meets all the criteria.

Build/Configuration: The build or configuration phase begins once the design is approved. In this phase, the SAP system is configured and customized according to the design specifications. This involves setting up modules, defining business processes, and developing any necessary custom code. The build phase is highly technical and requires collaboration between functional and technical teams to ensure the system operates as intended. This phase also includes data migration activities to ensure that historical data is accurately transferred to the new system.

Testing: Testing is a critical phase in SAP implementation to ensure that the configured system meets all the specified requirements and functions correctly. Various types of testing are conducted, including unit testing, integration testing, user acceptance testing (UAT), and performance testing. Any issues or bugs are identified and resolved during this phase, ensuring the system is robust and reliable. User involvement is crucial during UAT to validate that the system meets their needs and expectations.

Deployment: The final phase is deployment, where the system is moved to the production environment and goes live. This phase involves careful planning and coordination to minimize disruption to business operations. Activities include final data migration, user training, and system cutover. Post-deployment support is also provided to address issues arising after the system goes live. This phase ensures a smooth transition from the old system to the new SAP environment, enabling the organization to start reaping the new solution's benefits.

In summary, while SAP implementation methodologies may differ in specific practices and terminologies, they universally adhere to a structured approach encompassing requirements gathering, design, build/configuration, testing, and deployment. This common framework ensures that SAP implementations are systematic, thorough, and aligned with the organization's strategic goals, ultimately leading to successful outcomes.

Below is an example of SAP Implementation Methodology from an actual program:

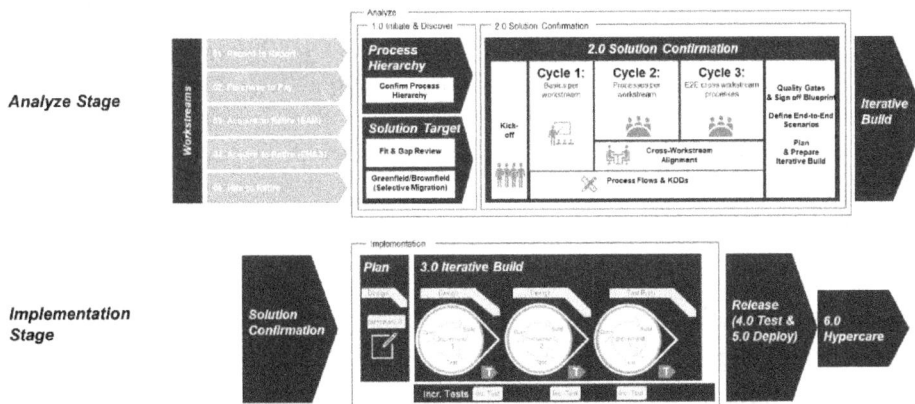

The above diagram depicts:

These stages are composed of the following Phases:
- Initiate & Discovery or *"Plan Phase"* (Plan & Solution Target review, Selective Migration assessment)
- Solution Confirmation or *"Design Phase"* (High-Level Design, Finalized Business Process Design)

- Iterative Build or *"Development Phase"* (Detailed Solution design/build/validate producing WRICEF-level functional and technical designs, configuration, integration development, unit testing, and string testing).
- *"Test Phase"* (Systems Integration Testing, User Acceptance Testing, Operational Readiness Testing, Test Automation foundation)
- *"Deploy Phase"* (Cutover, Production data load)
- Hypercare (Stabilization of critical business and system processes)

Defining Project Scope and Objectives

Understanding Business Needs

The first and most crucial step in an SAP implementation project is defining the project scope and objectives. This involves understanding the specific business needs and challenges the SAP system intends to address. The project scope outlines the boundaries of the project, including which business processes will be covered, what functionalities will be implemented, and what the desired outcomes are. Clear and well-defined project objectives are essential for guiding the project team and ensuring alignment with the organization's strategic goals.

Stakeholder Involvement

Engaging stakeholders from various departments is critical during this phase. Stakeholders include senior management, department heads, end-users, and IT staff. Their input is invaluable for identifying pain points, setting realistic expectations, and defining the project's success criteria. Conducting workshops and interviews with stakeholders helps gather detailed requirements and ensures that the project scope aligns with the organization's overall strategy.

Documenting Requirements

The next step is to document the business requirements and translate them into specific project objectives. This documentation should be thorough and detailed, covering all aspects of the business processes to be improved or automated. The requirements document serves as a reference point throughout the project, helping to manage scope creep and ensure that all parties clearly understand what the project aims to achieve.

Setting SMART Objectives

Project objectives should be Specific, Measurable, Achievable, Relevant, and Time-bound (SMART). For example, an objective might be to reduce the time required for monthly financial closing by 30% within six months of SAP implementation. SMART objectives provide clear targets for the project team and make it easier to measure success.

Scope Management

Scope management is a continuous process that begins with defining the project scope and continues throughout the project lifecycle. It involves monitoring the project to ensure that it stays within the defined boundaries and managing changes to the scope. Scope changes can arise due to evolving business needs or unforeseen challenges. A structured change management process helps assess the impact of scope changes on the project timeline, budget, and resources.

Building the Project Team

Roles and Responsibilities

Building a competent and cohesive project team is critical for the success of an SAP implementation. The project team should comprise individuals with diverse skills and expertise, including project management, business process knowledge, technical skills, and change management. Key roles in the project team include:

- **Project Sponsor:** A senior executive who provides strategic direction, secures funding, and resolves high-level issues.

- **Project Manager:** The person responsible for planning, executing, and closing the project. The project manager coordinates the team, manages resources, and ensures the project stays on track.

- **Business Analysts:** Individuals who understand the business processes and work closely with stakeholders to gather and document requirements.

- **SAP Consultants:** Experts in SAP modules and functionalities who provide technical guidance and configure the system.

- **IT Team:** Responsible for infrastructure setup, data migration, and system integration.

- **Change Management Team:** Focuses on communication, training, and supporting end-users through the transition.

- **End-Users:** Individuals from various departments who will use the SAP system. Their involvement is crucial for user acceptance testing and ensuring the system meets their needs.

Team Selection and Onboarding

Selecting the right team members involves considering their skills, experience, and availability. Team members should understand the business processes to be implemented and be capable of working collaboratively. Once selected, team members should be onboarded with a clear understanding of their roles, responsibilities, and the project objectives. Onboarding sessions should cover the project scope, timeline, key deliverables, and success criteria.

Establishing Governance Structures

Effective governance structures are essential for decision-making, risk management, and accountability. Governance structures include steering committees, project management offices (PMOs), and working groups. The steering committee comprises senior executives and key stakeholders who provide strategic oversight and make high-level decisions. The PMO supports the project manager in planning, monitoring, and controlling the project.

Working groups focus on specific aspects of the project, such as data migration or change management.

Team Collaboration and Communication

Collaboration and communication are vital for the success of the project team. Regular team meetings, status updates, and progress reports help keep everyone aligned and informed. Collaboration tools such as project management software, communication platforms, and document-sharing systems facilitate efficient teamwork. Clear communication channels and protocols ensure that information flows smoothly and issues are promptly addressed.

Training and Development

Training and development are essential for building the project team's capabilities. Team members may need training on SAP functionalities, project management methodologies, or specific business processes. Providing access to resources such as SAP Learning Hub, online courses, and workshops helps team members acquire the necessary skills and knowledge. Continuous learning and development ensure the team remains competent throughout the project lifecycle.

Initial Planning and Kickoff

Project Planning

Initial planning involves developing a detailed project plan that outlines the activities, timelines, resources, and milestones required to achieve the project objectives. The project plan serves as a roadmap for the project team, providing a clear path from project initiation to completion. Key components of the project plan include:

- **Work Breakdown Structure (WBS):** A hierarchical project decomposition into manageable tasks and activities.

- **Project Schedule:** A timeline that defines each task's start and end dates, dependencies, and critical milestones.

- **Resource Plan:** An allocation of resources, including personnel, equipment, and materials, required to complete the project tasks.

- **Budget:** An estimation of the costs associated with the project, including personnel, hardware, software, and other expenses.

- **Risk Management Plan:** A strategy for identifying, assessing, and mitigating potential risks that could impact the project.

Kickoff Meeting

The project kickoff meeting marks the project's official start and sets the stage for the project team's activities. The kickoff meeting brings together all stakeholders to review the project scope, objectives, and plan. Essential agenda items for the kickoff meeting include:

- **Introduction and Welcome:** An overview of the project and its importance to the organization.

- **Project Scope and Objectives:** A detailed review of the project scope, objectives, and key deliverables.

- **Project Plan:** Presentation of the project plan, including the schedule, milestones, and resource allocation.

- **Roles and Responsibilities:** Clarification of team members' roles and responsibilities.

- **Communication Plan:** Discuss communication protocols, reporting structures, and collaboration tools.

- **Risk Management:** Identification and discussion of potential risks and mitigation strategies.

The kickoff meeting is an opportunity to align all stakeholders, address any questions or concerns, and build enthusiasm for the project. It sets the project's tone and ensures everyone is on the same page. At a high level, the Phases for SAP implementation are listed below, which should be included in the Kick-Off meeting:

Detailed Requirement Analysis

Following the kickoff meeting, the project team conducts a detailed requirement analysis to refine and validate the business requirements gathered during the project initiation phase. This involves engaging stakeholders through workshops, interviews, and surveys to gather specific details about the business processes and functionalities to implement.

The requirement analysis phase aims to produce a comprehensive requirements specification document as a blueprint for system configuration and development. This document includes detailed descriptions of the business processes, data requirements, user interfaces, and integration points. It ensures that the project team understands what needs to be delivered and provides a basis for testing and validation.

System Design and Blueprinting

Based on the requirements specification, the project team develops a system design and blueprint that outlines how the SAP system will be configured and customized to meet the business needs. The system design includes:

- **Process Flows:** Visual representations of the business processes and how they will be executed in the SAP system.

- **Data Models:** Definitions of the data structures, including master data, transactional data, and relationships between data entities.

- **System Architecture:** An overview of the technical architecture, including hardware, software, and network components.

- **Integration Plan:** Details of how the SAP system will integrate with other systems and applications within the organization.

- **User Interfaces:** Design the user interfaces and screens with which users will interact.

The system blueprint is a detailed guide for the configuration and development phase, ensuring the implementation aligns with the business requirements.

Configuration and Development

The configuration and development phase involves setting up the SAP system according to the design and blueprint. This includes configuring the system settings, customizing functionalities, and developing any necessary custom code or extensions. Key activities in this phase include:

- **System Configuration:** Setting up the SAP modules, defining organizational structures, configuring workflows, and establishing data parameters.

- **Customization:** Developing custom code, reports, interfaces, and enhancements to meet specific business needs.

- **Data Migration:** Extracting, transforming, and loading data from legacy systems into the SAP system.

- **Integration:** Setting up interfaces and connections between the SAP system and other applications.

- **Testing:** Conducting unit, integration, and user acceptance testing to ensure the system functions correctly and meets the business requirements.

Training and Change Management

Training and change management are critical components of a successful SAP implementation. The project team must ensure that end-users are adequately trained on the new system and prepared for the changes in business processes. Key activities in this phase include:

- **Training Needs Assessment:** Identifying the training needs of different user groups and developing a training plan.

- **Training Development:** Creating training materials, including manuals, e-learning modules, and hands-on exercises.

- **Training Delivery:** Conducting training sessions, workshops, and support sessions for end-users.

- **Change Management:** Communicating the changes to stakeholders, addressing concerns, and providing ongoing support to ensure a smooth transition.

Go-Live and Support

The final phase of the SAP implementation project is the go-live, where the new system is deployed, and the organization transitions to the SAP environment. Key activities in this phase include:

- **Go-Live Preparation:** Conducting final testing, data validation, and system checks to ensure readiness for go-live.

- **Cutover Planning:** Developing a detailed plan for transitioning from the legacy system to the new SAP system, including data migration, system setup, and user support.

- **Go-Live:** Executing the cutover plan, transitioning to the new system, and providing immediate support to address any issues.

- **Post-Go-Live Support:** Offering ongoing support and monitoring to ensure the system operates smoothly and address post-implementation issues.

Key Deliverables

Key deliverables of this phase include the following:

Org Chart

The Organizational Chart outlines the project team structure, depicting roles, reporting lines, and key team members involved in the SAP implementation.

Program RACI

The Program RACI (Responsible, Accountable, Consulted, Informed) matrix defines the roles and responsibilities of project team members, ensuring clarity on who is responsible for, accountable for, consulted on, and informed about each task.

Governance Plan

The Governance Plan establishes the framework for decision-making, project oversight, and accountability. It details the processes, committees, and roles that will guide the project's execution and ensure alignment with organizational objectives.

Communication Plan

The Communication Plan outlines the strategy for effective communication throughout the SAP implementation. It identifies key stakeholders, communication channels, frequency, and content of communications to ensure transparency and stakeholder engagement.

Resource Plan, Including User/Team Access

The Resource Plan identifies the human and material resources required for the project, detailing roles, skills, and access levels. It ensures that team members have the necessary resources and system access to perform their tasks, including when resources are onboarding and offboarding. A team calendar and vacation plans should be documented.

Project Plan, Schedule, Milestones

The Project Plan provides a detailed timeline of the SAP implementation, including key activities, dependencies, and milestones. It serves as a roadmap to guide project execution and track progress.

Below is an example of a client project schedule:

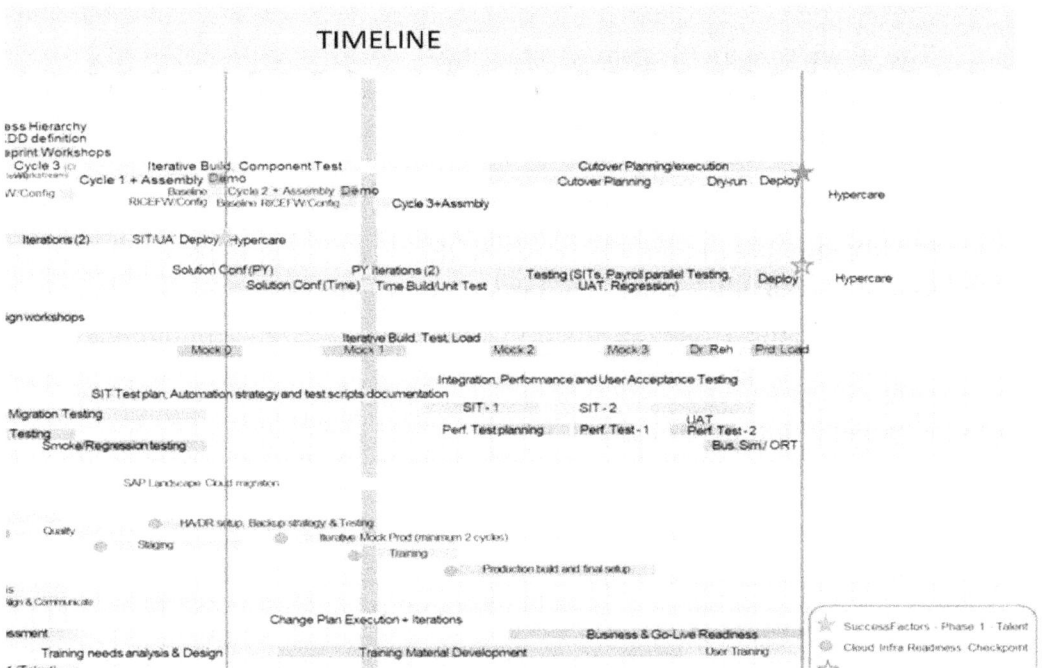

List of Deliverables

The List of Deliverables outlines all the tangible outputs to be produced during the SAP implementation. It includes specifications, due dates, and responsible parties for each deliverable.

RAID Log (Risks, Actions, Issues, Decisions)

The RAID Log comprehensively records the project's risks, actions, issues, and decisions. It facilitates risk management, action tracking, resolution, and decision-making documentation.

Team Collaboration Site

The Team Collaboration Site is an online platform where project team members can share documents, communicate, and collaborate in real time, ensuring efficient information flow and teamwork.

Environment / System Architecture

The Environment/System Architecture document describes the technical infrastructure for the SAP implementation, including hardware, software, network components, and their interactions.

Quality Assurance Plan

The Quality Assurance Plan outlines the processes and criteria for ensuring the SAP implementation meets quality standards. It includes testing strategies, quality control measures, and continuous improvement practices.

Change Request Process

The Change Request Process defines the procedures for managing project scope, schedule, or resource changes. It ensures that all changes are evaluated, approved, and documented systematically.

Demo Environment

The Demo Environment is a sandbox version of the SAP system for demonstrations, training, and testing. It allows stakeholders to interact with the system without affecting the live environment.

Procurement of Software/Hardware, BOM

The Procurement Plan details the necessary software and hardware acquisition, including the Bill of Materials (BOM). It ensures that all required components are procured timely and within budget.

Initial WRICEF List (If and Whatever is Available)

The Initial WRICEF List is a preliminary inventory of Workflow, Reports, Interfaces, Conversions, Enhancements, and Forms required for the SAP implementation. It serves as a starting point for detailed customization planning. Nite: sometimes, the WRICEF list is written as RICEFW or WRICEFX (X for UX). These deviations have the same meaning.

Status Report Template

The Status Report Template is a standardized document that regularly updates stakeholders on the project's progress. It includes vital information such as completed tasks, upcoming activities, the current status of deliverables, risks, issues, and any deviations from the project plan. This template ensures consistent and comprehensive reporting across all project updates.

Regular Team Meetings Scheduled

Regular Team Meetings refer to the pre-scheduled meetings for the project team, including frequency, participants, and agenda topics. These meetings facilitate ongoing communication, coordination, and issue resolution among team members, ensuring the project remains on track and promptly addresses any obstacles. As the program progresses, these will be updated.

Education of Program Team on Tools

This component involves training and educating the program team on effectively using the procured tools and software. It includes developing a training plan, scheduling training sessions, creating user guides and documentation, and providing ongoing support. The goal is to ensure that all team members are proficient in using the tools, enhancing productivity and project success.

Phase Entry & Exit Criteria

As part of the program, phase entry & exit criteria must be defined.

Below is an example from a company that developed such entry & exit criteria:

PHASE	EN/EX	CRITERIA
Plan	Exit	The Requirements Traceability Matrix has been updated as appropriate. The updated version has been reviewed and approved or is in the approval workflow as appropriate.
Plan	Exit	All milestone deliverables expected based on the deliverable matrix for the current phase ending have been approved or are in the approval workflow.
Initiate	Entry	Key stakeholders have been contacted & informed of their roles and associated responsibilities.

PHASE	EN/EX	CRITERIA
Initiate	Entry	Resources required for the upcoming stage are in place or ready for resource staffing expectations planned throughout the phase.
Initiate	Entry	Project Management Processes have been defined and are in place.
Initiate	Entry	Workplans, including dependencies, are ready for baseline and in place for the upcoming phase.
Initiate	Entry	Environments required for the Initiate Phase have been provisioned and are ready for use.
Initiate	Exit	Known, documented, and dispositioned detailed requirements have been completed, reviewed, and approved or are in the approval workflow. Non-dispositioned requirements have a resolution mitigation plan to be performed at the beginning of the upcoming phase and will not be included in the RICEFW estimate. They must go through the Change Request process to be brought into scope.
Initiate	Exit	The Requirements Traceability Matrix has been updated as appropriate. The updated version has been reviewed and approved or is in the approval workflow as appropriate.
Initiate	Exit	RICEFW Inventory is based on all known dispositioned requirements that have been completed, reviewed, and approved or are in the approval workflow. Non-dispositioned RICEFW has a resolution mitigation plan to be performed at the beginning of the upcoming phase. They must go through the Change Request process to be brought into scope.
Initiate	Exit	All milestone deliverables expected based on the deliverable matrix for the current phase ending have been approved or are in the approval workflow.
Initiate	Exit	Deployment Approach has been drafted (this will be refined in future phases).
DBV	Entry	The technical support (e.g., release strategy, security support, backup) required for the upcoming phase has been identified and agreed to.
DBV	Entry	Tools required for the upcoming phase are configured and accessible, including user roles and IDs.
DBV	Entry	Defect management process in place
DBV	Entry	Team members will receive orientation on DBV stage processes, procedures, and deliverable standards.
DBV	Entry	Environments required for the beginning of the DBV Phase have been provisioned and are ready for use.
DBV	Entry	Resources required for the upcoming stage are in place or ready for resource staffing expectations planned throughout the phase.
DBV	Entry	Workplans, including dependencies, are ready for baseline and in place for the upcoming phase.

PHASE	EN/EX	CRITERIA
DBV	Exit	The Validation Test Exit Criteria are at least 70% complete per the DBV approach document (or approval to proceed given from Project Leadership for any exit criteria that were not met).
DBV	Exit	70% of in-scope interfacing systems have been Validation tested and testing agreements (TPAs) drafted for Product Testing
DBV	Exit	Validation Test documentation is 100% complete, including expected and actual results and pass/fail information for Validation Test Scripts in QC.
DBV	Exit	The test team has received access to the application components.
Test	Entry	The meeting cadence has been defined for the upcoming phase.
Test	Entry	Security role design is complete for 70% of the roles for Release 2.
Test	Entry	Validation Test documentation is at least 70% complete, including expected and actual results and pass/fail information for Validation Test Scripts in QC.
Test	Entry	Unresolved defects for RICEFWs that have been Validation tested are fully documented, and plans are in place to address them in the Product Test.
Test	Entry	Design and build teams agree to design changes for RICEFW's completed or in progress, and project leadership has provided approval for anything closed.
Test	Entry	All parties agree to a precise mechanism for handling scope changes and a defined control process.
Test	Entry	The impacts of design changes are assessed, and the budgets, schedules, etc., are updated and tracked accordingly.
Test	Entry	Application code is component (unit) tested.
Test	Entry	Technical architecture components are reviewed and component (unit) tested.
Test	Entry	Technical architecture components and custom code comply with project coding and documentation standards.
Test	Entry	Environments required for the Test Phase have been provisioned and are ready for use.
Test	Entry	The test team has received the application components.
Test	Entry	The test team has received the technical architecture components
Test	Entry	Training deliverables required for product tests are approved or on pace per the training work plan.
Test	Entry	Technical components of the training and performance support have been provided to the OCM team per the work plan.

PHASE	EN/EX	CRITERIA
Test	Entry	For the first cycle of the product test, tests have been scripted, uploaded to HPQC, and assigned to users.
Test	Entry	QC tool is configured and accessible, including user roles and IDs.
Test	Entry	Defect management process in place.
Test	Entry	Supporting test data generation and management tool (i.e., master data generator)/jobs aids are ready.
Test	Entry	The high-level Product test plan/schedule and test resource staffing were defined and approved.
Test	Entry	Business requirements for Cycle 1 are mapped to Product Test scenarios
Test	Entry	Converted data loaded into the test environment and verified.
Test	Entry	All relevant transport requests have been moved into the Testing environment and verified.
Test	Entry	Appropriate authorization to test environments and HPQC has been given to the Test and Fix-It teams.
Test	Entry	Logistics for Product Test execution have been identified/confirmed.
DBV	Exit	Report build iterations are tracked to completion before the cycle 2 Product Test ends.
Test	Entry	Milestone deliverables expected by Product Test entry based on the deliverable matrix have been approved or are in the approval workflow.
Test	Entry	The freeze calendar Initial Draft has been started.
Test	Entry	Resources required for the upcoming stage are in place or ready for any resource staffing changes planned throughout the phase.
Test	Exit	The product Test Closure Memo was drafted and is in the approval workflow.
Test	Exit	95% of Test scripts fully executed across the Release* * A script will be deemed successfully executed as long as all steps have been executed and no Critical or High Business Severity defect remains open.
Test	Exit	The entire batch schedule unit was tested successfully.
Test	Exit	Any unresolved defects are fully documented and signed off by Test Leads and Release Leads. Review and transition plan with Delivery Leads for overall defect backlog in place for the beginning of the Deployment Phase.
Test	Exit	A product test review meeting has been scheduled or conducted with project leadership.

PHASE	EN/EX	CRITERIA
Deploy	Entry	Environments required for the Deploy Phase have been provisioned and are ready for use.
Deploy	Entry	Resources required for the upcoming stage are in place or ready for any resource staffing changes planned throughout the phase.
Deploy	Entry	Service Introduction organization and roles are defined.
Deploy	Entry	The training materials meet the users' needs as defined in the requirements.
Deploy	Entry	HPQC has been installed on laptops, and users have been trained on the use of HPQC with security roles appropriately assigned
Deploy	Entry	Converted data loaded into the test environment and verified by the fix-it team or planned for data load at the beginning of the phase.
Deploy	Entry	The Cutover Plan has been drafted and includes all the information required for the upcoming dress rehearsal.
Deploy	Entry	Business Readiness activity for capturing and handling Manual Conversion is in progress.
Deploy	Entry	Business Readiness activity for capturing and handling Interim Processes is in progress.
Deploy	Entry	Business Readiness activity for capturing and handling Manual Workarounds is in progress.
Deploy	Entry	Business Readiness activity for capturing and handling Business Recovery work is in progress.
Deploy	Entry	All milestone deliverables expected based on the deliverable matrix for the current phase ending have been approved or are in the approval workflow.
Deploy	Entry	The current version of the Freeze Calendar has been communicated to relevant stakeholders, and adherence monitoring is in progress.
Deploy	Entry	A Hypercare plan has been drafted.
Deploy	Exit	The application and the technology infrastructure have been tested for operability and rolled out.
Deploy	Exit	The support team has been trained, and the performance support materials have been provided.
Deploy	Exit	The change enablement team has transitioned the change enablement responsibilities to the organization needed to sustain the change's results.
Deploy	Exit	The handover documents are complete and meet the Application Management team's acceptance requirements.
Deploy	Exit	Service Level Agreement documentation has been updated to reflect the new service, and the service level has been agreed on.

PHASE	EN/EX	CRITERIA
Deploy	Exit	The application management team has accepted the new application and the supporting documentation and is ready to assume the new responsibility based on the knowledge transfer criteria.
Deploy	Exit	The program leadership team has accepted the final status information on the deployed application.
Deploy	Exit	The business has identified, tested, and accepted interim procedures, including training of impacted end users.
Deploy	Exit	>90% of workarounds due to defects or rejected SCRs identified, documented and communicated to business units
Deploy	Exit	Business Recovery manual procedures required during deployment have been defined and approved.
Deploy	Exit	Hypercare logistics documented, including command center, transition to stabilization, # of required participants, workstation and facilities, and resource support logistics
Deploy	Exit	All go-live criteria for the release deployment have been met, or a contingency plan has been drafted for the remaining criteria and approved by the Delivery Leads.

Kick-Off Deck

The Kick-Off Deck is a presentation used to launch the SAP implementation project. It provides an overview of the project objectives, scope, timeline, team roles, and critical milestones to align all stakeholders.

An SAP implementation project is a complex and multifaceted endeavor that requires careful planning, coordination, and execution. Defining the project scope and objectives, building a competent project team, and conducting thorough initial planning are essential to ensure successful implementation. By following a structured approach and engaging stakeholders throughout the process, organizations can achieve their SAP implementation goals, optimize their business processes, and realize significant benefits from their SAP investment.

Chapter 4: Business Blueprint or Explore Phase

Explore Phase

- **Objective**: To validate the solution requirements and finalize the design.
- **Activities**: In this phase, workshops are conducted to gather detailed business requirements and explore the standard SAP processes. The project team works to map these requirements to the SAP solution, identifying gaps and deciding on necessary customizations.
- **Deliverables**: Solution design, process flows, fit-gap analysis, and prioritized list of requirements.

Conducting Requirement Analysis

Understanding the Requirement Analysis Process

Requirement analysis is a critical step in the SAP implementation process, serving as the foundation for creating a robust and effective SAP system tailored to an organization's specific needs. This phase involves gathering detailed information about the business processes, identifying pain points, and understanding the current system landscape. The goal is ensuring the new SAP system aligns with business goals and delivers the desired outcomes.

Engaging Stakeholders

The requirement analysis phase begins with engaging stakeholders from various departments within the organization. Stakeholders typically include senior management, department heads, process owners, end-users, and IT staff. Their involvement is essential for capturing a comprehensive view of the business processes and requirements. Workshops, interviews, surveys, and questionnaires are commonly used to gather stakeholder information.

Mapping Current Business Processes

Understanding the current business processes is a crucial part of requirement analysis. This involves documenting how tasks are performed, what systems are currently used, and identifying any inefficiencies or issues. Process mapping techniques like flowcharts and process diagrams are valuable tools for visualizing business operations. These maps help identify areas for improvement and set the stage for defining future processes.

Identifying Business Requirements

Once the current processes are documented, the next step is identifying specific business requirements. These requirements can be categorized into functional and non-functional requirements. Functional requirements, such as particular functionalities, workflows, and data management, describe what the system should do. Non-functional requirements specify the system's performance criteria, such as scalability, security, and user experience.

Prioritizing Requirements

Not all requirements are equally important. It is essential to prioritize requirements based on their impact on business operations and strategic goals. Techniques like the MoSCoW method (Must have, Should have, Could have, and Won't have) can help prioritize requirements. High-priority requirements are critical for business operations, while lower-priority requirements are those that would be nice to have but are not essential.

Documenting Requirements

The outcome of the requirement analysis phase is a detailed requirements document that captures all the identified business needs. This document serves as a reference point throughout the project and ensures that the project team and stakeholders understand what the SAP system needs to achieve. The requirements document should include:

- Detailed descriptions of business processes

- Specific functional and non-functional requirements

- Prioritization of requirements

- Any constraints or assumptions

- Acceptance criteria for each requirement

Understanding Fit to Standard Concept and Running Facilitated Workshops

Definition and Overview

The Fit to Standard concept is pivotal in SAP implementation, especially within the SAP Activate methodology. It leverages SAP's predefined best practices and standard processes to minimize custom development. The idea is to fit the organization's processes to the standard functionalities provided by SAP rather than customizing SAP to fit the organization's existing processes.

Importance of Fit to Standard

Adopting the Fit to Standard approach offers several benefits:

- **Reduced Implementation Time**: Utilizing standard processes reduces the time required for customization.

- **Cost Efficiency**: Minimizing custom development lowers implementation and maintenance costs.

- **Best Practices**: Organizations benefit from SAP's industry best practices embedded in the standard processes.

- **Simplified Upgrades**: Standard processes ease the upgrade path, as customizations often complicate upgrades.

Steps in the Fit-to-Standard Process

a. Preparation

- **Understanding Organizational Requirements**: Conduct a thorough analysis of the organization's current processes and identify essential requirements.

- **SAP Best Practices Exploration**: Use the SAP Best Practices Explorer to learn about SAP's standard processes and functionalities.

b. Conducting Fit to Standard Workshops

- **Workshops Planning**: Schedule and plan workshops involving key stakeholders, business process owners, and SAP consultants.

- **Demonstration of Standard Processes**: Use a pre-configured SAP system to demonstrate the standard processes to the stakeholders.

- **Fit/Gap Analysis**: Conduct a detailed Fit/Gap analysis to identify where the organization's requirements align with the standard processes and where gaps exist.

c. Decision Making

- **Fit to Standard Decisions**: Adopt these processes in areas where the organization's requirements fit the standard methods.

- **Gap Handling**: Determine whether identified gaps can be addressed through minor adjustments or if custom development is necessary.

d. Implementation

- **Configuration**: Configure the SAP system according to the decisions made during the Fit to Standard workshops.

- **Testing**: Perform rigorous testing to ensure the configured processes meet the organizational requirements.

- **Training**: Train end-users on the new processes and system functionalities.

Best Practices for Fit to Standard

a. Early Engagement of Stakeholders

Engage key stakeholders and business process owners early to ensure their buy-in and support.

b. Comprehensive Preparation

To prepare thoroughly for Fit to Standard workshops, understand the organization's requirements and the capabilities of SAP's standard processes.

c. Clear Communication

Maintain clear and transparent communication with all stakeholders to manage expectations and facilitate decision-making.

d. Flexibility and Openness

Encourage flexibility and openness among stakeholders to adapt to new processes and ways of working that align with SAP's best practices.

e. Continuous Review

Continuously review and validate the decisions made during the Fit to Standard process to ensure alignment with organizational goals and objectives.

Running Facilitated Workshops

Definition and Purpose

Facilitated workshops are structured sessions designed to gather information, validate requirements, and make decisions in a collaborative environment. These workshops are crucial in SAP implementation for aligning stakeholders, understanding requirements, and ensuring the system configuration meets the organization's needs.

Types of Workshops

a. Discovery Workshops

- **Purpose**: To gather initial information about the organization's processes, requirements, and pain points.

- **Participants**: Key stakeholders, business process owners, and SAP consultants.

- **Activities**: High-level process walkthroughs, discussions on business goals and challenges, and identification of critical requirements.

b. Fit to Standard Workshops

- **Purpose**: To demonstrate SAP's standard processes and conduct a Fit/Gap analysis.

- **Participants**: Business process owners, key stakeholders, and SAP consultants.

- **Activities**: Demonstration of standard processes, detailed Fit/Gap analysis, and decision-making on process adoption.

c. Design Workshops

- **Purpose**: To design the solution based on the decisions made during the Fit to Standard workshops.

- **Participants**: SAP consultants, business process owners, and technical experts.

- **Activities**: Detailed design discussions, configuration planning, and documentation of design decisions.

d. Validation Workshops

- **Purpose**: To validate the configured solution against the requirements and ensure it meets the organization's needs.

- **Participants**: End-users, business process owners, and SAP consultants.

- **Activities**: System demonstrations, testing feedback sessions, and discussions on any required adjustments.

Below is a Design Approach for Fit to Standard workshops

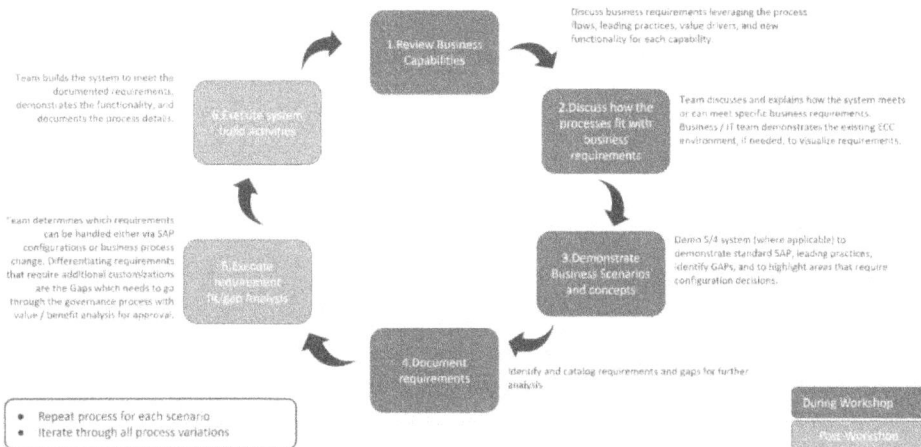

Best Practices for Running Facilitated Workshops

a. Clear Objectives

Define clear objectives for each workshop to ensure that all participants understand the purpose and desired outcomes.

b. Structured Agenda

Develop a structured agenda that outlines the topics to be covered, the sequence of activities, and the time allocated for each segment.

c. Pre-Workshop Preparation

Prepare thoroughly before each workshop by reviewing relevant materials, setting up necessary systems, and preparing demonstrations.

d. Skilled Facilitation

Utilize skilled facilitators who can guide discussions, manage time effectively, and ensure that all participants have the opportunity to contribute.

e. Active Participation

Encourage active participation from all attendees to gather diverse perspectives and ensure comprehensive discussions.

f. Documentation

Document critical discussions, decisions, and action items during the workshop to provide a clear record for future reference.

g. Follow-Up

Follow up on action items and decisions made during the workshop to ensure that they are implemented and that any outstanding issues are addressed.

Detailed Steps for Conducting Facilitated Workshops

a. Planning

- **Identify Objectives**: Clearly define the objectives and desired outcomes of the workshop.

- **Select Participants**: Identify and invite key stakeholders and subject matter experts.

- **Prepare Materials**: Prepare necessary materials, such as process maps, system demonstrations, and presentation slides.

- **Set Agenda**: Develop a detailed agenda outlining the sequence of activities and time allocations.

b. Execution

- **Kickoff**: Begin with an introduction, stating the objectives, agenda, and expected outcomes.

- **Facilitation**: Guide the discussions, ensuring all topics are covered and participants stay focused.

- **Demonstration**: Use system demonstrations to illustrate key points and facilitate discussions.

- **Engagement**: Encourage active participation and constructively manage conflicts or differing opinions.

c. Documentation

- **Record Discussions**: Document critical discussions, decisions, and action items.

- **Summarize Outcomes**: Summarize the workshop outcomes, including any decisions made and next steps.

d. Follow-Up

- **Action Items**: Ensure all action items are assigned to specific individuals and have clear deadlines.

- **Review**: Conduct a review session to follow up on action items and ensure that decisions are being implemented.

Implementing SAP effectively requires a thorough understanding of the Fit to Standard concept and the ability to run successfully facilitated workshops. Organizations can achieve a smooth and efficient implementation by leveraging SAP's predefined best practices and engaging stakeholders through structured workshops.

Adopting best practices such as early stakeholder engagement, clear communication, and comprehensive documentation further enhances the likelihood of success. With these approaches, organizations can ensure that their SAP implementation aligns with business objectives, maximizes efficiency, and delivers lasting value.

Creating the Business Blueprint Document

Purpose of the Business Blueprint

The Business Blueprint is a critical document in the SAP implementation process, serving as the foundation for the system design and configuration. It describes how the SAP system will support the business processes and meet the identified requirements. The Business Blueprint ensures that the project team and stakeholders have a shared understanding of the system's scope and functionalities.

Structure of the Business Blueprint

The Business Blueprint typically includes the following sections:

1. **Introduction and Overview**

   o Project objectives and scope

   o Summary of the business processes covered

   o Stakeholders involved

2. **Business Process Descriptions**

   o Detailed descriptions of each business process

   o Flowcharts and process diagrams

   o Roles and responsibilities within each process

3. **Functional Requirements**

   o Specific functionalities required for each process

- o Detailed descriptions of how the SAP system will support these functionalities

4. **Non-Functional Requirements**

- o Performance criteria

- o Security requirements

- o User experience considerations

5. **System Architecture**

- o Overview of the technical architecture

- o Hardware, software, and network components

6. **Integration Points**

- o Interfaces with other systems and applications

- o Data exchange requirements

7. **Customization and Development**

- o Any custom code or enhancements required

- o Reports and interfaces to be developed

8. **Testing and Validation**

- o Test plans and strategies

- o Acceptance criteria for each requirement

9. **Training and Change Management**

- o Training plans for end-users

- o Change management strategies

10. **Project Plan and Timeline**

- o Milestones and deliverables

- o Detailed project schedule

Developing the Business Blueprint

Developing the Business Blueprint is a collaborative effort involving the project team, stakeholders, and SAP consultants. The process begins with reviewing the requirements document and validating the information gathered during the requirement analysis phase. Workshops and stakeholder meetings are conducted to discuss and refine the business processes and requirements.

Detailing Business Processes

Each business process is documented in detail, including the steps involved, roles and responsibilities, and desired outcomes. Flowcharts and process diagrams visualize the processes, making identifying gaps or inefficiencies easier. The documentation should clearly describe how the SAP system will support each process, including any customizations or enhancements required.

Defining Functional Requirements

Functional requirements are detailed in the Business Blueprint, specifying the exact functionalities needed to support the business processes. This includes defining the data fields, workflows, user interfaces, and reports required for each process. The functional requirements should align with the business goals and ensure the system delivers the desired outcomes.

Addressing Non-Functional Requirements

The business blueprint also addresses non-functional requirements like performance, security, and user experience. These requirements are critical for ensuring the SAP system operates effectively and meets the organization's standards. The Blueprint should detail how these requirements will be met, including any configurations or customizations needed.

System Architecture and Integration

The Business Blueprint includes an overview of the system architecture, detailing the hardware, software, and network components required for the SAP system. It also outlines the integration points with other systems and applications, specifying how data will be exchanged and ensuring seamless connectivity.

The integration plan should address potential challenges and provide consistent and accurate solutions with data.

Customization and Development

The Business Blueprint details any custom code or enhancements required to meet the business requirements. This includes developing custom reports, interfaces, and user screens. The document should specify the development tasks, timelines, and resources needed to complete the customizations.

Testing and Validation

The Business Blueprint includes testing and validation plans to ensure the system meets the defined requirements. This includes unit testing, integration testing, and user acceptance testing. The acceptance criteria for each requirement are clearly defined, providing a basis for evaluating the system's performance.

Training and Change Management

The Business Blueprint also addresses training and change management. A detailed training plan is developed to ensure end-users are adequately trained on the new system. Change management strategies are outlined to help stakeholders transition smoothly to the latest SAP environment. This includes communication plans, support structures, and addressing resistance to change.

Finalizing the Business Blueprint

Once the Business Blueprint is developed, stakeholders review and validate it. Any feedback or revisions are incorporated into the document to reflect the business requirements and processes accurately. The final Business Blueprint serves as a blueprint for the system configuration and development phases, guiding the project team in building a system that meets the organization's needs.

Gap Analysis

Understanding Gap Analysis

Gap analysis is a critical step in the SAP implementation process. It is used to identify the differences between the current state of business processes and the desired future state as defined in the Business Blueprint. The goal is to identify any gaps or discrepancies that must be addressed to achieve the desired outcomes. Gap analysis helps ensure that the SAP system is configured to meet the organization's specific needs and that potential issues are identified and resolved early in the project.

Conducting Gap Analysis

Gap analysis involves comparing the current business processes and system functionalities with the requirements and future state defined in the Business Blueprint. The process typically includes the following steps:

1. **Review Current Processes:** Review the business processes and system functionalities documented during the requirement analysis phase. Understand how tasks are currently performed and identify any pain points or inefficiencies.

2. **Compare with Business Blueprint:** Compare the current processes and functionalities with the desired future state defined in the Business Blueprint. Identify any gaps or discrepancies between the current state and the requirements.

3. **Identify Gaps:** Document the gaps identified during the comparison. This includes any missing functionalities, process inefficiencies, or areas where the current system does not meet the requirements.

4. **Analyze Impact:** Assess the impact of each gap on the business operations and the overall project. Determine the priority of addressing each gap based on its impact and importance to the business.

5. **Develop Solutions:** Develop solutions to address the identified gaps. This may include configuring the SAP system, developing custom code, or modifying business processes to align with the requirements.

Types of Gaps

Gaps identified during the analysis can be categorized into several types:

- **Functional Gaps:** Missing or inadequate functionalities that the current system does not support but are required by the Business Blueprint.

- **Process Gaps:** Inefficiencies or issues in the current business processes must be addressed to achieve the desired future state.

- **Data Gaps:** Inconsistencies or inaccuracies in the current data must be resolved for accurate reporting and analysis.

- **Technical Gaps:** Technical limitations or challenges must be overcome to implement the desired functionalities or processes.

- **Compliance Gaps:** Areas where the current system does not meet regulatory or compliance requirements.

Documenting and Prioritizing Gaps

Documenting the identified gaps is essential for developing a comprehensive plan. Each gap should be described in detail, including its impact on business operations and the proposed solution. The gaps should be prioritized based on their importance and the urgency of addressing them. High-priority gaps significantly impact business operations or are critical for achieving the project objectives.

Developing a Gap Resolution Plan

A gap resolution plan is developed to address the identified gaps. The plan should include:

- **Solutions:** Detailed descriptions of the solutions to address each gap, including system configurations, customizations, or process changes.

- **Resources:** Allocation of resources required to implement the solutions, including personnel, time, and budget.

- **Timeline:** A timeline for implementing the solutions, including key milestones and deadlines.

- **Risks and Mitigations:** Identification of potential risks associated with addressing the gaps and strategies for mitigating those risks.

Implementing the Gap Resolution Plan

The project team implements the solutions once the gap resolution plan is developed. This involves configuring the SAP system, creating custom code, and modifying business processes as required. Regular monitoring and reporting are essential to track progress and ensure that the solutions are implemented effectively.

Testing and Validation

Testing and validation are critical to ensure that the solutions effectively address the identified gaps. This includes conducting unit testing, integration testing, and user acceptance testing to verify that the system meets the requirements and functions as expected. Any issues identified during testing should be addressed promptly to ensure a smooth implementation.

Continuous Improvement

Gap analysis is not a one-time activity but a continuous process throughout the SAP implementation project. As the project progresses, new gaps may be identified, and existing gaps may evolve. Constant monitoring and analysis help ensure that the project stays on track and that any issues are addressed promptly. Regular reviews and updates to the gap resolution plan ensure the project team remains aligned with the project objectives and business goals.

Key Deliverables

Key deliverables of this phase include the following:

Workshop Schedules and Agendas

Scheduled workshops with detailed agendas to facilitate Fit to Standard analysis and requirement gathering sessions with stakeholders.

Fit/Gap Analysis Report

Documentation of the Fit to Standard workshop results, identifying areas where the organization's requirements align with SAP standard processes and where gaps exist.

Business Process Hierarchy (BPH)

The Business Process Hierarchy (BPH) is a structured representation of all organizational business processes organized in a hierarchical format. In the context of SAP implementation, the BPH serves as a blueprint that maps out the various business processes and their sub-processes, showing how they interact and relate to each other within the SAP system.

Business Requirements Document (BRD)

A comprehensive document outlining the specific business needs and functionalities to be addressed by the SAP implementation.

WRICEF List

The SAP implementation requires an inventory of Workflow, Reports, Interfaces, Conversions, Enhancements, and Forms. This should include an estimate for developing WRICEF objects.

Business Process Diagrams (BPD)

Visual representations of current and future state business processes, highlighting how SAP will support these processes.

Functional Specification Document (FSD)

The Functional Specification Document (FSD) is a comprehensive document that outlines the functional requirements and detailed business processes that a specific SAP customization or development will address. It serves as a bridge between business requirements and technical development, ensuring that the technical team understands the functional needs of the end-users.

Technical Design Document (TDD)

The Technical Design Document (TDD) is a detailed technical blueprint that outlines how the functional requirements specified in the FSD will be technically implemented within the SAP system. It provides the technical team with the necessary information to develop and configure the solution.

Data Migration Plan

A strategy for migrating data from legacy systems to SAP, including data cleansing and enrichment activities.

Change Management Plan

A strategy for managing organizational change, including stakeholder engagement, communication, and training activities to facilitate the transition to the new system.

Technical Architecture Document

A document describing the technical infrastructure for the SAP implementation, including hardware, software, and network components.

Demo Environment Setup

A sandbox version of the SAP system is configured for demonstrations, training, and testing.

The Business Blueprint or Explore Phase is a critical stage in the SAP implementation process, laying the foundation for a successful project. Conducting a thorough requirement analysis ensures the project team understands the business needs and requirements.

Creating a comprehensive Business Blueprint document provides a clear roadmap for the system configuration and development phases. Gap analysis helps identify and address discrepancies between the current and desired future, ensuring that the SAP system meets the organization's needs and delivers the desired outcomes. Organizations can achieve their SAP implementation goals and drive significant business improvements by following a structured approach and engaging stakeholders.

Chapter 5: Project Realization Phase or Build/Test Phase

Realize Phase

- **Objective**: Configure and build the solution based on the approved design.
- **Activities**: This phase involves configuring the SAP system according to the business requirements, developing custom enhancements, and migrating data. It also includes rigorous testing to ensure the solution meets the specified requirements. Iterative cycles of build and test are conducted to refine the solution.
- **Deliverables**: Configured system, completed custom developments, migrated data, and tested solution.

The Project Realization Phase is a critical stage in the SAP implementation process where the design and plans laid out in the earlier phases are brought to life. This phase focuses on configuring the SAP modules according to the business requirements, developing custom functionalities to address unique needs, and ensuring that data is accurately migrated from legacy systems to the new SAP environment. Each of these tasks requires meticulous planning, execution, and testing to ensure the successful deployment of the SAP system.

Configuring SAP Modules

Overview of Configuration

Configuration in SAP refers to setting up the system to reflect the business processes and requirements defined during the blueprint phase. Unlike customization, which involves writing new code, configuration uses the standard tools and options SAP provides to adjust the system. This process consists of setting parameters, defining rules, and creating organizational structures that align with the company's operational needs.

Steps in Configuring SAP Modules

1. **Organizational Structure Setup**

   o **Define Organizational Units:** The first step involves defining the organizational units such as company codes, plants, sales organizations, and purchasing organizations. These units form the backbone of the SAP system and dictate how data flows through various processes.

   o **Assign Organizational Units:** Once defined, these units need to be assigned to each other to reflect the actual business structure. For example, a sales organization is linked to a company code, and a plant is assigned to a purchasing organization.

2. **Controller Data Configuration**

   o **Material Master:** This involves setting up the material master data, which includes all the information related to materials that a company procures, manufactures, stores, and ships. Parameters such as material type, industry sector, and material group are configured.

- o **Customer and Vendor Controller:** Configuration of customer and vendor master data involves defining attributes such as account groups, payment terms, and partner functions.

3. **Process Configuration**

- o **Procurement Process:** Configuring the procurement process includes setting up procurement types, defining purchase order types, and establishing release procedures. It ensures that procurement activities are streamlined and align with the company's policies.

- o **Sales and Distribution Process:** This involves configuring sales order types, delivery types, billing types, and pricing procedures. Each step in the sales process is mapped to ensure seamless operations from order creation to delivery and billing.

- o **Production Planning:** Configuration involves defining production types, setting up BOMs (Bill of Materials), routing, and work centers. This ensures efficient planning, scheduling, and execution of manufacturing activities.

4. **Financial Configuration**

- o **General Ledger:** This involves setting up the chart of accounts, defining fiscal year variants, and configuring tax settings. The general ledger configuration is crucial for accurate financial reporting and compliance.

- o **Accounts Payable and Receivable:** Configuration includes setting up vendor and customer accounts, payment terms, and dunning procedures. It ensures effective management of payables and receivables.

- o **Controlling:** In the controlling module, cost, profit-center accounting, and internal orders are configured to provide detailed insights into costs and profitability.

5. **Integration Points Configuration**

   o **Cross-Module Configuration:** Many business processes span multiple modules, and configuring these integration points is crucial. For example, the integration between MM (Materials Management) and FI (Financial Accounting) ensures that goods movements impact financial accounts appropriately.

   o **Interface Setup:** Configuring interfaces with external or other SAP systems is part of this step. This ensures seamless data exchange and process continuity across systems.

Testing Configuration

After configuring the SAP modules, thorough testing ensures the setup meets the business requirements. This involves unit testing, integration testing, and user acceptance testing (UAT). Each configuration setting is validated to ensure it works as expected and supports the business processes efficiently.

Custom Development
Need for Custom Development

While SAP provides a comprehensive set of standard functionalities, specific business requirements often cannot be met through standard configuration alone. Custom development involves creating or modifying new functionalities to meet these unique needs. This can include custom reports, interfaces, enhancements, and forms.

Steps in Custom Development

1. **Requirements Gathering**

   o Detailed discussions with business stakeholders to understand the requirements for custom development.

o Document the requirements with precise specifications, including expected outputs, data sources, and user interfaces.

2. **Design and Prototyping**

   o **Technical Design:** Creating a technical design document outlining the custom solution's architecture. This includes data models, integration points, and user interfaces.

   o **Prototyping:** Developing prototypes to demonstrate the concept and gather feedback from stakeholders. Prototyping helps validate the design and identify potential issues early in development.

3. **Development**

   o **Coding:** Writing the code to develop the custom solution using ABAP (Advanced Business Application Programming) for SAP. This can involve creating new programs, modifying standard programs, or developing custom reports.

   o **User Exits and BAdIs:** Implementing user exits and Business Add-Ins (BAdIs) to enhance standard SAP functionality without modifying the standard code. This approach ensures that customizations are maintainable and upgrade-friendly.

   o **Forms and Reports:** Developing custom forms using SAPscript or SmartForms and creating reports using tools like SAP Query or ABAP List Viewer (ALV).

4. **Testing and Validation**

   o **Unit Testing:** Testing individual components of the custom development to ensure they work as expected.

   o **Integration Testing:** Ensuring the custom solutions integrate seamlessly with other SAP modules and external systems.

     o **User Acceptance Testing (UAT):** Conducting UAT with end-users to validate that the custom developments meet their needs and expectations.

5. **Deployment**

     o **Transport Management:** Using SAP's transport management system to move custom developments from the development environment to the quality assurance (QA) and production environments.

     o **Post-Deployment Support:** Providing support to address any issues that arise after deployment and making necessary adjustments based on user feedback.

Best Practices in Custom Development

- **Minimal Customization:** Aim to minimize custom development by leveraging standard SAP functionalities as much as possible. This reduces complexity and maintenance effort.

- **Documentation:** Maintain comprehensive documentation of all custom developments, including technical specifications, design documents, and testing results.

- **Code Reviews:** Conduct regular code reviews to ensure custom developments adhere to coding standards and best practices.

- **Performance Optimization:** Optimize custom code for performance to ensure it does not negatively impact system performance.

Below is a Development Approach from a customer

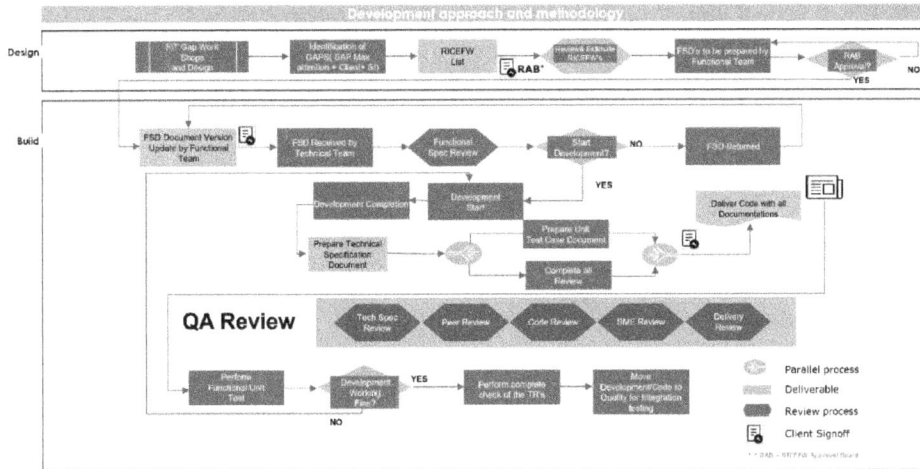

Data Migration and Management

Importance of Data Migration

Data migration is crucial to the SAP implementation process, involving data transfer from legacy systems to the new SAP environment. Accurate and efficient data migration is essential for ensuring data integrity and enabling smooth business operations. Poor data migration can lead to inconsistencies, operational disruptions, and user dissatisfaction.

Steps in Data Migration

1. **Data Assessment and Mapping**

   o **Data Inventory:** Conducting a comprehensive data inventory in the legacy systems. This includes identifying the data types, volumes, and sources.

   o **Data Mapping:** Mapping data from legacy systems to the corresponding data fields in SAP. This involves defining transformation rules to ensure data is correctly formatted and structured for the SAP system.

2. **Data Cleansing**

   o **Data Quality Assessment:** Assessing the quality of data in the legacy systems to identify any inaccuracies, duplicates, or incomplete records.

   o **Data Cleansing Activities:** Performing data cleansing activities to correct errors, remove duplicates, and fill in missing information. Clean data is critical for ensuring the accuracy and reliability of the SAP system.

3. **Data Extraction**

   o **Extraction Methods:** Extracting data from legacy systems using appropriate methods and tools. This can include database queries, ETL (Extract, Transform, Load) tools, or custom extraction programs.

   o **Data Staging:** Staging the extracted data in a temporary storage area to review and validate it before being loaded into SAP.

4. **Data Transformation**

   o **Transformation Rules:** Applying transformation rules to convert data into the required format for SAP. This can involve data type conversions, field mappings, and aggregations.

   o **Validation Checks:** Performing validation checks to ensure the transformed data meets the required standards and business rules.

5. **Data Loading**

   o **Loading Methods:** Loading the transformed data into the SAP system using appropriate loading methods. This can include direct input methods, batch input, or data migration tools like LSMW (Legacy System Migration Workbench) or SAP Data Services.

- o **Loading Strategies:** Developing loading strategies to minimize the impact on business operations. This can include phased loading, parallel processing, and scheduling data loads during off-peak hours.

6. **Data Validation and Reconciliation**

   - o **Validation Processes:** Conducting validation processes to ensure data has been accurately migrated to the SAP system. This involves comparing data in SAP with the source data to identify discrepancies.

   - o **Reconciliation Reports:** Generating reconciliation reports to document the validation results and confirm that data migration has been successful.

7. **Data Maintenance**

   - o **Ongoing Data Quality:** Implement ongoing data quality management processes to ensure data remains accurate and consistent.

   - o **Data Governance:** Establishing data governance practices to define data ownership, standards, and management policies.

Challenges in Data Migration

- **Data Quality Issues:** Poor data quality in legacy systems can lead to inaccurate or incomplete data migration. Data cleansing is essential to address these issues.

- **Complex Data Structures:** Complex data structures and relationships in legacy systems can make data mapping and transformation challenging.

- **Data Volume:** Large data volumes can impact the performance and timing of data migration activities. Effective planning and execution strategies are required to manage large data volumes.

- **System Downtime:** Minimizing system downtime during data migration is critical to ensure business continuity.

Careful scheduling and phased migration approaches can help mitigate this risk.

Tools and Technologies for Data Migration

- **SAP Data Services:** A comprehensive data integration and transformation tool supporting data migration, quality, and governance.

- **LSMW (Legacy System Migration Workbench):** A tool SAP provides for migrating data from legacy systems to SAP. It supports data mapping, transformation, and loading activities.

- **ETL Tools:** Tools like Informatica, Talend, and Microsoft SQL Server Integration Services (SSIS) are commonly used for data extraction, transformation, and loading.

Best Practices in Data Migration

- **Early Planning:** Start planning data migration activities early in the project to ensure adequate data assessment, cleansing, and validation time.

- **Stakeholder Involvement:** Involve business stakeholders in data migration activities to ensure data requirements are accurately captured and validated.

- **Incremental Migration:** Use incremental migration approaches to minimize risk and validate data migration activities in stages.

- **Comprehensive Testing:** Conduct thorough testing and validation of data migration activities to ensure data accuracy and integrity.

- **Continuous Improvement:** Monitor and improve data migration processes to address issues and enhance data quality.

Key Deliverables

Configured System:

- Detailed configuration of the SAP modules based on the business blueprint.
- Documentation of configuration settings and rationale.

Custom Developments:

- Development of custom enhancements, interfaces, reports, and workflows (RICEFW objects).
- Technical specifications for custom developments.
- Unit testing of custom developments to ensure they function as expected.

Data Migration:

- Data migration plan detailing the approach, tools, and processes for migrating data from legacy systems to SAP.
- Data mapping documents outlining the source-to-target data transformation rules.
- Execution of data migration cycles to validate data integrity and accuracy.
- Data migration test results and sign-off.

Integration Testing:

- Test scripts and scenarios for integration testing, ensuring end-to-end business processes function across different SAP modules and external systems.
- Execution of integration tests and documentation of test results.
- Resolution of integration issues identified during testing.

User Acceptance Testing (UAT):

- The UAT plan defines the scope, objectives, and approach for user acceptance testing.
- Development of UAT test cases and scenarios based on business requirements.

- Execution of UAT by end-users and documentation of feedback and test results.
- Resolution of defects and issues identified during UAT.

Training Materials & Training:

- Development of end-user training materials, including user manuals, quick reference guides, and training presentations.
- Deliver end-user training sessions to ensure users are comfortable with the new system.

Cutover Plan:

- Detailed cutover plan outlining the activities, sequence, and responsibilities for transitioning from the legacy system to the new SAP system.
- Executing mock cutover rehearsals to validate the plan and address potential issues.

Technical Documentation:

- Comprehensive technical documentation covering system configuration, custom developments, data migration, integration points, and testing results.
- Technical architecture diagrams and infrastructure documentation.

System Testing and Validation:

- Execution of various types of testing, including unit testing, integration testing, regression testing, performance testing, and security testing.
- Documentation of test cases, test results, and issue logs.

Issue Resolution and Change Management:

- Tracking and resolving issues and defects identified during the build and test phases.
- Management of change requests and updates to the system configuration and custom developments.

The Project Realization Phase is a critical stage in the SAP implementation process, where the system is configured, custom developments are created, and data is migrated to the new environment. Each activity requires careful planning, execution, and validation to ensure that the SAP system meets the business requirements and supports efficient operations. By following best practices and engaging stakeholders throughout the process, organizations can achieve a successful SAP implementation and realize significant benefits from their investment.

Chapter 6: Go Live Preparation or Deploy Phase

Deploy Phase

- **Objective**: To transition the solution to the production environment and ensure it is fully operational.
- **Activities**: Activities in this phase include final data migration, user training, system cutover, and go-live support. The focus is on ensuring a smooth transition with minimal disruption to business operations. Post-go-live support is also provided to address any issues that arise after deployment.
- **Deliverables**: Go-live plan, trained users, migrated data, and operational SAP system in the production environment.

The go-live phase of an SAP implementation is the culmination of months, if not years, of planning, development, and testing. It marks the transition from project to operational mode, where the SAP system becomes the organization's record system. This chapter provides detailed guidance on final preparations, cutover planning and execution, and managing the go-live process to ensure a smooth and successful transition.

Final Preparations

Overview of Final Preparations
Final preparations involve completing all necessary activities before the go-live date to ensure the system, users, and support teams are ready for the transition. This phase is critical for identifying and mitigating any last-minute issues that could impact the success of the go-live.

Key Activities in Final Preparations
1. **System Readiness:**
    o **System Testing:** Conduct final rounds of system testing, including regression testing, performance testing, and stress testing, to ensure the system operates correctly under expected workloads.
    o **Data Migration Validation:** Verify that all data has been accurately migrated from legacy systems to the SAP system. Perform data validation checks to ensure data integrity and completeness.
    o **Configuration Verification:** Review and verify all system configurations to ensure they align with business requirements and processes.
2. **User Readiness:**
    o **Training Completion:** Ensure all end-users have completed the necessary training programs and are comfortable using the SAP system.
    o **User Acceptance Testing (UAT):** Conduct final UAT sessions to confirm that the system meets user expectations and business requirements.
3. **Support Readiness:**
    o **Support Team Training:** Provide comprehensive training to the support team, including help desk personnel and system administrators, to prepare them for post-go-live support.
    o **Support Processes:** Establish and document support processes, including incident management, problem resolution, and escalation procedures.
4. **Communication:**
    o **Go-Live Announcements:** Communicate the go-live date and key milestones to all stakeholders, including employees, customers, and partners.

o **User Guides and Resources:** Distribute user guides, quick reference materials, and other resources to assist users during the transition.

Best Practices for Final Preparations

1. **Thorough Testing:** Conduct exhaustive testing to identify and resolve issues before going live.
2. **Comprehensive Training:** Ensure all users and support personnel are adequately trained and prepared for the new system.
3. **Clear Communication:** Maintain clear and open communication with all stakeholders to keep them informed and engaged.
4. **Risk Mitigation:** Identify potential risks and develop mitigation plans to address them proactively.

Below is a sample from a project that used the Go Live Readiness check across ten dimensions.

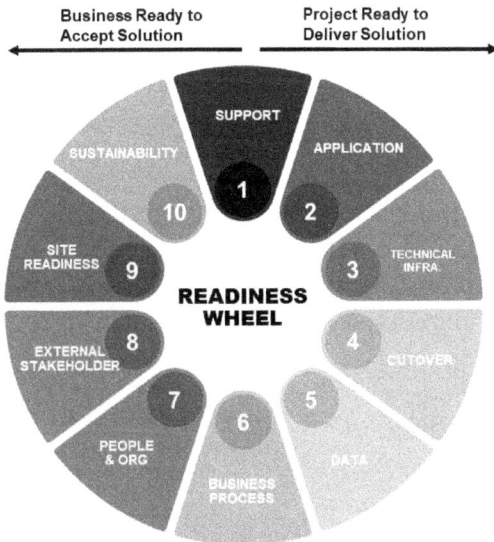

In this particular example, the project Go Live readiness was checked against the following dimensions:

- Support Readiness (Support teams in place and minimum levels of KT completed, business staffing in place)

- Application Readiness (Testing results, defects volumes meet maximum threshold)
- Technical Readiness (Environmental stability, system performance service levels)
- Cutover / Deployment Readiness (cutover plan tested, dress rehearsal executed with accepted results)
- Data Readiness (data quality, conversion error rate, and conversion window)
- Business Process (business processes verified/practiced, procedures updated as applicable, Controls & Financial Reporting Readiness SOX compliance met, internal controls verified by audit, month-end close practiced)
- People & Org (Business Readiness, change impacts understood, proficiency levels)
- External Stakeholder (Regulatory, Financial/Investor, customers, suppliers and other external stakeholder communications complete)
- Site Readiness (physical and virtual Hypercare and support sites prepared)
- Sustainability (transition to long-term support operating model in place)

Cutover Planning and Execution

Overview of Cutover Planning

Cutover planning involves defining and coordinating the activities required to transition from the legacy to the SAP system. This phase is critical for ensuring a smooth and controlled switch-over, minimizing disruption to business operations.

Critical Components of Cutover Planning

1. **Cutover Strategy:**
   - **Big Bang vs. Phased:** Decide whether to adopt a Big Bang approach (all systems go live simultaneously) or a phased approach (systems go live in stages).
   - **Weekend vs. Weekday:** Determine the optimal time for the cutover, considering business operations and the need to minimize disruption.

2. **Cutover Plan:**
   o **Detailed Tasks:** Develop a detailed cutover plan that outlines all tasks to be performed, including data migration, system configuration, user access setup, and system validation.
   o **Roles and Responsibilities:** Assign clear roles and responsibilities for each task, ensuring all team members understand their duties.
3. **Data Migration:**
   o **Final Data Load:** Plan the final data load from legacy systems to the SAP system, ensuring that all data is accurately transferred and validated.
   o **Data Reconciliation:** Perform data reconciliation to verify the accuracy and completeness of the migrated data.
4. **System Configuration:**
   o **Final Configurations:** Implement final system configurations, including security settings, user roles, and access permissions.
   o **System Validation:** Conduct system validation to ensure all configurations are correct and the system is ready for use.
5. **Communication:**
   o **Cutover Schedule:** Communicate the cutover schedule to all stakeholders, including key milestones and expected downtime.
   o **Progress Updates:** Provide regular progress updates throughout the cutover process to keep stakeholders informed.

Steps in Cutover Execution

1. **Pre-Cutover Activities:**
   o **Data Backup:** Perform a full backup of all systems and data to ensure recovery in case of any issues.
   o **System Freeze:** Implement a system freeze to prevent any changes to the legacy system during the cutover process.
2. **Cutover Activities:**
   o **Data Migration:** Execute the final tasks, ensuring data is accurately transferred and validated.

- o **System Configuration:** Complete any remaining system configurations and validate the settings.
- o **System Testing:** Conduct final system testing to ensure all components function correctly.

3. **Post-Cutover Activities:**
   - o **System Validation:** Perform comprehensive system validation to ensure the SAP system is fully operational and meets business requirements.
   - o **User Access:** Enable user access to the SAP system and verify that all users can log in and perform their tasks.
   - o **Data Reconciliation:** Conduct data reconciliation to verify the accuracy and completeness of the migrated data.

Below is a visual of the Cutover Strategy

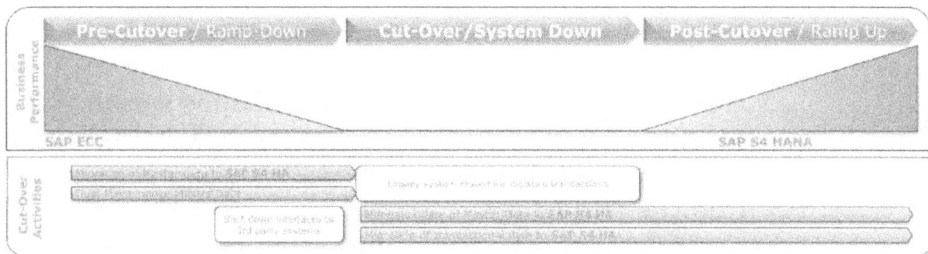

Best Practices for Cutover Planning and Execution

1. **Detailed Planning:** Develop a detailed cutover plan that outlines all tasks, roles, and responsibilities.
2. **Clear Communication:** Communicate the cutover plan and schedule to all stakeholders to ensure alignment and readiness.
3. **Risk Management:** Identify potential risks and develop mitigation strategies to address them proactively.
4. **Backup and Recovery:** Implement robust backup and recovery procedures to ensure data integrity and system availability.

Managing Go-Live

Overview of Managing Go-Live

Managing the go-live process involves overseeing the transition to the new SAP system and ensuring that all aspects of the system are functioning correctly. This phase requires close monitoring, immediate issue resolution, and ongoing support to ensure a smooth transition.

Key Activities in Managing Go-Live

1. **Monitoring and Support:**
   - **Go-Live Command Center:** Establish a go-live command center to monitor the system and coordinate support activities.
   - **Real-Time Monitoring:** Implement real-time monitoring tools to track system performance, user activity, and data integrity.

2. **Issue Resolution:**
   - **Incident Management:** Set up an incident management process to quickly identify, prioritize, and resolve issues.
   - **Support Teams:** Ensure that support teams are available around the clock to address any issues.

3. **User Support:**
   - **Help Desk:** Establish a help desk to provide immediate assistance to users experiencing issues or needing guidance.
   - **User Guides:** Distribute user guides, quick reference materials, and other resources to assist users.

4. **Communication:**
   - **Status Updates:** Provide regular status updates to stakeholders on the progress of the go-live process.
   - **Feedback Mechanisms:** Implement feedback mechanisms to gather input from users and address their concerns.

5. **Post-Go-Live Activities:**
   - **Stabilization Period:** Plan a stabilization period during which the system is closely monitored and any issues are addressed promptly.
   - **Performance Optimization:** Conduct performance optimization activities to ensure the system operates efficiently.

o **Continuous Improvement:** Gather user feedback and improve the system based on input.

Best Practices for Managing Go-Live

1. **Proactive Monitoring:** Implement real-time monitoring tools to track system performance and quickly identify issues.
2. **Robust Support:** Ensure that support teams are available 24/7 to provide immediate assistance and resolve issues.
3. **Clear Communication:** Maintain open and transparent communication with all stakeholders throughout the go-live process.
4. **User Feedback:** Gather feedback from users to identify areas for improvement and address their concerns promptly.
5. **Continuous Improvement:** Use feedback and performance data to improve the system and enhance user satisfaction continuously.

Case Studies and Examples

Case Study 1: Manufacturing Company Go-Live
Overview: A manufacturing company implemented SAP across its global operations. The go-live involved transitioning from multiple legacy systems to a unified SAP system.
Approach:
- **Final Preparations:** Conducted extensive system testing, completed user training, and established support processes.
- **Cutover Planning:** Developed a detailed cutover plan with a big bang approach, ensuring all tasks and responsibilities were clearly defined.
- **Managing Go-Live:** Established a go-live command center, implemented real-time monitoring, and provided robust user support.
Outcome:
- **Smooth Transition:** Achieved a smooth transition with minimal disruption to business operations.
- **Issue Resolution:** Quickly resolved any issues during the go-live period.
- **User Satisfaction:** Improved user satisfaction through practical training and support.

Case Study 2: Retail Chain Go-Live

Overview: A retail chain implemented SAP across its stores and distribution centers. The go-live involved a phased rollout to manage the transition and minimize disruption.

Approach:

- **Final Preparations:** Completed user training, conducted UAT, and established support teams.
- **Cutover Planning:** Developed a phased cutover plan, rolling out the system in stages across different regions.
- **Managing Go-Live:** Monitored the system closely, provided user support, and gathered feedback to improve the system.

Outcome:

- **Successful Rollout:** Successfully rolled out the system across all stores and distribution centers.
- **Improved Efficiency:** Enhanced operational efficiency through streamlined processes and real-time data access.
- **User Engagement:** Increased user engagement and satisfaction through continuous support and feedback.

Conclusion

Go-live preparation is a critical phase in the SAP implementation, requiring meticulous planning, coordination, and execution. By conducting thorough final preparations, developing and executing a detailed cutover plan, and effectively managing the go-live process, organizations can ensure a smooth and successful transition to the new SAP system. Adhering to best practices in these areas helps minimize disruption, address issues promptly, and achieve the desired business outcomes.

Chapter 7: Post Go Live Support & Hypercare, or Run Phase

Run Phase

- **Objective:** To operate and continuously improve the SAP solution.
- **Activities:** This phase encompasses the ongoing support and optimization of the SAP system. It includes monitoring system performance, managing incidents, applying updates, and identifying opportunities for improvement.
- **Deliverables:** Stable and optimized SAP environment, continuous improvement plan, and ongoing support documentation.

After the go-live phase, the focus shifts to ensuring the stability and performance of the new SAP system, providing ongoing support and maintenance, and facilitating knowledge transfer to the internal teams. This chapter explores the stabilization phase, continuing support and maintenance, and the importance of knowledge transfer in ensuring a smooth and sustainable SAP implementation.

Stabilization Phase

Overview of the Stabilization Phase

The stabilization phase, also known as the Hypercare phase, immediately follows the go-live of an SAP system. This period is crucial for addressing any issues arising as users begin working with the new system, ensuring that it operates smoothly, and confirming that it meets the business requirements.

Key Activities in the Stabilization Phase

1. **Intensive Monitoring:**
   o **System Performance:** Monitor system performance closely to identify and address speed, responsiveness, and functionality issues.
   o **User Activity:** Track user activity to ensure users can perform their tasks without encountering errors or delays.
   o **Data Integrity:** Verify the integrity of data being processed and stored in the system, ensuring no data loss or corruption.

2. **Issue Resolution:**
   o **Incident Management:** Set up an incident management process to quickly identify, log, and prioritize issues reported by users.
   o **Quick Response:** Ensure that support teams are prepared to respond quickly to issues, providing immediate fixes or workarounds.
   o **Root Cause Analysis:** Conduct root cause analysis for recurring issues to identify underlying problems and implement permanent solutions.

3. **User Support:**
   o **Help Desk:** Establish a help desk to provide users with immediate assistance and guidance as they navigate the new system.
   o **User Training:** Offer refresher training sessions and workshops to help users become more comfortable and proficient with the system.
   o **Feedback Collection:** Gather feedback from users to identify pain points and areas for improvement.

4. **System Adjustments:**
   - **Configuration Tweaks:** Make necessary adjustments to system configurations to better align with user needs and business processes.
   - **Performance Optimization:** Optimize system settings and processes to enhance performance and efficiency.

Below is a visual of Hypercare

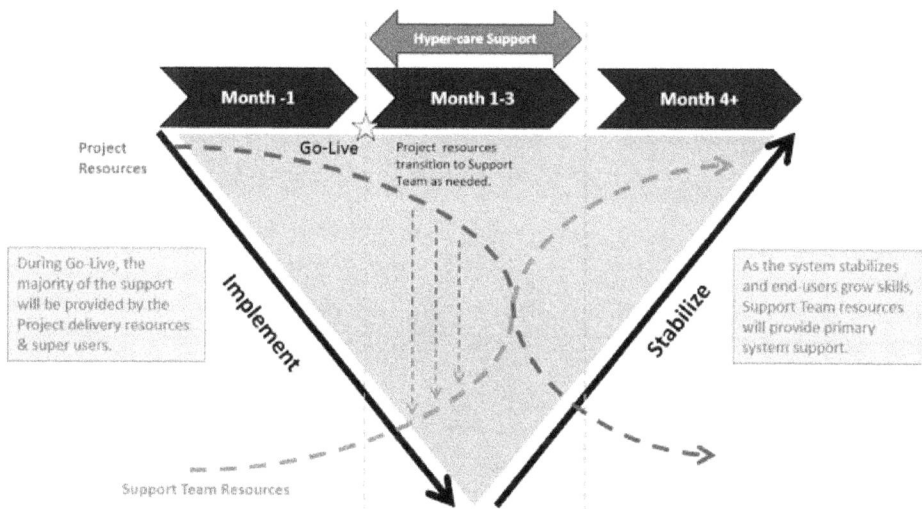

During Go-Live, the majority of the support will be provided by the Project delivery resources & super users.

As the system stabilizes and end-users grow skills, Support Team resources will provide primary system support.

Project resources transition to Support Team as needed.

Best Practices for the Stabilization Phase

1. **Define Hypercare exit criteria.**
2. **Proactive Monitoring:** Implement robust monitoring tools and practices to identify and address issues before they impact users.
3. **Clear Communication:** Maintain open lines of communication with users, providing regular updates on system status and issue resolution progress. Communicate expectations of the Hypercare period with stakeholders.
4. Provide training for new processes, interim processes, and expected challenges to prepare trainers for end-user training delivery and training of "floor walkers" and super users.

Familiarize the project team with Hypercare management tools and methodologies.

5. **Dedicated Support Teams:** Assign dedicated support teams to handle stabilization activities, ensuring quick response and resolution.
6. **Comprehensive Documentation:** Document all issues, resolutions, and adjustments made during the stabilization phase for future reference.
7. **Continuous Improvement:** Use feedback and data collected during stabilization to improve system performance and user satisfaction.

Below is an example of the Hypercare model used for a client that is composed of multiple levels of support:

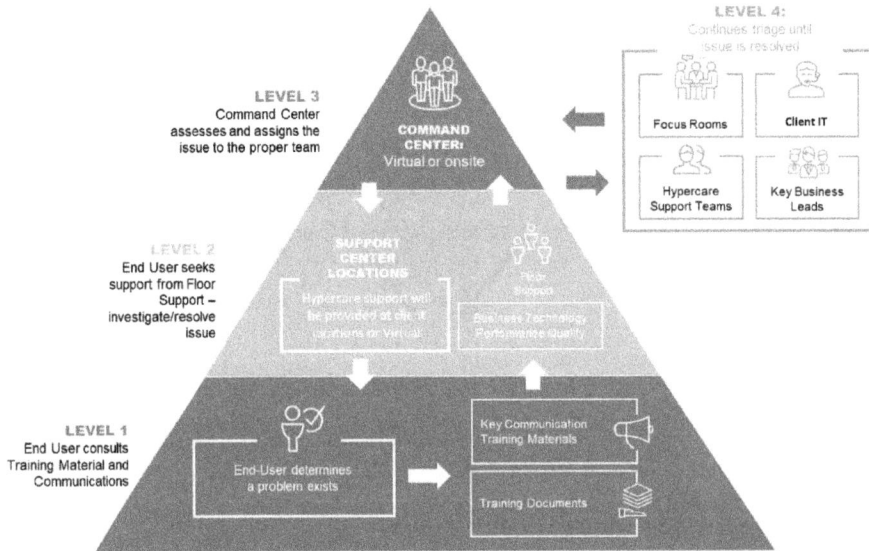

Hypercare Duration

One common question that is asked is how long Hypercare should last. The duration of the Hypercare phase for an SAP project implementation typically varies based on the complexity and scale of the project, but it generally lasts between **4 to 12 weeks**. Here are some considerations that can affect the length of the Hypercare period:

- **Project Size and Complexity**: Larger and more complex projects may require a more extended Hypercare phase to ensure all aspects of the system are functioning correctly.
- **User Adoption and Training**: If users need additional time to adapt to the new system and require more extensive training, the Hypercare period might be extended.
- **System Stability**: Ensuring the system is stable, and all major issues are resolved before ending Hypercare is crucial. If there are significant issues, the Hypercare phase may be prolonged.
- **Business Cycles**: Aligning the Hypercare period with business cycles (e.g., end-of-quarter and peak business periods) can influence the duration.

While the standard duration is around 4 to 12 weeks, assessing the project's specific needs and circumstances is essential to determine the appropriate length of the Hypercare phase. Hypercare should, at minimum, close one complete cycle of financial close activity.

Ongoing Support and Maintenance

Overview of Ongoing Support and Maintenance
Ongoing support and maintenance are essential to ensure the long-term success and sustainability of the SAP system. This involves regular system updates, issue resolution, performance monitoring, and user support to keep the system running smoothly and efficiently.

Critical Components of Ongoing Support and Maintenance

1. **Help Desk Support:**
   o **User Assistance:** Provide users with ongoing assistance through a dedicated help desk, addressing queries and resolving issues promptly.
   o **Incident Management:** Maintain an incident management system to log, track, and prioritize issues reported by users.
2. **System Monitoring:**
   o **Performance Monitoring:** Continuously monitor system performance to identify and address performance-related issues.

- o **Security Monitoring:** Implement security monitoring to detect and prevent unauthorized access, data breaches, and other security threats.

3. **Regular Updates and Patches:**
   - o **Software Updates:** Keep the SAP system up-to-date with the latest software updates and patches released by SAP.
   - o **Testing:** Conduct thorough testing of updates and patches in a non-production environment before applying them to the live system.

4. **Preventive Maintenance:**
   - o **System Health Checks:** Perform regular system health checks to identify and address potential issues proactively.
   - o **Database Maintenance:** Ensure that databases are regularly maintained, including tasks such as indexing, cleanup, and optimization.

5. **Performance Optimization:**
   - o **System Tuning:** Continuously tune system settings and configurations to enhance performance and efficiency.
   - o **Capacity Planning:** Monitor system usage and plan for future capacity needs to ensure the system can handle increased workloads.

6. **User Training and Support:**
   - o **Ongoing Training:** Provide ongoing training opportunities for users to enhance their SAP system skills and knowledge.
   - o **User Guides and Documentation:** Maintain and update user guides, manuals, and other documentation to support users.

Best Practices for Ongoing Support and Maintenance

1. **Proactive Approach:** Adopt a proactive approach to support and maintenance, identifying and addressing potential issues before they impact users.
2. **Regular Updates:** Stay current with SAP updates and patches, applying them promptly to ensure the system remains secure and efficient.

3. **Comprehensive Monitoring:** Implement comprehensive monitoring tools and practices to track system performance, security, and user activity.
4. **User-Centric Support:** Focus on providing user-centric support, ensuring users have the resources and assistance to perform their tasks effectively.
5. **Continuous Improvement:** Use data and feedback from support and maintenance activities to improve system performance and user satisfaction.

Knowledge Transfer

Overview of Knowledge Transfer

Knowledge transfer transfers critical information, skills, and expertise from the implementation team to the internal team responsible for managing and supporting the SAP system. This ensures the internal team is well-equipped to maintain and enhance the system after completing the implementation project.

Key Components of Knowledge Transfer

1. **Documentation:**
   o **System Documentation:** Provide comprehensive documentation of the SAP system, including configurations, customizations, integrations, and workflows.
   o **Process Documentation:** Document key business processes and how they are implemented in the SAP system.
2. **Training Programs:**
   o **Technical Training:** Offer technical training programs for the internal IT team, covering system administration, configuration, and troubleshooting.
   o **Functional Training:** Provide functional training for business users, focusing on how to use the system to perform their daily tasks.

3. **Workshops and Hands-On Training:**
   - o **Workshops:** Conduct workshops to provide hands-on training and practical experience with the SAP system.
   - o **Mentorship:** Implement a mentorship program where experienced team members mentor new users and administrators.
4. **Knowledge Repositories:**
   - o **Knowledge Base:** Create a knowledge base with articles, FAQs, and best practices to support users and administrators.
   - o **Collaboration Tools:** Use tools like wikis, forums, and document-sharing platforms to facilitate knowledge sharing.
5. **Support Transition:**
   - o **Shadowing:** Allow the internal team to shadow the implementation team during stabilization to gain practical experience.
   - o **Gradual Transition:** Implement a gradual transition of responsibilities from the implementation team to the internal team, ensuring a smooth handover.

Best Practices for Knowledge Transfer

1. **Comprehensive Documentation:** Ensure all system configurations, customizations, and processes are thoroughly documented and accessible to the internal team.
2. **Structured Training:** Develop structured training programs that cover the SAP system's technical and functional aspects.
3. **Hands-On Experience:** Provide opportunities for hands-on experience through workshops, shadowing, and mentorship programs.
4. **Ongoing Learning:** Encourage ongoing learning and knowledge sharing within the organization.
5. **Clear Communication:** Maintain clear and open communication between the implementation and internal teams to ensure a smooth knowledge transfer process.

Below is an example of a Knowledge Transfer that was performed with a client:

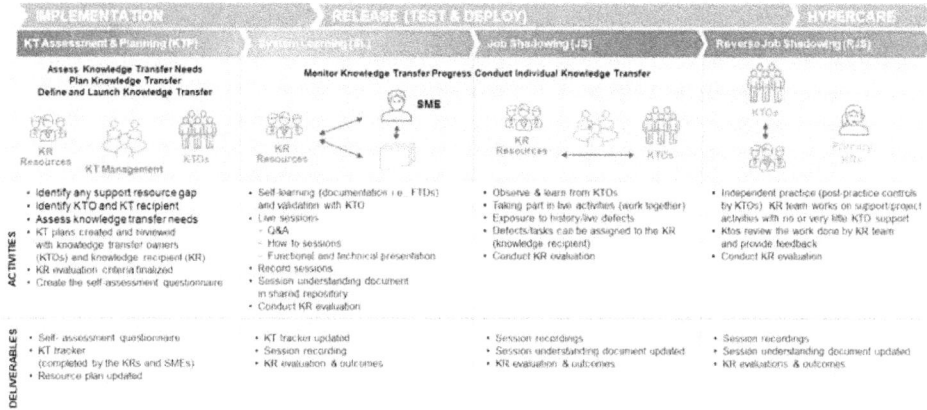

Case Studies and Examples

Case Study 1: Global Pharmaceutical Company
Overview: A global pharmaceutical company implemented SAP across its operations. The post-go-live support and hypercare phase focused on ensuring system stability, providing ongoing support, and transferring knowledge to the internal team.
Approach:
- **Stabilization Phase:** Conducted intensive monitoring, provided immediate issue resolution, and offered refresher training sessions.
- **Ongoing Support:** Established a help desk, performed regular system updates, and conducted preventive maintenance.
- **Knowledge Transfer:** Provided comprehensive documentation, conducted technical and functional training programs, and implemented a mentorship program.

Outcome:
- **Smooth Transition:** Achieved a smooth transition with minimal disruption to business operations.
- **Enhanced Support:** Improved support capabilities through effective knowledge transfer and ongoing training.
- **Sustainable Operations:** Ensured the long-term sustainability of the SAP system through proactive maintenance and continuous improvement.

Case Study 2: Retail Chain

Overview: A retail chain implemented SAP across its stores and distribution centers. The focus was stabilizing the system, providing ongoing support, and ensuring knowledge transfer to internal teams.

Approach:

- **Stabilization Phase:** Monitored system performance, promptly addressed user issues, and optimized system.
- **Ongoing Support:** Provided user assistance through a help desk, applied regular updates, and optimized system performance.
- **Knowledge Transfer:** Developed comprehensive documentation, offered hands-on training workshops, and created a knowledge base.

Outcome:

- **Improved Efficiency:** Enhanced operational efficiency through proactive support and maintenance.
- **Empowered Team:** Empowered the internal team with the knowledge and skills needed to manage the SAP system effectively.
- **Continuous Improvement:** Achieved continuous improvement through regular feedback and system optimization.

Conclusion

The post-go-live support and Hypercare phase is critical for ensuring the stability and success of the SAP system after implementation. By focusing on the stabilization phase, providing ongoing support and maintenance, and facilitating effective knowledge transfer, organizations can achieve a smooth transition, maintain system performance, and empower their internal teams to manage and optimize the SAP system. Adhering to best practices in these areas ensures that the SAP system delivers long-term value and supports the organization's strategic objectives.

PART C – ELEMENTS OF SAP IMPLEMENTATION

Chapter 8: Customization and Enhancements

Customization and enhancements are integral to the SAP implementation process, enabling organizations to tailor the system to their unique business needs and processes. This chapter delves into how businesses can effectively customize SAP, utilize enhancements and exits, and adhere to best practices for custom development.

Customizing SAP for Business Needs

Understanding Customization

Customization involves configuring the SAP system to align with an organization's requirements and processes. While SAP provides a wide range of standard functionalities that cater to everyday business processes, customization ensures that the system fully supports a business's unique aspects.

Types of Customizations

1. Configuration Customization

   o Organizational Structures: Defining company codes, plants, sales organizations, and other organizational units to reflect the business hierarchy.

   o Master Data Configuration: Setting up master data elements such as customer, vendor, material masters, and chart of accounts.

   o Process Customization: Adjusting processes like order-to-cash, procure-to-pay, and production planning to align with business workflows.

2. User Interface Customization

   o Screen Layouts: Modifying screen layouts to include or exclude specific fields based on user roles and requirements.

- o Personalization: Users can personalize their dashboards and reports to quickly access frequently used functionalities.

3. Reports and Analytics Customization

- o Custom Reports: Developing custom reports to meet specific reporting requirements that standard SAP reports do not cover.

- o KPIs and Dashboards: Setting up key performance indicators (KPIs) and dashboards to provide real-time insights into business performance.

Steps in Customizing SAP

1. Requirement Gathering

- o Engage stakeholders to understand their specific needs and requirements.

- o Document the customization requirements, including desired functionalities, process flows, and reporting needs.

2. Configuration and Setup

- o Use the SAP Implementation Guide (IMG) to navigate the configuration settings.

- o Define organizational structures, set up master data, and configure business processes per the requirements.

3. Validation and Testing

- o Conduct thorough testing to ensure the customized settings meet the business requirements.

- o Perform unit, integration, and user acceptance testing to validate the customizations.

4. Documentation and Training

- o Document the customization settings and changes made to the standard SAP configuration.

- o Provide training to end-users to ensure they understand how to use the customized functionalities.

Using SAP Enhancements and Exits

Introduction to Enhancements and Exits

SAP provides several mechanisms to enhance and extend its standard functionalities without modifying the core code. Enhancements and exits allow businesses to add custom logic or functionality to SAP standard processes, ensuring the system meets specific business needs.

Types of Enhancements and Exits

1. User Exits

- o Definition: User exits are predefined points in SAP standard programs where custom code can be inserted. They are implemented using function modules and can be used to add or modify standard SAP functionality.

- o Example: Adding custom validation logic during the sales order creation process.

2. Customer Exits

- o Definition: Customer exits are similar to user exits but are implemented using function modules that are part of the SAP enhancement framework. They are more structured and easier to manage.

- o Example: Enhancing the SAP standard screen to include additional fields.

3. Business Add-Ins (BAdIs)

   o Definition: BAdIs are more advanced enhancement techniques that allow multiple implementations. They provide greater flexibility and can be used to enhance standard SAP applications and processes.

   o Example: Modifying the behavior of the materials management module to accommodate specific business rules.

4. Enhancement Points

   o Definition: Enhancement points are locations in the SAP standard code where custom code can be inserted using the enhancement framework. They are used to enhance or modify standard processes without changing the original code.

   o Example: Adding custom logic to the SAP standard purchase order approval process.

Steps to Implement Enhancements and Exits

1. Identify Enhancement Opportunities

   o Analyze business processes to identify areas where enhancements are needed.

   o Review SAP standard processes and determine the appropriate enhancement or exit point.

2. Develop Custom Logic

   o Write the custom code or logic needed to achieve the desired functionality.

   o Use SAP's development tools, such as ABAP Workbench, to create and test the custom code.

3. Implement Enhancements

   o Implement the custom logic using user exits, customer exits, BAdIs, or enhancement points.

      o Ensure that the enhancements are implemented in a way that does not affect the standard SAP functionality.

4. Test and Validate

      o Conduct thorough testing to ensure that the enhancements work as expected.

      o Perform unit, integration, and user acceptance testing to validate the custom enhancements.

5. Documentation and Deployment

      o Document the enhancements and custom logic for future reference.

      o Deploy the enhancements to the production environment and provide support as needed.

Best Practices for Custom Development

Minimizing Customization

While customization is sometimes necessary, minimizing it to avoid complexity and maintenance challenges is best. Rely on standard SAP functionalities as much as possible and only customize when necessary.

Adhering to SAP Standards

Ensure all custom developments adhere to SAP's coding standards and best practices. This includes using naming conventions, following coding guidelines, and documenting the code thoroughly.

Comprehensive Documentation

Maintain detailed documentation for all custom developments, including technical specifications, design documents, and testing results. Documentation is essential for future maintenance and troubleshooting.

Regular Code Reviews

Conduct regular code reviews to ensure that custom developments meet quality standards and not introduce performance issues. Code reviews help identify potential problems early and ensure the code is maintainable.

Performance Optimization

Optimize custom code for performance to ensure it does not negatively impact the overall system performance. This includes efficient database queries, proper indexing, and minimizing resource-intensive operations.

Change Management

Implement a robust change management process to manage custom developments. This includes tracking changes, managing versions, and ensuring that changes are tested thoroughly before deployment.

Testing and Quality Assurance

Ensure comprehensive testing and quality assurance for all custom developments. This includes unit, integration, and user acceptance testing to validate that the customizations meet business requirements and function correctly.

Continuous Improvement

Adopt a continuous improvement approach to custom development. Regularly review and refine customizations to ensure they remain relevant and practical as business needs evolve.

Leveraging SAP Tools

Utilize SAP's development tools and frameworks for custom development. Tools like ABAP Workbench, SAP Web IDE, and SAP Cloud Platform provide robust environments for developing, testing, and deploying custom solutions.

Training and Knowledge Transfer

Provide training and knowledge transfer to ensure the development team is well-versed in SAP customization techniques and best practices. Continuous learning and development help maintain high standards in custom development.

Aligning with Business Goals

Ensure all custom developments align with the organization's strategic goals and objectives. Customizations should add value to the business and support its mission and vision.

Security Considerations

Incorporate security considerations into custom development. Ensure that custom code does not introduce vulnerabilities and meets data security and compliance requirements.

Scalability and Flexibility

Design custom developments with scalability and flexibility in mind. Custom solutions should be able to handle increased workloads and adapt to changing business needs without requiring extensive rework.

Integration with Standard Processes

Ensure that custom developments integrate seamlessly with standard SAP processes. This minimizes disruption and ensures that custom solutions complement the standard functionality.

End-User Involvement

Involve end-users in the development process to ensure that custom solutions meet their needs and expectations. End-user feedback is invaluable for refining and validating customizations.

Monitoring and Maintenance

Implement monitoring and maintenance processes to ensure custom developments function correctly and efficiently. Regularly review and update custom solutions to address any issues and improve performance.

Collaboration and Communication

Foster collaboration and communication between the development team, business stakeholders, and end-users. Clear communication ensures that everyone is aligned and that custom developments meet business needs.

Leveraging Industry Best Practices

Stay updated with industry best practices and incorporate them into custom development processes. This helps ensure that custom solutions are innovative, efficient, and effective.

Project Management

Use effective project management techniques to plan, execute, and monitor custom development projects. This includes setting clear objectives, defining timelines, and managing resources to ensure successful outcomes.

Post-Implementation Support

Provide post-implementation support to address any issues after custom solutions are deployed. This ensures a smooth transition and helps maintain user satisfaction.

Customization and enhancements are critical for tailoring the SAP system to meet specific business needs. By following best practices, organizations can ensure that custom developments add value, support business processes, and integrate seamlessly with standard SAP functionalities. Proper planning, execution, and monitoring of customization efforts help achieve successful SAP implementations and drive significant business improvements.

When Custom Becomes Critical: A Lesson in Balancing Innovation with Integrity

I still remember a pivotal moment during a global S/4HANA rollout for a manufacturing client operating across 12 countries. The business was adamant about replicating their legacy rebate calculation engine—an intricate, homegrown system with decades of exceptions, overrides, and manual checks. Standard SAP rebate functionality could cover 80% of their use cases, but the remaining 20% became the battleground for customization. The business insisted that without a carbon copy of the old logic, financial reconciliation would collapse. As delivery director, I knew that giving in to every customization request risked turning a modern ERP into a legacy trap. After a series of structured Fit-to-Standard workshops and simulations, we negotiated a hybrid approach: leverage standard rebate groups with a BAdI enhancement for edge cases, paired with change management training to modernize the process logic. We saved six months of unnecessary custom code and reduced technical debt without sacrificing compliance.

Another instance taught me the high cost of customization without governance. In an earlier project, I inherited an implementation where the previous team had allowed dozens of user exits to be activated without documentation or central review. What looked like a simple upgrade turned into a minefield—every enhancement had dependencies buried in core processes, and regression testing became a nightmare. We had to pause the project and build a "custom object rescue squad" to catalog, analyze, and validate every enhancement. That experience reinforced a hard truth: in SAP, custom code is not free—it's an ongoing liability unless it's reviewed, justified, and aligned with business value. From that point on, I made code review boards a standard governance checkpoint in every S/4 program I led.

Chapter 9: WRICEF Objects

Introduction to WRICEF Objects

WRICEF stands for Workflows, Reports, Interfaces, Conversions, Enhancements, and Forms. These objects are crucial components of SAP implementations, enabling organizations to tailor the SAP system to their unique business requirements. Understanding and effectively managing WRICEF objects is essential for a successful SAP project. This chapter provides a detailed overview of each WRICEF component, discusses best practices for their development and implementation, and explores their critical role in ensuring a tailored and effective SAP solution.

Workflows

Overview of Workflows

SAP business workflows automate processes by coordinating tasks, data, and people. They ensure processes are executed consistently and efficiently, reducing manual effort and improving productivity. SAP Business Workflow allows the design and implementation of complex workflows that integrate various SAP modules.

Critical Components of SAP Workflows

1. Tasks: Individual units of work assigned to users or roles.

2. Events: Triggers that initiate workflows based on specific conditions or actions.

3. Agents: Users or roles responsible for executing tasks within the workflow.

4. Rules: Define conditions and logic for workflow execution.

5. Containers: Data storage elements used to pass information between tasks.

Best Practices for Workflows

1. Simplify Workflows: Keep workflows as simple as possible. Complex workflows are more complicated to manage and maintain.

2. Reuse Standard Workflows: Leverage SAP's standard workflows whenever possible to reduce development time and effort.

3. Clear Documentation: Document each workflow step, including tasks, events, agents, and rules.

4. Testing: Rigorously test workflows to ensure they function correctly and handle all possible scenarios.

5. User Training: Train end-users on workflow usage and monitor their performance to ensure efficiency.

Reports

Overview of Reports

SAP reports provide critical insights into business data, enabling decision-makers to analyze performance, identify trends, and make informed decisions. SAP offers various tools for creating reports, including SAP Query, ABAP List Viewer (ALV), and SAP BusinessObjects.

Types of Reports

1. Standard Reports: Predefined reports provided by SAP to cover everyday business needs.

2. Custom Reports: Tailored reports developed to meet specific business requirements.

Best Practices for Reports

1. Define Clear Objectives: Clearly define the purpose and objectives of each report.

2. Leverage Standard Reports: Use standard reports to save development time.

3. Optimize Performance: Ensure reports are optimized for performance to handle large data volumes efficiently.

4. User-Friendly Design: Design reports to be user-friendly, with intuitive layouts and clear visuals.

5. Data Accuracy: Validate data accuracy by cross-referencing report outputs with source data.

Interfaces

Overview of Interfaces

Interfaces enable communication between SAP and external systems, facilitating seamless data exchange and integration. Interfaces can be inbound (data coming into SAP) or outbound (data going out of SAP).

Types of Interfaces

1. File-Based Interfaces: Exchange data using flat files or XML files.

2. Real-Time Interfaces: Use middleware or APIs to enable real-time data exchange.

3. Batch Interfaces: Transfer data in batches at scheduled intervals.

Best Practices for Interfaces

1. Standard Protocols: Use standard protocols (e.g., HTTP, FTP, SOAP, REST) to ensure compatibility and ease of integration.

2. Data Validation: Implement robust data validation to ensure data integrity during transfer.

3. Error Handling: Develop comprehensive error-handling mechanisms to manage failures and retries.

4. Performance Optimization: Optimize interfaces for performance to minimize latency and ensure timely data exchange.

5. Documentation: Document interface specifications, including data formats, transfer protocols, and error handling procedures.

Conversions

Overview of Conversions

Data conversions involve transforming data from legacy systems to SAP during implementation. This ensures that historical data is accurately and efficiently transferred to the new SAP environment.

Steps in Data Conversion

1. Data Mapping: Define mapping rules to convert legacy data to SAP fields.

2. Data Extraction: Extract data from legacy systems.

3. Data Transformation: Apply transformation rules to convert extracted data into the required SAP format.

4. Data Loading: Load the transformed data into the SAP system.

5. Data Validation: Validate the loaded data to ensure accuracy and completeness.

Best Practices for Conversions

1. Early Planning: Start planning data conversion activities early in the project.

2. Data Cleansing: Cleanse legacy data to remove duplicates, errors, and inconsistencies before conversion.

3. Incremental Loading: Use incremental loading to manage large data volumes and reduce risk.

4. Testing: Conduct thorough testing to validate data accuracy and completeness.

5. Stakeholder Involvement: Involve business stakeholders in the data validation to ensure data meets business requirements.

Enhancements

Overview of Enhancements

Enhancements allow organizations to extend SAP standard functionalities to meet specific business needs without modifying the core SAP code. SAP provides various enhancement techniques, including user exits, customer exits, Business Add-Ins (BAdIs), and enhancement points.

Types of Enhancements

1. User Exits Predefined points in SAP standard programs where custom code can be inserted.

2. Customer Exits Function modules that allow custom code to be added to SAP standard programs.

3. BAdIs: Advanced enhancement techniques that support multiple implementations.

4. Enhancement Points: Locations in the SAP standard code where custom logic can be inserted.

Best Practices for Enhancements

1. Minimize Enhancements: Minimize enhancements to reduce complexity and maintenance efforts.

2. Leverage Standard Options: Use standard SAP enhancement options whenever possible.

3. Documentation: Document each enhancement, including the purpose, logic, and impact on the system.

4. Testing: Conduct thorough testing to ensure enhancements work as expected and not disrupt standard functionalities.

5. Code Reviews: Perform regular code reviews to ensure adherence to coding standards and best practices.

Forms

Overview of Forms

SAP forms create business documents such as invoices, purchase orders, and delivery notes. SAP provides various tools for form development, including SAPscript, Smart Forms, and Adobe Forms.

Types of Forms

1. SAPscript: A legacy form development tool used for simple forms.

2. Smart Forms: An advanced tool that offers more flexibility and functionality than SAPscript.

3. Adobe Forms: The most advanced form development tool, providing extensive design and layout capabilities.

Best Practices for Forms

1. Select the Right Tool: Based on the complexity and requirements of the form, choose the appropriate form development tool.

2. Standard Templates: Use standard templates as a starting point to ensure consistency and reduce development time.

3. User-Friendly Design: Design user-friendly forms with clear layouts and easy-to-read information.

4. Testing: Test forms thoroughly to ensure data is displayed correctly and that the form meets business requirements.

5. Version Control: Implement version control for forms to manage changes and maintain consistency.

Minimizing WRICEF Objects in Standard SAP Deployment

Fit to Standard Approach

a. Leveraging Standard Processes

- **Business Process Alignment**: As much as possible, align business processes with standard SAP processes. Conduct Fit to Standard workshops to identify areas where standard methods can be adopted.

- **Change Management**: Implement a robust change management program to help stakeholders adapt to new processes and minimize resistance to standardization.

b. Gap Analysis

- **Detailed Fit/Gap Analysis**: Perform a detailed Fit/Gap analysis to identify where the organization's requirements differ from standard SAP processes. Focus on understanding the criticality of each gap.

- **Prioritization**: Prioritize gaps based on business impact and feasibility of adopting standard processes. Address high-priority gaps first and explore workarounds or minor adjustments for lower-priority gaps.

Reducing Custom Development

a. Enhancements and Extensions

- **Use of Enhancement Framework**: Utilize the SAP Enhancement Framework for necessary customizations, ensuring they are implemented in a controlled and maintainable manner.

- **Avoiding Hard Coding**: Avoid hard-coding business logic into the system. Instead, use the configuration and customization options SAP provides to achieve flexibility.

b. Custom Reports and Forms

- **Standard Reporting Tools**: Leverage standard reporting tools such as SAP Query, ALV, and CDS Views to create custom reports without extensive development.

- **Form Customization**: Customize standard forms using SAP's design tools rather than developing entirely new forms.

Efficient Interface Management

a. Standard Integration Solutions

- **SAP Integration Suite**: Use the SAP Integration Suite and other standard integration tools to interface with external systems, reducing the need for custom interface development.

- **Middleware Solutions**: Explore middleware solutions like SAP PI/PO (Process Integration/Process Orchestration) for seamless data integration and process automation.

Data Governance

- **Data Standards**: Establish data standards and governance policies to ensure data exchange between systems' consistency and quality.

- **Interface Monitoring**: Implement robust monitoring and error-handling mechanisms to ensure the reliability of interfaces and minimize downtime.

Efficient Data Migration

a. Standard Migration Tools

- **SAP Migration Cockpit**: Use the SAP Migration Cockpit and other standard migration tools to facilitate data migration, reducing the need for custom conversion programs.

- **Incremental Approach**: Adopt an incremental migration approach to minimize disruption and allow for thorough validation at each stage.

b. Data Quality Management

- **Data Cleansing**: Perform data cleansing and enrichment activities to improve data quality before migration.

- **Validation and Reconciliation**: Conduct thorough data validation and reconciliation to ensure the accuracy and completeness of migrated data.

Below is an example of a Day in the Life of a WRICEF Object

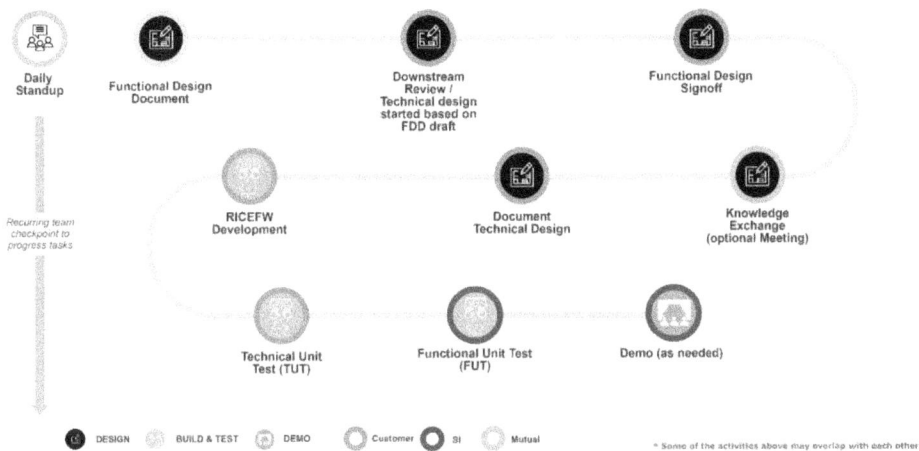

Continuous Improvement and Review

a. Periodic Review

- **Regular Review Sessions**: Conduct regular review sessions to evaluate the effectiveness of WRICEF objects and identify opportunities for improvement.

- **Stakeholder Feedback**: Gather feedback from stakeholders and end-users to understand their needs and challenges and make necessary adjustments.

b. Continuous Training

- **Training Programs**: Implement continuous training programs to keep the project team and end-users updated on best practices and new SAP functionalities.

- **Knowledge Sharing**: Foster a culture of sharing and collaboration to disseminate best practices throughout the organization.

Below is a workflow for the WRICEF Approval process

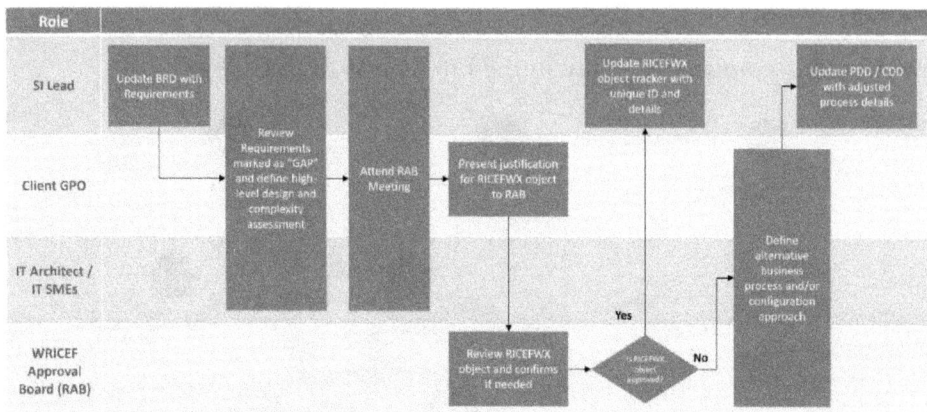

WRICEF objects are essential components of SAP implementations, providing the flexibility and customization needed to tailor the SAP system to specific business requirements. Organizations can ensure a successful SAP implementation that meets their unique needs and drives business value by understanding the purpose and best practices for workflows, reports, interfaces, conversions, enhancements, and forms. Effective management of WRICEF objects involves careful planning, thorough testing, and continuous improvement to maintain a robust and efficient SAP environment.

When WRICEF Runs Wild: Taming the Customization Beast Before It Consumes Your Project

At a global pharmaceutical client, we initially scoped 140 WRICEF objects during the Explore phase — seemingly manageable. But by

Realize, that number had ballooned to over 300, many of which were unnecessary variations or duplicate requests driven by siloed teams. Each functional area thought their report or interface was "business critical," and no clear WRICEF governance framework existed to challenge or consolidate. The PMO flagged it late, when development timelines were already slipping and UAT was imminent. I stepped in to conduct a WRICEF rationalization sprint, gathering all object owners, developers, and business leads into focused sessions. We categorized objects by business value and risk, eliminated 90 redundant items, and postponed 30 others for post-go-live. That one-week intervention helped stabilize the timeline and taught the team a powerful lesson: unchecked WRICEF sprawl is often the hidden killer of project velocity.

Another engagement involved a retail client where interface complexity became the Achilles' heel. The project aimed to integrate SAP S/4 with ten third-party logistics and POS systems using custom interfaces. Rather than using SAP Integration Suite or IDoc standards, previous architects had pushed for heavily customized REST APIs without proper middleware orchestration. As a result, error-handling was inconsistent, logs were unreadable, and interface failures went undetected until end-of-day batch reconciliations. We paused all custom interface builds and reestablished a central Integration Control Board. By enforcing interface templates, standardized error-handling frameworks, and automated alerts, we reduced interface failures by 80% within a month. That experience cemented my belief that WRICEF governance isn't just a technical discipline—it's a strategic imperative to prevent system chaos and protect business continuity.

Chapter 10: Mobile and Remote Access

The increasing reliance on mobile and remote workforces has made mobile and remote access solutions a critical component of SAP implementations. This chapter focuses on how organizations can leverage SAP mobile solutions, configure remote access, and ensure security in mobile deployments to support a flexible and efficient workforce.

SAP Mobile Solutions

Overview of SAP Mobile Solutions

SAP offers various mobile solutions that enable employees to access SAP systems and perform business functions on mobile devices. These solutions enhance productivity, improve decision-making, and support real-time business operations from anywhere. Critical SAP mobile solutions include SAP Fiori, SAP Mobile Platform, and SAP Cloud Platform Mobile Services.

SAP Fiori

SAP Fiori is a user experience (UX) design that provides a simple and intuitive interface for SAP applications across various devices, including desktops, tablets, and smartphones. SAP Fiori apps are role-based and responsive and offer a consistent experience across different devices.

- **Key Features of SAP Fiori:**
    - Role-based access tailored to specific user needs.
    - Responsive design that adapts to different screen sizes.
    - Simple and intuitive user interface.
    - Real-time access to SAP data and processes.

SAP Mobile Platform

The SAP Mobile Platform is a comprehensive solution for developing, deploying, and managing mobile applications. It supports integrating SAP and non-SAP systems, providing a unified platform for mobile app development.

- **Key Features of SAP Mobile Platform:**
    - Support multiple mobile operating systems (iOS, Android, Windows).
    - Integration with SAP and third-party systems.
    - Tools for developing, testing, and deploying mobile apps.
    - Centralized management and security for mobile applications.

SAP Cloud Platform Mobile Services

SAP Cloud Platform Mobile Services offer cloud-based solutions for developing and managing mobile apps. These services provide the flexibility and scalability needed to support mobile initiatives in the cloud.

- **Key Features of SAP Cloud Platform Mobile Services:**
    - Cloud-based development and deployment of mobile apps.
    - Integration with SAP Cloud Platform and other SAP systems.
    - Tools for managing mobile app lifecycle and performance.
    - Enhanced security features for mobile deployments.

Implementing SAP Mobile Solutions

1. **Assess Business Requirements:**
    - Identify business processes that can benefit from mobile access.

o Engage stakeholders to gather requirements and define use cases.

2. **Select the Right Solution:**

   o Choose the appropriate SAP mobile solution based on business needs and technical requirements.

   o Consider user roles, device compatibility, and integration needs.

3. **Develop and Customize Apps:**

   o Use SAP Fiori or SAP Mobile Platform to develop custom mobile apps.

   o Ensure that apps are user-friendly, responsive, and meet business requirements.

4. **Test and Validate:**

   o Conduct thorough testing to ensure mobile apps function correctly and provide the desired user experience.

   o Perform usability testing to gather feedback from end-users.

5. **Deploy and Manage:**

   o Deploy mobile apps using SAP Mobile Platform or SAP Cloud Platform Mobile Services.

   o Implement centralized management and monitoring to ensure app performance and security.

Configuring Remote Access

Overview of Remote Access

Remote access enables employees to connect to SAP systems from remote locations, facilitating flexible work arrangements and improving productivity. Configuring remote access involves securing secure connections, ensuring reliable performance, and providing user support.

Remote Access Solutions

1. **SAP GUI for HTML (SAP Web GUI):**

    o   Provides web-based access to SAP systems using a browser.

    o   Suitable for users who need occasional or lightweight access to SAP applications.

2. **SAP Business Client:**

    o   A desktop application integrating SAP GUI and web content into a single interface.

    o   Provides a consistent user experience for accessing SAP systems and web applications.

3. **SAP Fiori Launchpad:**

    o   A web-based portal that provides access to SAP Fiori and other web-based applications.

    o   Offers a role-based, personalized user experience.

4. **VPN (Virtual Private Network):**

    o   Establishes a secure connection between remote users and the corporate network.

    o   Ensures data privacy and security during remote access.

Steps to Configure Remote Access

1. **Define Access Requirements:**

    o   Identify user groups and their specific access needs.

    o   Determine the level of access required for different roles.

2. **Select Remote Access Solutions:**

   o Choose the appropriate remote access solution based on user requirements and technical capabilities.

   o Consider factors like ease of use, security, and integration with existing systems.

3. **Set Up Infrastructure:**

   o Configure the necessary infrastructure to support remote access, including VPN, SAP Web Dispatcher, and reverse proxy servers.

   o Ensure that network bandwidth and performance are sufficient to support remote connections.

4. **Implement Security Measures:**

   o Implement security measures such as encryption, multi-factor authentication, and role-based access control to protect remote connections.

   o Use firewalls and intrusion detection systems to monitor and secure remote access.

5. **Test and Validate:**

   o Conduct thorough testing to ensure that remote access solutions work as expected.

   o Perform load testing to ensure the infrastructure can handle the expected number of remote users.

6. **User Training and Support:**

   o Provide training to end-users on how to access SAP systems remotely.

   o Set up a helpdesk or support team to assist users with remote access issues.

Ensuring Security in Mobile Deployments

Importance of Security

Security is a critical concern in mobile deployments, as mobile devices are often exposed to various threats, including data breaches, malware, and unauthorized access. Ensuring security in mobile deployments involves implementing robust security measures to protect data, devices, and network connections.

Security Challenges in Mobile Deployments

1. **Device Security:**

   o Mobile devices are susceptible to loss, theft, and unauthorized access.

   o Ensuring device security is essential to protect sensitive data.

2. **Data Security:**

   o Data transmitted between mobile devices and SAP systems must be encrypted to prevent interception and tampering.

   o Ensuring data security involves protecting data at rest and in transit.

3. **Application Security:**

   o Mobile applications must be secure to prevent vulnerabilities that attackers could exploit.

   o Ensuring application security involves secure coding practices and regular security testing.

4. **Network Security:**

   o Network connections used by mobile devices must be secure to prevent unauthorized access and data breaches.

o Ensuring network security involves using secure communication protocols and network monitoring.

Best Practices for Mobile Security

1. **Device Management:**

   o Implement Mobile Device Management (MDM) solutions to manage and secure mobile devices.

   o Enforce security policies such as password protection, device encryption, and remote wipe capabilities.

2. **Data Encryption:**

   o Encrypt data at rest on mobile devices and in transit between devices and SAP systems.

   o Use robust encryption algorithms and ensure that encryption keys are securely managed.

3. **Secure Authentication:**

   o Implement multi-factor authentication (MFA) to enhance user authentication security.

   o Use secure authentication methods such as biometrics, one-time passwords (OTPs), and hardware tokens.

4. **Application Security:**

   o Follow secure coding practices to develop secure mobile applications.

   o Conduct regular security testing, including vulnerability assessments and penetration testing.

5. **Network Security:**

   o Use Virtual Private Networks (VPNs) to secure network connections between mobile devices and SAP systems.

- o Implement firewalls, intrusion detection systems (IDS), and intrusion prevention systems (IPS) to monitor and secure network traffic.

6. **User Awareness and Training:**

- o Educate users on mobile security best practices, such as recognizing phishing attempts and avoiding insecure networks.

- o Provide training on securely accessing SAP systems and handling sensitive data.

7. **Regular Updates and Patching:**

- o Ensure that mobile devices, operating systems, and applications are regularly updated with the latest security patches.

- o Implement automated patch management solutions to streamline the update process.

8. **Access Control:**

- o Implement role-based access control (RBAC) to restrict access to SAP systems and data based on user roles.

- o Regularly review and update access permissions to ensure that users have the appropriate level of access.

9. **Monitoring and Incident Response:**

- o Implement real-time monitoring solutions to detect and respond to security incidents.

- o Develop and test incident response plans to ensure the organization can effectively respond to security breaches.

10. **Compliance and Regulations:**

- o Ensure mobile deployments comply with relevant regulations and industry standards, such as GDPR, HIPAA, and ISO 27001.

    o   Conduct regular audits and assessments to verify compliance and identify areas for improvement.

Conclusion

Integrating mobile and remote access solutions into SAP implementations is essential for supporting a flexible and efficient workforce. Organizations can ensure their employees can access SAP systems and perform business functions from anywhere by leveraging SAP mobile solutions, configuring secure remote access, and implementing robust security measures. Adhering to best practices in mobile deployments enhances productivity, protects sensitive data, and ensures compliance with regulatory requirements. Following this chapter's guidelines and best practices, organizations can successfully implement mobile and remote access solutions that meet their needs and drive significant business improvements.

Chapter 11: System Integration

System integration is critical to SAP implementation, ensuring the new SAP system works seamlessly with existing legacy systems and other enterprise applications. Effective integration facilitates smooth data flow, process automation, and enhanced operational efficiency. This chapter delves into the strategies and best practices for integrating SAP with legacy systems, the use of middleware and integration tools, and the importance of testing integration points.

Integration with Legacy Systems

Understanding Legacy Systems

Legacy systems are the existing software applications and infrastructure an organization has used before implementing SAP. These systems often hold critical data and support essential business processes. Integrating SAP with legacy systems is crucial in ensuring the continuity of operations and leveraging historical data.

Challenges of Integrating Legacy Systems

1. **Data Consistency:** Data consistency between SAP and legacy systems can be challenging due to data formats and structure differences.

2. **System Compatibility:** Legacy systems may use outdated technologies incompatible with modern SAP solutions.

3. **Performance Issues:** Integration can introduce performance bottlenecks if not adequately designed.

4. **Complexity:** Integrating multiple legacy systems with SAP can be complex and require significant development and testing effort.

Strategies for Integrating Legacy Systems

1. **Data Mapping and Transformation:**

   o **Data Mapping:** Identify corresponding data fields between SAP and legacy systems. Define how data will be mapped from one system to the other.

   o **Data Transformation:** Implement transformation rules to convert data formats and structures to ensure compatibility.

2. **Integration Methods:**

   o **Batch Integration:** Batch processing transfers data between SAP and legacy systems at scheduled intervals. This method is suitable for non-time-critical data transfers.

   o **Real-Time Integration:** Implement real-time data synchronization for time-sensitive processes using APIs or middleware solutions.

   o **Data Replication:** Data replication tools maintain a synchronized copy of data between SAP and legacy systems.

3. **Interface Development:**

   o **Custom Interfaces:** Develop custom interfaces using SAP's ABAP or other programming languages to facilitate data exchange between SAP and legacy systems.

   o **Standard Interfaces:** Leverage SAP's standard interfaces and integration tools, such as IDocs (Intermediate Documents) and BAPIs (Business Application Programming Interfaces), to streamline integration efforts.

4. **Phased Integration Approach:**

   o **Incremental Integration:** Implement integration in phases, starting with critical processes and expanding to other areas gradually. This approach helps manage complexity and reduces risk.

- o **Parallel Run:** Run SAP and legacy systems in parallel during the initial integration phases to ensure data consistency and system stability.

5. **Data Validation and Reconciliation:**

- o **Validation Rules:** Implement data validation rules to ensure data integrity during integration.

- o **Reconciliation Processes:** Develop reconciliation processes to compare data between SAP and legacy systems and identify discrepancies.

Best Practices for Integrating Legacy Systems

1. **Stakeholder Involvement:** Involve key stakeholders from both business and IT departments in the integration planning and execution phases.

2. **Documentation:** Maintain comprehensive documentation of data mappings, transformation rules, and interface specifications.

3. **Performance Optimization:** Optimize integration processes to minimize performance impact on SAP and legacy systems.

4. **Regular Monitoring:** Implement monitoring tools to track integration performance and identify issues promptly.

5. **Continuous Improvement:** Regularly review and refine integration processes to address changing business requirements and technological advancements.

Middleware and Tools

Role of Middleware in Integration

Middleware is an intermediary layer that facilitates communication and data exchange between different systems, including SAP and legacy systems. It helps bridge the gap between incompatible systems and simplifies integration by providing standardized interfaces and protocols.

Types of Middleware Solutions

1. **Enterprise Service Bus (ESB):**

   o **Functionality:** ESB provides a centralized platform for integrating various applications and systems. It supports message routing, transformation, and protocol mediation.

   o **Examples:** Apache Camel, MuleSoft, IBM Integration Bus.

2. **API Management Platforms:**

   o **Functionality:** API management platforms enable the creation, deployment, and management of APIs. They provide tools for securing, monitoring, and versioning APIs.

   o **Examples:** SAP API Management, Apigee, AWS API Gateway.

3. **Data Integration Tools:**

   o **Functionality:** Data integration tools facilitate data extraction, transformation, and loading (ETL) between different systems. They support batch and real-time data integration.

   o **Examples:** SAP Data Services, Informatica, Talend.

4. **Message Queuing Systems:**

   o **Functionality:** Message queuing systems enable asynchronous communication between systems by placing messages in a queue until they are processed. This ensures reliable data exchange.

   o **Examples:** RabbitMQ, Apache Kafka, Amazon SQS.

Choosing the Right Middleware

Selecting the appropriate middleware solution depends on several factors, including the complexity of integration, the volume of data, real-time processing requirements, and budget constraints. Key considerations include:

1. **Scalability:** Ensure the middleware can handle the expected volume of data and transactions.

2. **Compatibility:** Verify that the middleware supports the required protocols and data formats for SAP and legacy systems.

3. **Security:** Choose a solution that provides robust security features, such as encryption, authentication, and access control.

4. **Ease of Use:** Consider the middleware solution's ease of configuration, deployment, and management.

5. **Support and Maintenance:** Evaluate the middleware vendor's level of support and maintenance.

Implementing Middleware for Integration

1. **Planning and Design:**

   o **Integration Architecture:** Design the integration architecture, specifying how middleware will connect SAP and legacy systems.

   o **Data Flow Diagrams:** Create data flow diagrams to visualize data movement between systems.

2. **Configuration:**

  o **Middleware Setup:** Install and configure the solution based on the integration requirements.

  o **Connectivity:** Set up connections between middleware, SAP, and legacy systems.

3. **Development:**

  o **Integration Logic:** Develop the integration logic, including message routing, data transformation, and protocol mediation.

  o **APIs and Connectors:** Create APIs and connectors to facilitate system communication.

4. **Testing:**

  o **Unit Testing:** Test individual components of the integration logic to ensure they function correctly.

  o **Integration Testing:** Conduct end-to-end testing to validate the entire integration process.

5. **Deployment and Monitoring:**

  o **Deployment:** Deploy the integration solution in the production environment.

  o **Monitoring:** Implement monitoring tools to track the performance and reliability of the integration.

Best Practices for Middleware Implementation

1. **Standardization:** Use standardized protocols and data formats to simplify integration and improve interoperability.

2. **Reuse:** Leverage reusable components and templates to reduce development time and effort.

3. **Scalability:** Design the integration solution to scale quickly with the growth of data and transaction volumes.

4. **Security:** Implement robust security measures to protect data during transmission and storage.

5. **Documentation:** Maintain detailed documentation of the integration architecture, data flows, and configuration settings.

Testing Integration Points

Importance of Testing Integration Points

Testing integration points is crucial to ensure the integrated systems function correctly, data is accurately exchanged, and business processes run smoothly. Thorough testing helps identify and resolve issues before the system goes live, reducing the risk of disruptions.

Types of Integration Testing

1. **Unit Testing:**

    o **Focus:** Testing individual components or modules of the integration logic to ensure they work as expected.

    o **Objective:** Validate that each component functions correctly in isolation.

2. **Interface Testing:**

    o **Focus:** Testing the interfaces between SAP and legacy systems to ensure they communicate correctly.

    o **Objective:** Verify that data is accurately exchanged and transformed between systems.

3. **End-to-End Testing:**

    o **Focus:** Testing the entire integration process from start to finish, covering all systems and interfaces involved.

- Objective: Ensure integrated business processes function correctly and data flows seamlessly between systems.

4. **Performance Testing:**

   - **Focus:** Assessing the performance of the integration solution under various loads and conditions.

   - **Objective:** Ensure the integration can handle the expected volume of data and transactions without performance degradation.

5. **User Acceptance Testing (UAT):**

   - **Focus:** Involving end-users in testing the integrated system to ensure it meets their requirements and expectations.

   - **Objective:** Validate that the integration supports business processes and delivers the desired outcomes.

Steps for Testing Integration Points

1. **Test Planning:**

   - **Test Strategy:** Develop a comprehensive test strategy outlining the objectives, scope, and approach for integration testing.

   - **Test Scenarios:** Define test scenarios and use cases covering all integration aspects.

2. **Test Environment Setup:**

   - **Test Data:** Prepare test data that accurately represents real-world data scenarios.

   - **Test Environment:** Set up a dedicated test environment that mirrors the production environment as closely as possible.

3. **Test Execution:**

   - **Unit Testing:** Execute unit tests to validate individual components of the integration logic.

   - **Interface Testing:** Perform interface tests to verify data exchange and transformation.

   - **End-to-end Testing:** Conduct end-to-end tests to validate the entire integration process.

4. **Performance Testing:**

   - **Load Testing:** Simulate different loads to assess the performance of the integration solution.

   - **Stress Testing:** Evaluate how the integration handles peak loads and identify performance bottlenecks.

5. **User Acceptance Testing (UAT):**

   - **End-User Involvement:** Engage end-users in testing to ensure the integration meets their needs.

   - **Feedback and Refinement:** Gather end-user feedback and refine the integration solution based on their input.

6. **Issue Resolution:**

   - **Bug Tracking:** Bug tracking tools document and track issues identified during testing.

   - **Issue Resolution:** Prioritize and resolve issues and retest to ensure they are fixed.

7. **Test Documentation:**

   - **Test Results:** Document test results, including pass/fail status and any issues identified.

   - **Test Reports:** Prepare test reports summarizing the testing activities, findings, and recommendations.

Best Practices for Testing Integration Points

1. **Comprehensive Coverage:** Ensure test scenarios cover all integration points, data flows, and business processes.

2. **Realistic Test Data:** Use realistic test data that accurately represents the data used in production.

3. **Automated Testing:** Implement automated tools to streamline and accelerate the testing process.

4. **Continuous Testing:** Adopt a continuous testing approach to validate integration points throughout the development lifecycle.

5. **Collaboration:** Foster collaboration between development, testing, and business teams to ensure comprehensive and practical testing.

6. **Performance Monitoring:** Continuously monitor the performance of integration points in production to identify and address any issues promptly.

Where Failure Finds a Foothold: The High-Stakes Reality of Integration & Boundary Systems

Integration and boundary systems have consistently been the most underestimated—and riskiest—workstreams in every SAP program I've led. On one global rollout, the team focused heavily on finance and supply chain design while pushing interface development to the back of the queue. The assumption was that legacy systems would "just plug in" using existing specs. But the specs were outdated, middleware versions were mismatched, and critical interface logic was hard-coded in undocumented scripts from systems two decades old. We didn't fully grasp the extent of the issue until system integration testing, when orders started disappearing mid-transit between SAP and the legacy order management platform. We lost three weeks and had to spin up a cross-functional "Integration SWAT team" to triage failures, rewrite connectors, and implement real-time message tracking via PI. That moment cemented a rule I now carry into every S/4 implementation: if you're not actively managing integration from Day 1, you're managing a future crisis.

In another project for a logistics provider, over 60 interfaces were classified as "boundary" scope — defined as sitting between SAP and satellite systems like telematics, weighbridge software, and route optimizers. Because they didn't touch SAP core, they were deprioritized during planning and assigned to a single offshore developer with limited access to business SMEs. It wasn't until user acceptance testing that the gaps became apparent: incorrect timestamps, duplicated loads, and misrouted orders stemming from faulty assumptions about message sequencing. We were forced to delay go-live by six weeks, a painful lesson in the false sense of safety that "non-core" interfaces can give. Boundary systems *are* core to business operations, and they deserve the same rigor, traceability, and executive oversight as any finance configuration or warehouse process. From that point forward, I made it policy to assign an Integration Lead at the same level of accountability as Functional and Technical Leads — and to never treat interfaces as an afterthought.

Conclusion

System integration is vital to SAP implementation, ensuring seamless data flow and process automation between SAP and legacy systems. Organizations can achieve a successful SAP implementation that supports efficient and reliable business operations by effectively integrating legacy systems, leveraging middleware and integration tools, and rigorously testing integration points. Adhering to best practices in these areas helps minimize risks, optimize performance, and ensure that the integrated system meets the organization's needs and delivers significant business value.

Chapter 12: Testing & Quality Assurance

Testing and Quality Assurance (QA) are critical components of the SAP implementation process. They ensure that the SAP system meets business requirements, functions correctly, and provides a reliable platform for business operations. This chapter provides a detailed overview of the different types of testing involved in SAP implementation, including unit testing, integration testing, and user acceptance testing (UAT). Each section will outline the objectives, methodologies, and best practices to ensure a successful SAP implementation.

Unit Testing

Overview of Unit Testing

Unit testing is the first level of testing in the SAP implementation process. It involves testing individual components or modules of the SAP system to ensure they function correctly in isolation. The primary goal of unit testing is to validate that each element performs as expected and to identify any defects at an early stage.

Objectives of Unit Testing

1. **Verify Functionality:** Ensure that each component of the SAP system performs its intended functions correctly.

2. **Identify Defects:** Detect and fix defects early in the development cycle to reduce the cost and effort of later-stage bug fixes.

3. **Validate Code Changes:** Confirm that recent code changes do not introduce new defects or negatively impact existing functionality.

Methodologies for Unit Testing

1. **Manual Testing:** Involves manually executing test cases to verify the functionality of individual components. While

time-consuming, it is effective for complex scenarios that are difficult to automate.

2. **Automated Testing:** Automated tools execute test cases, compare actual outcomes with expected results, and generate reports. Automated testing is efficient for repetitive and regression testing tasks.

Below is a typical Testing V-Model

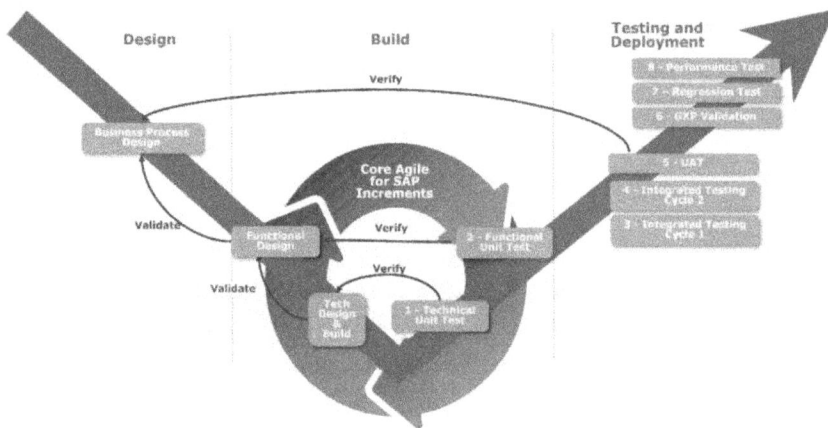

Steps in Unit Testing

1. **Develop Test Cases:**

   o Identify test scenarios for each component based on functional specifications.

   o Create detailed test cases that outline the input data, execution steps, and expected results.

2. **Set Up Test Environment:**

   o Prepare the test environment, including the necessary hardware, software, and data.

    o Ensure the environment is isolated from the development and production environments to prevent interference.

3. **Execute Test Cases:**

    o Execute each test case and record the results.

    o Compare the actual outcomes with the expected results to identify any discrepancies.

4. **Document and Track Defects:**

    o Document any defects identified during testing, including detailed descriptions and steps to reproduce the issue.

    o Use a defect tracking tool to manage and prioritize defect resolution.

5. **Retest and Validate Fixes:**

    o Retest the components after defects are fixed to ensure the issues are resolved.

    o Validate that the fixes do not introduce new defects or negatively impact other functionalities.

Best Practices for Unit Testing

1. **Early Involvement:** Begin unit testing once individual components are developed to identify and fix defects early.

2. **Comprehensive Test Coverage:** Ensure test cases cover all possible scenarios, including edge cases and negative testing.

3. **Automate Where Possible:** Use automated testing tools to increase efficiency and reduce the risk of human error.

4. **Maintain Test Scripts:** Regularly update and maintain test scripts to reflect changes in requirements and code.

5. **Continuous Integration:** Integrate unit testing into the continuous integration (CI) pipeline to automatically test code changes and provide immediate feedback.

Integration Testing

Overview of Integration Testing

Integration testing follows unit testing and involves testing the interactions between different components or modules of the SAP system. The primary goal is to ensure that integrated components work together as expected and data flows correctly between them.

Objectives of Integration Testing

1. **Verify Interactions:** Ensure that integrated components communicate and interact correctly.

2. **Validate Data Flow:** Confirm that data is accurately exchanged between modules and systems.

3. **Identify Interface Issues:** Detect and resolve any issues related to interfaces, data mappings, and integrations.

Methodologies for Integration Testing

1. **Top-Down Integration Testing:** Tests the higher-level components first and then integrates and tests lower-level components.

2. **Bottom-Up Integration Testing:** Tests the lower-level components first and then integrates and tests higher-level components.

3. **Big Bang Integration Testing:** Integrates and tests all components simultaneously. This approach can be risky if issues are widespread.

4. **Incremental Integration Testing:** This method integrates and tests components incrementally in a phased manner, which helps isolate issues more effectively.

Steps in Integration Testing

1. **Define Integration Scenarios:**

    o Identify key integration points and data flows between components.

o Develop integration scenarios that outline the expected interactions and data exchanges.

2. **Develop Test Cases:**

   o Create detailed test cases for each integration scenario, specifying the input data, execution steps, and expected outcomes.

   o Include both positive and negative test cases to validate interactions thoroughly.

3. **Set Up Test Environment:**

   o Configure the test environment to simulate the integrated system, including necessary hardware, software, and data.

   o Ensure the environment accurately reflects the production setup to identify real-world issues.

4. **Execute Test Cases:**

   o Execute integration test cases and document the results.

   o Monitor data flow and interactions between components to identify any discrepancies.

5. **Document and Track Defects:**

   o Document any defects identified during integration testing, including detailed descriptions and steps to reproduce the issue.

   o Use a defect tracking tool to manage and prioritize defect resolution.

6. **Retest and Validate Fixes:**

   o Retest the integration scenarios after defects are fixed to ensure the issues are resolved.

   o Validate that the fixes do not introduce new defects or negatively impact other functionalities.

Below is an example of a testing timeline

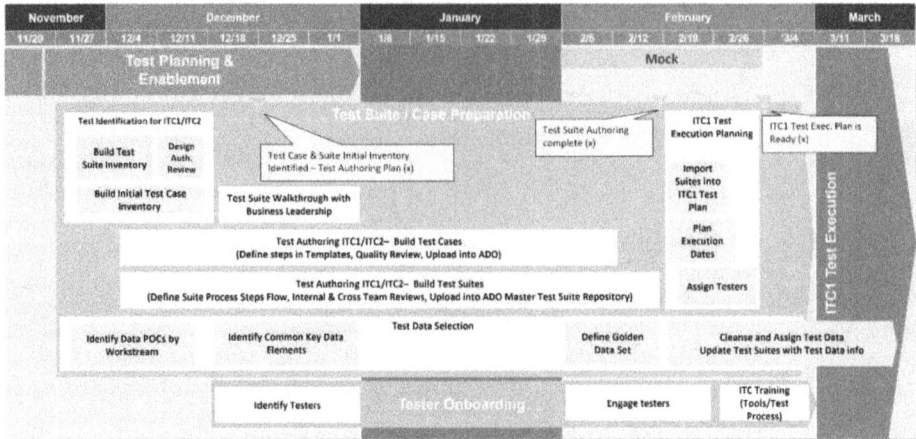

Best Practices for Integration Testing

1. **Comprehensive Test Coverage:** Ensure test cases cover all possible integration scenarios, including edge cases and negative testing.

2. **Incremental Approach:** Use an incremental approach to integration testing to isolate and resolve issues more effectively.

3. **Automate Where Possible:** Use automated testing tools to increase efficiency and reduce the risk of human error.

4. **Maintain Test Scripts:** Regularly update and maintain test scripts to reflect changes in requirements and code.

5. **Collaboration:** Foster collaboration between development, testing, and business teams to ensure comprehensive and practical testing.

User Acceptance Testing (UAT)

Overview of User Acceptance Testing (UAT)

User Acceptance Testing (UAT) is the final testing phase before the SAP system goes live. It involves testing the system from an end-user perspective to ensure it meets business requirements and is ready for production use. UAT is conducted by business users and stakeholders who validate that the system performs as expected in real-world scenarios.

Objectives of User Acceptance Testing

1. **Validate Business Requirements:** Ensure that the SAP system meets the business requirements and effectively supports business processes.

2. **Identify Usability Issues:** Detect and resolve any usability issues impacting end-user productivity.

3. **Gain User Buy-In:** Obtain acceptance and approval from business users and stakeholders for the system to go live.

Methodologies for User Acceptance Testing

1. **Scenario-Based Testing:** Develop test scenarios based on real-world business processes and use cases. This approach ensures that the system is tested in the context of actual business operations.

2. **Exploratory Testing:** Allow end-users to explore the system freely to identify any issues or unexpected behavior that predefined test cases may not cover.

3. **Formal Testing:** Conduct structured testing sessions with predefined test cases and scripts to ensure comprehensive coverage of business requirements.

Steps in User Acceptance Testing

1. **Develop UAT Plan:**

   o Define the scope and objectives of UAT, including the specific business processes and requirements to be tested.

   o Develop a detailed UAT plan outlining the test scenarios, cases, and acceptance criteria.

2. **Prepare Test Environment:**

   o Set up a dedicated UAT environment that mirrors the production environment as closely as possible.

   o Ensure that the necessary hardware, software, and data are available for testing.

3. **Identify UAT Participants:**

   o Select business users and stakeholders to participate in UAT based on their roles and responsibilities.

   o Provide training and support to ensure participants understand the UAT process and their responsibilities.

4. **Execute Test Cases:**

   o Execute UAT test cases and document the results.

   o Encourage participants to explore the system and report any issues or feedback.

5. **Document and Track Defects:**

   o Document any defects identified during UAT, including detailed descriptions and steps to reproduce the issue.

   o Use a defect tracking tool to manage and prioritize defect resolution.

6. **Retest and Validate Fixes:**

   o Retest the system after defects are fixed to ensure that the issues are resolved.

   o Validate that the fixes do not introduce new defects or negatively impact other functionalities.

7. **Obtain User Acceptance:**

   o Obtain formal acceptance and approval from business users and stakeholders for the system to go live.

   o Document the acceptance and approval process to ensure transparency and accountability.

Best Practices for User Acceptance Testing

1. **Early Involvement:** To meet their requirements and expectations, involve business users and stakeholders early in the UAT planning process.

2. **Realistic Scenarios:** Develop realistic test scenarios based on actual business processes and use cases to ensure comprehensive coverage.

3. **Clear Communication:** Communicate the UAT process, objectives, and expectations clearly to all participants.

4. Provide training and support to UAT participants to ensure they understand the system and their testing responsibilities.

5. **Encourage Feedback:** Encourage participants to provide feedback and report any issues or concerns during UAT.

6. **Track and Resolve Defects:** Use a defect tracking tool to document, prioritize, and resolve defects identified during UAT.

7. **Obtain Formal Acceptance:** Ensure formal acceptance and approval are obtained from business users and stakeholders before the system goes live.

Test Phases

During an ERP implementation, there are different functional and technical test phases. All testing should be done using pre-defined test scripts from a testing tool.

Functional Phases:
1. Unit Testing
2. Assembly Testing (also known as String Test)
3. Product Testing (also known as Integration Test)
4. Operational Readiness Testing: includes UAT, Parallel/Compare Test, Operations Test, and Deployment Test

Technical Phases:
1. Performance Testing
2. Disaster Recovery Testing
3. Conversion Testing
4. Hardware Testing

Starting with the Unit Test, all test phases undergo a planning and coordination approach, including environment and data needs, resourcing, scheduling, script writing and execution planning, dependency coordination, etc. The figure below summarizes the key activities required to prepare for each phase.

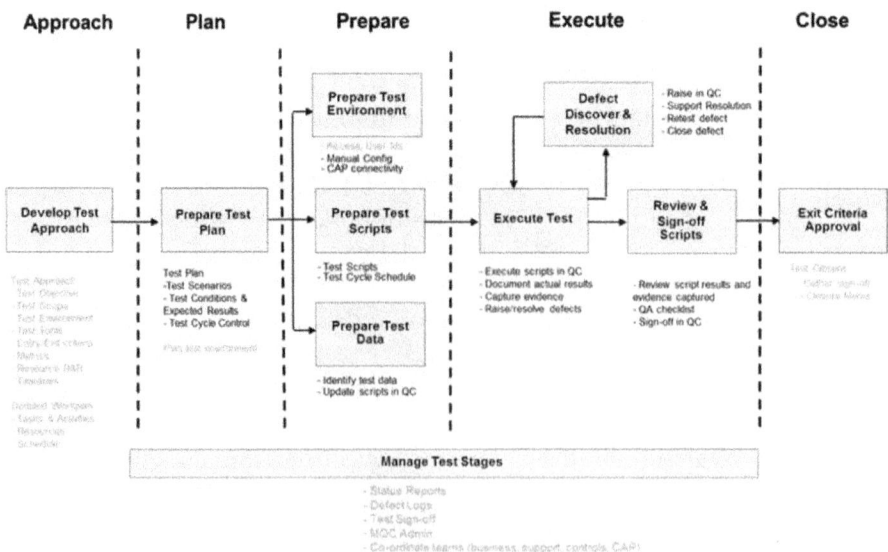

Where It Breaks Is Where You Didn't Test: Making QA a Gate, Not a Checkbox

In one of my earliest SAP programs, the client insisted on compressing the test cycle to "save time." Integration Testing was rushed, UAT was treated as a formality, and the program leadership bypassed the Exit Gate because no critical defects were "blocking" go-live—at least, not visibly. Within 72 hours of cutover, the system crashed under batch load conditions no one had stress-tested, invoices failed to generate, and master data discrepancies created a week-long backlog in warehouse fulfillment. It cost the company over $4 million in emergency remediation and lost revenue in the first month alone. That experience forever changed how I view testing: it's not a box to tick—it's your insurance policy. From that point forward, I made testing gate reviews a formal, signed checkpoint with executive visibility, and I insisted that no go-live decision be made without passing through every exit gate with clear evidence, not assumptions.

What many underestimate is that quality is not just about finding defects—it's about making informed decisions. I've seen projects where entry and exit criteria were vague, undocumented, or bypassed to meet artificial deadlines. The result? A chain of unvalidated assumptions stretching from Unit Test all the way to UAT. In contrast, the most successful programs I've led had a rigorous gating model: no test phase began without a readiness checklist, and no phase exited without stakeholder signoff, defect trend analysis, and test coverage metrics. These weren't bureaucratic hoops—they were project health indicators. Every Go/No-Go decision was backed by structured QA reporting, heatmaps of remaining risk, and business owner signoff. Testing must have a seat at the leadership table, not just the project room. Because in ERP, what you don't test isn't invisible—it's just waiting to fail in production.

Conclusion

Testing and Quality Assurance are essential components of the SAP implementation process. They ensure the system meets business requirements, functions correctly, and provides a reliable platform for business operations. Unit testing, integration testing, and user acceptance testing (UAT) each play a critical role in validating different aspects of the system and identifying defects early in the process. By following best practices and involving key stakeholders throughout the testing phases, organizations can achieve a successful SAP implementation that delivers significant business value and supports efficient and reliable business operations.

Chapter 13: Change Management

Implementing an SAP system is a technical challenge and a significant organizational change. Effective change management ensures a smooth transition to the new system, and employees are well-prepared and supportive of the latest processes and tools. This chapter focuses on managing organizational change, developing training and support strategies, and creating comprehensive communication plans to facilitate a successful SAP implementation. Change management is usually referenced as Organizational Change Management (OCM) in these implementations.

Managing Organizational Change

Understanding Organizational Change

Organizational change involves transitioning individuals, teams, and organizations from a current state to a desired future state. This means shifting from existing systems and processes to the new SAP environment in the context of SAP implementation. Effective change management minimizes resistance, reduces downtime, and ensures the new system delivers its intended benefits.

Critical Principles of Change Management

1. **Leadership Commitment:** Successful change management requires strong commitment and support from senior leadership. Leaders must champion the change, allocate necessary resources, and actively engage with employees throughout the transition.
2. **Employee Involvement:** Involving employees in the change process helps to build ownership and reduce resistance. Employees should be engaged early, and their feedback should be incorporated into the planning and implementation phases.
3. **Clear Vision and Objectives:** Clearly articulate the vision and objectives of the SAP implementation. Employees must understand why the change is happening and how it will benefit the organization and themselves.

4. **Structured Approach:** Use a structured approach to manage change. This includes defining change management processes, setting milestones, and measuring progress.

Steps to Manage Organizational Change

1. **Assess Readiness for Change:**
   o Conduct a change readiness assessment to understand the organization's capacity for change.
   o Identify potential barriers and enablers for the SAP implementation.
2. **Develop a Change Management Strategy:**
   o Define the change management objectives, scope, and approach.
   o Develop a detailed change management plan that includes timelines, responsibilities, and resources.
3. **Engage Stakeholders:**
   o Identify key stakeholders and understand their concerns and expectations.
   o Develop a stakeholder engagement plan to keep stakeholders informed and involved.
4. **Build a Change Management Team:**
   o Establish a dedicated change management team to lead and coordinate change activities.
   o Ensure the team includes representatives from different departments and levels.
5. **Communicate the Vision:**
   o Develop a clear and compelling vision for the SAP implementation.
   o Communicate the vision and objectives to all employees through various channels.
6. **Address Resistance:**
   o Identify potential sources of resistance and develop strategies to address them.
   o Provide support and resources to help employees adapt to the change.
7. **Monitor and Evaluate Progress:**
   o Regularly monitor the progress of change management activities.
   o Use feedback and metrics to evaluate the effectiveness of change management efforts and make adjustments as needed.

Best Practices for Managing Organizational Change

1. **Leadership Involvement:** Ensure senior leaders actively participate in the change management process.
2. **Employee Engagement:** Engage employees early and involve them in decision-making and problem-solving.
3. **Transparent Communication:** Communicate openly and honestly about the changes, including the benefits and challenges.
4. **Flexibility:** Be flexible and adaptable in your approach to change management. Be prepared to adjust strategies based on feedback and changing circumstances.
5. **Support Systems:** Provide support systems such as help desks, counseling, and peer support groups to help employees navigate the change.

Training and Support Strategies

Importance of Training and Support

Training and support are critical components of change management. Practical training ensures employees have the knowledge and skills to use the new SAP system, and ongoing support helps employees resolve issues and improve their proficiency with the system.

Developing a Training Strategy
1. **Conduct Training Needs Assessment:**
   o Identify the training needs of different user groups based on their roles and responsibilities.
   o Assess employees' current skill levels and determine the gaps that must be addressed.
2. **Define Training Objectives:**
   o Clearly define the objectives of the training program.
   o Ensure that the training objectives align with the overall goals of the SAP implementation.
3. **Design Training Programs:**
   o Develop training programs that cover all aspects of the SAP system, including system functionality, business processes, and best practices.

o   Use various training methods, such as instructor-led training, e-learning, hands-on practice, and workshops.

4. **Develop Training Materials:**
    o   Create comprehensive training materials, including user manuals, quick reference guides, and online tutorials.
    o   Ensure that training materials are accessible and easy to understand.
5. **Implement Training Programs:**
    o   Schedule and deliver training sessions for different user groups.
    o   Provide opportunities for hands-on practice and real-world scenarios to reinforce learning.
6. **Evaluate Training Effectiveness:**
    o   Use feedback surveys, assessments, and performance metrics to evaluate the effectiveness of the training programs.
    o   Make improvements to the training programs based on the feedback and evaluation results.

Providing Ongoing Support

1. **Establish a Support Team:**
    o   Create a dedicated support team to assist employees with issues related to the SAP system.
    o   Ensure that the support team is knowledgeable and responsive.
2. **Set Up a Help Desk:**
    o   Establish a help desk to provide immediate assistance to employees.
    o   Use a ticketing system to track and manage support requests.
3. **Create Support Resources:**
    o   Develop a knowledge base with articles, FAQs, and troubleshooting guides.
    o   Provide access to online forums and discussion groups where employees can share tips and solutions.

4. **Offer Continuous Learning Opportunities:**
   o Provide opportunities for continuous learning, such as advanced training sessions, webinars, and workshops.
   o Encourage employees to pursue SAP certification and professional development.
5. **Monitor and Improve Support Services:**
   o Regularly monitor the performance of support services using metrics such as response times and user satisfaction.
   o Use feedback to improve support services and address any gaps continuously.

Best Practices for Training and Support

1. **Tailored Training:** Tailor training programs to the specific needs of different user groups.
2. **Interactive Learning:** Use interactive and hands-on learning methods to engage employees and reinforce learning.
3. **Accessible Resources:** Ensure training materials and support resources are easily accessible to all employees.
4. **Continuous Improvement:** Regularly update training programs and support services based on feedback and changing needs.
5. **Encourage Self-Service:** Encourage employees to use self-service support resources like knowledge bases and online tutorials.

Communication Plans

Importance of Communication in Change Management

Effective communication is essential for managing organizational change. It helps build awareness, reduce uncertainty, and foster a positive attitude towards the new SAP system. A well-structured communication plan ensures that all stakeholders are informed, engaged, and supportive throughout the SAP implementation process.

Developing a Communication Plan

1. **Define Communication Objectives:**
    o   Clearly define the objectives of the communication plan.
    o   Ensure that the objectives align with the overall goals of the SAP implementation.
2. **Identify Stakeholders:**
    o   Identify all stakeholders affected by the SAP implementation, including employees, managers, customers, and partners.
    o   Understand the information needs and concerns of different stakeholder groups.
3. **Develop Key Messages:**
    o   Develop clear and consistent vital messages that convey the SAP implementation's vision, objectives, and benefits.
    o   Address potential concerns and provide reassurance.
4. **Select Communication Channels:**
    o   Choose appropriate communication channels for reaching different stakeholder groups.
    o   Use a mix of channels, such as emails, newsletters, intranet, town hall meetings, and social media.
5. **Create a Communication Schedule:**
    o   Develop a detailed communication schedule that outlines the timing and frequency of communication activities.
    o   Ensure that communication is ongoing and regular throughout the SAP implementation process.
6. **Assign Communication Responsibilities:**
    o   Assign responsibilities for communication activities to specific individuals or teams.
    o   Ensure that communication responsibilities are clearly defined and understood.

Executing the Communication Plan

1. **Launch Communication Campaign:**
    o   Launch a communication campaign to introduce the SAP implementation and build awareness.
    o   Use engaging and creative methods to capture attention and generate interest.

2. **Provide Regular Updates:**
   - Provide regular updates on the progress of the SAP implementation, including milestones achieved and upcoming activities.
   - Use visuals and storytelling to make updates more engaging and relatable.
3. **Engage Stakeholders:**
   - Engage stakeholders through interactive communication methods like Q&A sessions, feedback surveys, and focus groups.
   - Address questions and concerns promptly and transparently.
4. **Celebrate Successes:**
   - Celebrate milestones and successes throughout the SAP implementation process.
   - Recognize and reward contributions and achievements.
5. **Evaluate Communication Effectiveness:**
   - Use feedback surveys, focus groups, and performance metrics to evaluate the effectiveness of communication activities.
   - Make improvements to the communication plan based on the feedback and evaluation results.

Best Practices for Communication Plans

1. **Clarity and Consistency:** Ensure all communication is clear, consistent, and aligned with the vision and objectives.
2. **Timeliness:** Provide timely updates and information to keep stakeholders informed and engaged.
3. **Transparency:** Be transparent about challenges and progress to build trust and credibility.
4. **Two-Way Communication:** Encourage two-way communication and actively seek stakeholder feedback.
5. **Customization:** Tailor communication messages and channels to different stakeholder groups' specific needs and preferences.

Below is an example of an OCM approach that was used for a client:

Change Planning	Leadership Enablement & Coaching	Stakeholder Engagement & Communications	Organization Alignment	Change Measurement	Training & Performance Support	Business Readiness & Adoption
Identify people, process, technology, and data changes, as well as impacted stakeholders, to define a change strategy and approach that will build commitment for the program.	Aligning leaders to the new vision, coaching them to champion the change, and enabling them to manage to the new ways of working	Communications and engagement activities delivered at the right time, in the right way, and to the right people with a focus on "what's in it for me" and business value messaging.	Define the impacts of the program by organization and role and map end users to the appropriate system access and permissions	Continuously track and measure change adoption metrics to inform and refine change plan.	Just-in-time training utilizing multiple delivery methods based on the content and stakeholder needs.	Define and measure change readiness criteria to inform decision making and quickly respond to trends and challenges.

Change management should also be aligned against the entire project timeline, similar to below:

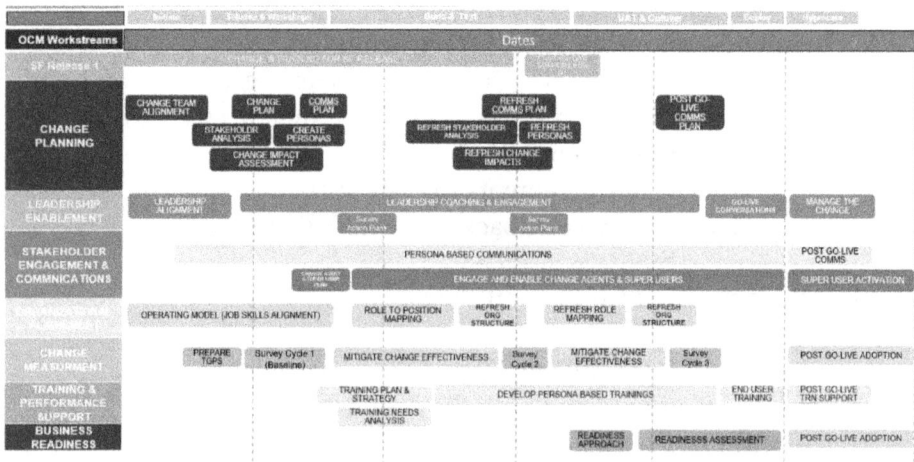

Change Isn't a Sidecar — It's the Steering Wheel: Embedding OCM in Business Transformation

In today's landscape, change management isn't a supporting function — it *is* the function that determines whether digital transformation becomes operational reality or remains a glossy slide deck. I've seen this play out firsthand in a financial services company undergoing a global SAP rollout while simultaneously launching a broader Business Transformation Office. The executive team understood that ERP alone wouldn't fix fragmented processes, cultural inertia, or siloed accountability. So instead of treating Organizational Change Management (OCM) as a back-office HR task, they embedded change leads into every workstream from day one. These leads weren't just managing training and communications—they were shaping how SAP enabled the business to work differently. The result? A smoother transition, faster adoption, and a culture that saw change as strategic rather than disruptive.

Contrast that with earlier projects where OCM was activated too late or under-resourced—often seen as "soft" work in a "technical" project. In one such case, the system was configured flawlessly, data migrated without error, and performance metrics met. But on Day 1, plant supervisors were printing work orders because no one trusted the new digital process. Why? No one had adequately prepared the users for the shift in accountability, nor aligned job roles with new system behaviors. That go-live became a recovery exercise in retroactive change management. The lesson? No matter how brilliant the technology, the business doesn't transform until people do. Companies that recognize this—especially those undergoing enterprise-wide transformation—are now building OCM into their program governance as a core capability, not an afterthought. When change is planned, resourced, and measured like any other workstream, that's when SAP becomes a business enabler—not just a system upgrade.

Conclusion

Change management is a critical component of SAP implementation, ensuring a smooth transition to the new system and that employees are well-prepared and supportive. Organizations can achieve a successful SAP implementation that delivers significant business value by effectively managing organizational change, developing comprehensive training and support strategies, and implementing a structured communication plan. Adhering to best practices in these areas helps minimize resistance, reduce downtime, and ensure that the new SAP system meets its intended objectives.

Chapter 14: Data Management and Migration

Effective data management and migration are crucial for the success of an SAP implementation. They ensure that data is accurately cleansed, migrated, validated, and reconciled, guarantee that the new system operates smoothly, and provide reliable information for business operations. This chapter focuses on data cleansing and preparation, data migration techniques, and validation and reconciliation processes. Each section will provide detailed guidance and best practices to ensure a successful data migration.

Data Cleansing and Preparation

Overview of Data Cleansing

Data cleansing involves identifying and correcting errors and inconsistencies in data to ensure it is accurate, complete, and ready for migration to the SAP system. This process is essential for maintaining data integrity and reliability in the new environment.

Steps in Data Cleansing

1. **Data Profiling:**

    o **Definition:** Data profiling involves analyzing the existing data to understand its structure, quality, and content. This step helps identify duplicates, missing values, and inconsistent formats.

    o **Tools:** Data profiling tools are used to automate the analysis and generate reports on data quality.

2. **Identifying Data Issues:**

    o **Data Quality Rules:** Define data quality rules to identify duplicates, missing values, incorrect formats, and inconsistencies.

    o **Data Audits:** Conduct audits to identify deviations from data quality rules.

3. **Correcting Data Issues:**

   o **Data Standardization:** Standardize data formats and structures to ensure consistency across the dataset.

   o **Deduplication:** Remove duplicate records to ensure each data entry is unique.

   o **Data Enrichment:** Enhance data by filling in missing values and adding relevant information.

4. **Data Validation:**

   o **Validation Rules:** Define validation rules to ensure data meets the required standards.

   o **Automated Validation:** Automated tools check data against validation rules and identify any remaining issues.

5. **Documentation:**

   o **Data Cleansing Log:** Maintain a log of data cleansing activities, including identified issues, corrective actions, and validation results.

Best Practices for Data Cleansing

1. **Early Start:** Begin data cleansing early in the project to allow sufficient time for thorough cleansing and validation.

2. **Involve Stakeholders:** Engage data owners and business users in the data cleansing process to ensure that data is accurate and relevant.

3. **Automate Where Possible:** Use automated tools to streamline data profiling, cleansing, and validation processes.

4. **Iterative Process:** Approach data cleansing as an iterative process, revisiting and refining data quality as needed.

5. **Document Changes:** Maintain detailed documentation of data cleansing activities and changes made to the data.

Data Migration Techniques

Overview of Data Migration

Data migration involves transferring data from legacy systems to the new SAP environment. This process must be meticulously planned and executed to ensure that data is accurately and efficiently migrated without loss or corruption.

Data Migration Strategies

1. **Big Bang Migration:**

   o **Definition:** All data is migrated to the new system in a single, concentrated effort, typically during a downtime or cutover.

   o **Advantages:** Faster transition to the new system, without long-term synchronization between old and new systems.

   o **Disadvantages:** High risk due to the large volume of data being moved at once, requiring extensive planning and testing.

2. **Incremental Migration:**

   o **Definition:** Data is migrated in phases, with subsets of data moved over time.

   o **Advantages:** Lower risk, as issues can be identified and resolved in smaller batches; less downtime required.

   o **Disadvantages:** Longer migration period, requiring synchronization between old and new systems during the transition.

Steps in Data Migration

1. **Planning and Assessment:**

- o **Data Inventory:** Conduct a thorough inventory of the data to be migrated, including data types, volumes, and sources.

- o **Migration Scope:** Define the scope of the migration, including which data sets will be moved and in what order.

2. **Data Mapping and Transformation:**

- o **Data Mapping:** Map data fields from legacy systems to corresponding fields in the SAP system.

- o **Transformation Rules:** Define transformation rules to convert data formats and structures as needed for the new system.

3. **Data Extraction:**

- o **Extraction Methods:** Use appropriate methods and tools to extract data from legacy systems, such as database queries, ETL (Extract, Transform, Load) tools, or custom extraction scripts.

4. **Data Loading:**

- o **Loading Methods:** Load the extracted and transformed data into the SAP system using direct input, batch input, or data migration tools like LSMW (Legacy System Migration Workbench) or SAP Data Services.

- o **Phased Loading:** Consider phased loading strategies to minimize downtime and reduce risk.

5. **Data Validation and Reconciliation:**

- o **Validation:** Validate the loaded data to ensure accuracy and completeness.

- o **Reconciliation:** Reconcile data between legacy and SAP systems to identify and resolve discrepancies.

Data Migration Tools

1. **LSMW (Legacy System Migration Workbench):**

   o **Overview:** An SAP tool designed to facilitate data migration from legacy systems to SAP.

   o **Features:** Supports data mapping, transformation, and loading; handles large volumes of data efficiently.

2. **SAP Data Services:**

   o **Overview:** A comprehensive data integration and transformation tool supporting data migration, quality, and governance.

   o **Features:** Provides robust ETL capabilities, data profiling, and validation tools.

3. **Third-Party ETL Tools:**

   o **Examples:** Informatica, Talend, Microsoft SQL Server Integration Services (SSIS).

   o **Features:** Provide advanced data extraction, transformation, and loading capabilities; support integration with various data sources and targets.

Best Practices for Data Migration

1. **Thorough Planning:** Develop a detailed migration plan that outlines the scope, sequence, and methods for migrating data.

2. **Risk Management:** Identify potential risks and develop mitigation strategies.

3. **Data Quality:** Ensure data is cleansed and validated before migration to maintain data integrity.

4. **Phased Approach:** Consider a phased migration approach to reduce risk and manage the transition effectively.

5. **Testing:** Conduct extensive testing at each stage of the migration process to identify and resolve issues.

6. **Backup and Recovery:** Implement robust backup and recovery procedures to protect data during migration.

Validation and Reconciliation

Overview of Validation and Reconciliation

Validation and reconciliation are critical steps in the data migration to ensure that data has been accurately and wholly transferred from legacy systems to the SAP environment. These steps help verify data integrity, consistency, and accuracy, reducing the risk of data-related issues post-migration.

Validation Processes

1. **Data Validation Rules:**

   o **Definition:** Define validation rules to check the migrated data's accuracy, completeness, and consistency.

   o **Types of Rules:** Include format checks, range checks, cross-field validations, and referential integrity checks.

2. **Automated Validation Tools:**

   o **Usage:** Automate validation tools to systematically apply validation rules and identify data issues.

   o **Examples:** SAP Data Services, custom validation scripts.

3. **Manual Validation:**

   o **Purpose:** Perform manual validation for complex data scenarios that cannot be easily automated.

o **Approach:** Review sample data sets, conduct spot checks, and verify data against source records.

4. **Data Comparison:**

o **Methods:** Compare legacy and SAP systems data to ensure accuracy.

o **Tools:** Use data comparison tools to automate and simplify the comparison process.

Reconciliation Processes

1. **Reconciliation Reports:**

o **Definition:** Generate reconciliation reports comparing data between legacy and SAP systems.

o **Metrics:** Include metrics such as record counts, totals, and critical field values to identify discrepancies.

2. **Issue Identification:**

o **Process:** Identify discrepancies and categorize them based on their severity and impact.

o **Types of Issues:** Common issues include missing records, duplicate records, data format mismatches, and value discrepancies.

3. **Issue Resolution:**

o **Approach:** Develop a systematic approach to resolve identified issues.

o **Techniques:** Techniques include data correction, re-migration of specific data sets, and adjustments to transformation rules.

4. **Documentation:**

o **Logs:** Maintain detailed logs of validation and reconciliation activities, including identified issues and corrective actions taken.

  ○ **Reports:** Prepare comprehensive reports summarizing the validation and reconciliation results.

Best Practices for Validation and Reconciliation

1. **Early and Continuous Validation:** Begin validation early in the data migration process and continue it throughout the migration to identify and resolve issues promptly.

2. **Automate Where Possible:** Automate validation and comparison tools to increase efficiency and accuracy.

3. **Involve Data Owners:** Engage data owners and business users in the validation and reconciliation process to ensure data meets business requirements.

4. **Comprehensive Documentation:** Maintain detailed documentation of validation rules, reconciliation processes, identified issues, and resolution actions.

5. **Iterative Approach:** Use an iterative approach to validation and reconciliation, revisiting and refining data quality as needed.

Below is a Data Migration Approach of a customer

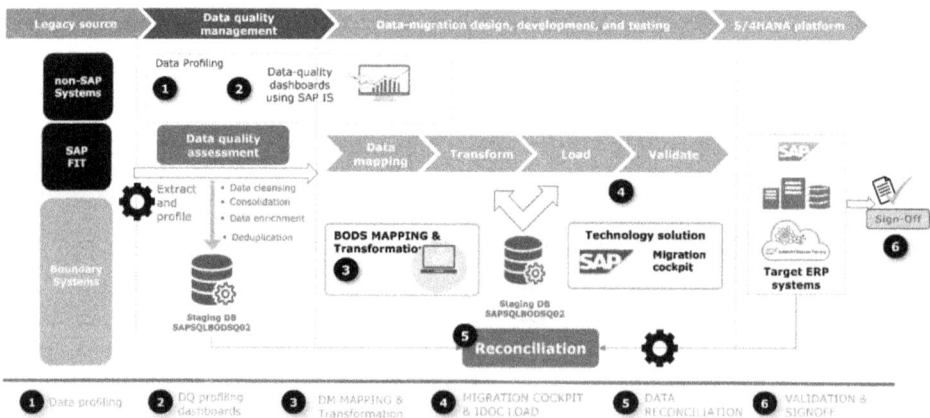

Where Programs Go to Die: Treating Data as a First-Class Workstream, Not a Last-Minute Task

Data is often labeled the "lifeblood" of an organization—but in an SAP implementation, it's also the greatest hidden risk. I've watched otherwise sound projects stumble in the final mile because data quality, transformation logic, or meta-data alignment were underestimated. In one global program, the business insisted that "most of the data is clean," and data cleansing was pushed to Realize. But when we hit mock conversion, 40% of vendor records were unusable, material master data was duplicative across plants, and customer hierarchies weren't defined consistently. What followed was a six-week triage operation, where business SMEs were pulled from operations to manually correct thousands of records. That delay could have been avoided had we started data profiling and cleansing during pre-project planning. Data is never just technical—it's organizational memory, operational structure, and compliance framework. If you don't start managing it early, it will own your timeline and budget by go-live.

Success in data migration doesn't just come from tools like LSMW or SAP Data Services—it comes from discipline. The most successful implementations I've led treated data as a fully accountable workstream, with dedicated data leads, business data owners, and integrated quality gates across each test cycle. We conducted metadata harmonization workshops early, developed transformation rules with full business sign-off, and implemented mock loads with reconciliation dashboards before SIT even began. We didn't just validate row counts—we reconciled financials, inventory positions, and customer balances across systems with documented evidence. We didn't wait for Go/No-Go to ask if data was ready—we built data readiness into our cutover criteria from day one. When programs take that level of ownership, data becomes an enabler, not an obstacle. But when it's treated like a back-end task, it's almost always the reason a project fails to land cleanly.

Conclusion

Data management and migration are critical components of SAP implementation, requiring meticulous planning, execution, and validation to ensure the new system's success. By thoroughly cleansing and preparing data, employing effective data migration techniques, and rigorously validating and reconciling data, organizations can achieve a smooth and reliable transition to the SAP environment. Adhering to best practices in each of these areas helps ensure data integrity, reduces risk, and supports the overall success of the SAP implementation.

Chapter 15: SAP Analytics and Reporting

Effective analytics and reporting are crucial components of SAP implementation, enabling organizations to derive insights from their data, make informed decisions, and monitor business performance. This chapter delves into the introduction to SAP Business Intelligence (BI) and Business Warehouse (BW), creating reports and dashboards, and data visualization techniques. Each section will provide detailed guidance and best practices to ensure successful SAP analytics and reporting.

Introduction to SAP BI/BW

Overview of SAP Business Intelligence (BI)

SAP Business Intelligence (BI) is a suite of tools and technologies that enable organizations to collect, process, analyze, and present data to support decision-making. It encompasses various components, including data warehousing, integration, analytics, and reporting.

Overview of SAP Business Warehouse (BW)

SAP Business Warehouse (BW) is integral to SAP's BI suite. It is a comprehensive data warehousing solution that enables organizations to consolidate data from various sources, perform complex analyses, and generate reports. SAP BW provides a robust platform for data modeling, ETL (Extract, Transform, Load) processes, and analytics.

Critical Components of SAP BI/BW

1. **Data Warehouse:**

    o **Definition:** A central repository that stores integrated data from multiple sources, including SAP and non-SAP systems.

○ **Function:** Supports data consolidation, historical analysis, and reporting.

2. **ETL Processes:**

   ○ **Definition:** ETL stands for Extract, Transform, Load, a process used to extract data from source systems, transform it into a suitable format, and load it into the data warehouse.

   ○ **Function:** Ensures data consistency, quality, and integration.

3. **Data Modeling:**

   ○ **Definition:** Defining data structures, relationships, and hierarchies in the data warehouse.

   ○ **Function:** Supports efficient data storage, retrieval, and analysis.

4. **Analytics and Reporting Tools:**

   ○ **Definition:** Tools and applications that enable users to analyze data, create reports, and visualize information.

   ○ **Examples:** SAP BusinessObjects, SAP Lumira, SAP Analytics Cloud.

Benefits of SAP BI/BW

1. **Integrated Data:** Consolidates data from various sources, providing a unified view of business operations.

2. **Advanced Analytics:** Supports complex analyses, including predictive and trend analyses.

3. **Real-Time Reporting:** Enables real-time access to data and insights, facilitating timely decision-making.

4. **Scalability:** Scales to accommodate growing data volumes and evolving business needs.

5. **User-Friendly Tools:** Provides intuitive tools for report creation, data visualization, and dashboard design.

Best Practices for Implementing SAP BI/BW

1. **Define Clear Objectives:** Clearly define the objectives and goals of the BI/BW implementation to ensure alignment with business needs.

2. **Engage Stakeholders:** Involve key stakeholders in the planning and implementation process to gather requirements and ensure buy-in.

3. **Data Governance:** Implement robust practices to ensure data quality, consistency, and security.

4. **Incremental Implementation:** Implement BI/BW components incrementally, starting with high-priority areas and expanding over time.

5. **Training and Support:** Provide training and support to users to ensure effective utilization of BI/BW tools and capabilities.

Creating Reports and Dashboards

Introduction to Reporting and Dashboards

Reports and dashboards are essential tools for presenting data and insights to users. Reports provide detailed information and analysis, while dashboards visually overview critical metrics and performance indicators.

Steps to Create Reports in SAP

1. **Gather Requirements:**

   o **Stakeholder Engagement:** Engage with stakeholders to understand their reporting needs and requirements.

   o **Define Metrics:** Identify the key metrics and performance indicators to be included in the reports.

2. **Data Source Identification:**

   o **Source Systems:** Identify the source systems and data sources for the required data.

   o **Data Extraction:** Define the data extraction process to retrieve data from source systems.

3. **Data Modeling:**

   o **Data Structures:** Design data structures and models to support efficient data retrieval and analysis.

   o **Data Integration:** Integrate data from multiple sources to provide a comprehensive view.

4. **Report Design:**

   o **Report Layout:** Design the report layout, including tables, charts, and visual elements.

   o **Filters and Parameters:** Implement filters and parameters to enable users to customize the report.

5. **Report Development:**

   o **Tools:** To develop the report, use SAP reporting tools such as SAP BusinessObjects, SAP Lumira, or SAP Analytics Cloud.

   o **Testing:** Test the report to ensure accuracy and performance.

6. **Report Deployment:**

   o **Distribution:** Define the distribution and access methods for the report, such as email, web portal, or mobile app.

   o **Security:** Implement security measures to control access to sensitive data.

Steps to Create Dashboards in SAP

1. **Define Objectives:**

    o   **Stakeholder Engagement:** Engage with stakeholders to understand the objectives and goals of the dashboard.

    o   **Key Metrics:** Identify the key metrics and performance indicators to be displayed on the dashboard.

2. **Data Source Identification:**

    o   **Source Systems:** Identify the source systems and data sources for the required data.

    o   **Data Integration:** Integrate data from multiple sources to provide a comprehensive view.

3. **Dashboard Design:**

    o   **Layout:** Design the dashboard layout, including the arrangement of charts, graphs, and visual elements.

    o   **Visualization Types:** Choose appropriate visualization types (e.g., bar charts, line charts, pie charts) based on the data and objectives.

4. **Dashboard Development:**

    o   **Tools:** SAP dashboard tools such as SAP BusinessObjects Dashboards, SAP Lumira, or SAP Analytics Cloud can be used to develop the dashboard.

    o   **Interactivity:** Implement interactive elements such as filters, drill-downs, and hover effects to enhance user experience.

5. **Testing and Validation:**

    o   **Functionality:** Test the dashboard to ensure all elements function correctly and provide accurate data.

- o **Performance:** Test the dashboard's performance to ensure it loads quickly and handles large data volumes.

6. **Dashboard Deployment:**

   - o **Access Methods:** Define the access methods for the dashboard, such as web portal, mobile app, or embedded in other applications.

   - o **User Training:** Provide training to users on how to navigate and use the dashboard effectively.

Best Practices for Creating Reports and Dashboards

1. **User-Centric Design:** Design reports and dashboards with the end-user in mind, ensuring they are easy to understand and navigate.

2. **Consistent Layout:** Maintain a consistent layout and design across reports and dashboards to enhance usability.

3. **Real-Time Data:** Ensure that reports and dashboards provide real-time or near-real-time data to support timely decision-making.

4. **Performance Optimization:** Optimize the performance of reports and dashboards to ensure quick loading times and responsiveness.

5. **Security and Access Control:** Implement robust security measures to control access to sensitive data and ensure compliance with data privacy regulations.

Data Visualization Techniques

Importance of Data Visualization

Data visualization is the graphical representation of data to make complex information more accessible, understandable, and usable. Effective data visualization techniques can highlight trends, patterns, and outliers, enabling users to gain insights and make informed decisions.

Fundamental Principles of Data Visualization

1. **Simplicity:** Keep visualizations simple and uncluttered to make the data understandable.

2. **Clarity:** Use clear and concise labels, legends, and titles to provide context and enhance comprehension.

3. **Relevance:** Ensure visualizations are relevant to the objectives and provide meaningful insights.

4. **Consistency:** Maintain consistency in design elements such as colors, fonts, and chart types to enhance readability.

Types of Data Visualizations

1. **Bar Charts:**

   o **Purpose:** Compare values across different categories.

   o **Best Use:** Suitable for comparing discrete data points, such as sales by region or product category.

2. **Line Charts:**

   o **Purpose:** Show trends and changes over time.

   o **Best Use:** Ideal for visualizing time series data, such as monthly sales or stock prices.

3. **Pie Charts:**

   o **Purpose:** Show the proportions of different categories within a whole.

   o **Best Use:** Suitable for displaying percentage distribution, such as market share or budget allocation.

4. **Scatter Plots:**

   o **Purpose:** Show relationships between two variables.

- Best Use: Useful for identifying correlations, such as the relationship between sales and advertising spending.

5. **Heat Maps:**

   - **Purpose:** Show data density and distribution.

   - **Best Use:** Ideal for visualizing data intensity, such as website traffic or sales by location.

6. **Histograms:**

   - **Purpose:** Show the distribution of data values.

   - **Best Use:** Suitable for displaying frequency distributions, such as test scores or age groups.

Data Visualization Best Practices

1. **Choose the Right Chart Type:** Based on the data and insights you want to convey, select the appropriate chart type.

2. **Use Colors Effectively:** Use colors to highlight key data points and differentiate between categories. Avoid using too many colors, which can be distracting.

3. **Provide Context:** Include labels, legends, and titles to provide context and make the visualization easy to understand.

4. **Avoid Overloading:** Avoid cluttering visualizations with too much information. Focus on the most critical data points and insights.

5. **Interactive Elements:** Incorporate interactive elements such as filters, drill-downs, and tooltips to enhance user engagement and exploration.

Tools for Data Visualization in SAP

1. **SAP Lumira:**

   - **Overview:** A data visualization tool that enables users to create interactive visualizations and stories.

- o **Features:** Supports visualization types, data integration capabilities, and sharing options.

2. **SAP Analytics Cloud:**

   - o **Overview:** A cloud-based analytics solution that provides data visualization, planning, and predictive analytics capabilities.

   - o **Features:** Offers intuitive visualization tools, real-time data access, and collaboration features.

3. **SAP BusinessObjects Dashboards:**

   - o **Overview:** A dashboard design tool that allows users to create interactive and visually appealing dashboards.

   - o **Features:** Provides a variety of visualization components, data connectivity options, and customization capabilities.

4. **SAP Crystal Reports:**

   - o **Overview:** A reporting tool that enables users to design and generate formatted reports with embedded visualizations.

   - o **Features:** Supports various data sources, formatting options, and distribution methods.

When Reporting Becomes a Program: Managing Scope Before It Manages You

Reporting is one of the most deceptively complex workstreams in any SAP implementation. On the surface, it's just "showing data." But what many companies don't anticipate is that they're not starting from zero—they're replacing thousands of legacy reports accumulated over decades. In one financial services program I led, the team initially estimated 200 reports would need rebuilding. After engaging the business, that list exploded to over 1,400—including dozens of one-off spreadsheets, locally stored macros, and shadow databases used by individual departments. The real challenge wasn't technical — it was cultural. Every team had its own definition of "critical," and without a strong governance model, reporting quickly began to consume project time and resources. We had to stand up a dedicated Reporting Governance Board with business data stewards and finance leads just to rationalize, prioritize, and standardize what was truly required for Day 1. Without this structure, the reporting scope would have delayed the go-live and left key users without trusted data.

Another often overlooked dimension is the intersection of SAP reporting with legacy data access and enterprise data warehousing strategies. Many organizations expect the new SAP system to replace their entire BI landscape overnight — but reality is more nuanced. Data warehousing remains essential for historical reporting, cross-system analytics, and preserving compliance records. In one manufacturing client, we treated the SAP reporting scope as a mini-program: we created workstreams for operational reports, KPIs, dashboards, legacy access, and external regulatory extracts. We aligned each to a strategic data architecture roadmap and ensured every report had a clear owner, defined purpose, and future-state platform. Success depended on a few critical factors: starting reporting discussions in Explore (not Realize), using a report rationalization template, involving end-users in design reviews, and building mock reports with real data during UAT. Treat reporting like the enterprise deliverable it is — or you'll be scrambling at cutover, wondering why no one trusts what the new system says.

Conclusion

SAP analytics and reporting are critical in helping organizations leverage their data to make informed decisions and drive business performance. Organizations can gain valuable insights and achieve their strategic objectives by utilizing SAP BI/BW, creating insightful reports and dashboards, and employing robust data visualization techniques. Adhering to best practices in each area ensures that analytics and reporting efforts are aligned with business needs, user-friendly, and impactful.

Chapter 16: SAP FIORI & UX

SAP Fiori represents a significant advancement in SAP's user experience (UX) strategy, offering a modern, intuitive, and responsive interface for SAP applications. This chapter explores the fundamentals of SAP Fiori, designing and deploying Fiori applications, and best practices for enhancing user experience in SAP implementations.

Introduction to SAP Fiori

Overview of SAP Fiori

SAP Fiori is a design system that provides a consistent and coherent user experience across all SAP applications. Fiori is based on modern web technologies and is designed to be role-based, simplifying tasks and increasing productivity. The Fiori design principles focus on providing a simple, intuitive, and responsive user experience.

Key Features of SAP Fiori

1. **Role-Based:** Fiori applications are designed for specific user roles, ensuring users can access the tools and information relevant to their tasks.
2. **Responsive:** Fiori applications are designed to work seamlessly across different devices, including desktops, tablets, and smartphones.
3. **Simple:** The user interface is clean and straightforward, reducing complexity and making it easy for users to navigate and complete tasks.
4. **Coherent:** Fiori provides a consistent user experience across all applications, ensuring users can easily switch between tasks without confusion.
5. **Delightful:** Fiori aims to provide an enjoyable user experience, with attention to design details that enhance usability and satisfaction.

Benefits of SAP Fiori

1. **Increased Productivity:** Fiori applications help users complete tasks more efficiently by providing a tailored user experience.
2. **Improved User Adoption:** The intuitive design of Fiori applications makes it easier for users to learn and adopt new SAP solutions.
3. **Enhanced Mobility:** Fiori applications' responsive design ensures that users can access SAP systems from any device, supporting mobile and remote work.
4. **Consistency:** A consistent user experience across all SAP applications reduces training requirements and improves user satisfaction.

Designing SAP Fiori Applications

Fiori Design Guidelines
SAP provides comprehensive design guidelines to help developers create Fiori applications that adhere to simplicity, responsiveness, and coherence principles. These guidelines cover various design aspects, including layout, navigation, controls, and interaction patterns.

1. **Layout:**
   o **Responsive Grid Layout:** A responsive grid layout ensures the application adapts to different screen sizes and orientations.
   o **Flexible Column Layout:** Implement a flexible column layout to provide a consistent structure for different views and components.
2. **Navigation:**
   o **Simple Navigation:** Use simple and intuitive navigation patterns like the Fiori launchpad to help users find and access applications quickly.
   o **Bread Crumbs:** Implement breadcrumbs to provide context and allow users to navigate back to previous screens.

3. **Controls:**
   - o **Consistent Controls:** Use Fiori control libraries to ensure consistency in the appearance and behavior of UI elements.
   - o **Input Controls:** Provide appropriate input controls, such as dropdowns, radio buttons, and checkboxes, to capture user input efficiently.
4. **Interaction Patterns:**
   - o **Action Buttons:** Place action buttons in prominent locations to make it easy for users to perform tasks.
   - o **Feedback Mechanisms:** Implement feedback mechanisms, such as success messages and error alerts, to keep users informed about the status of their actions.

Steps to Design Fiori Applications

1. **Requirement Gathering:**
   - o **User Roles:** Identify the user roles and personas that will use the Fiori application.
   - o **User Needs:** Gather requirements and understand the users' specific needs and pain points.
2. **Wireframing:**
   - o **Sketches:** Create initial sketches and wireframes to visualize the layout and structure of the application.
   - o **Feedback:** Review wireframes with stakeholders and gather feedback to refine the design.
3. **Prototyping:**
   - o **Interactive Prototypes:** Develop interactive prototypes using tools like SAP Fiori Design Studio or third-party prototyping tools.
   - o **Usability Testing:** Conduct usability testing with end-users to validate the design and identify areas for improvement.
4. **Visual Design:**
   - o **Styling:** Apply visual design elements, such as colors, fonts, and icons, to create a polished and professional look.
   - o **Branding:** Ensure the application aligns with the organization's branding guidelines.

5. **Development:**
   - o **SAPUI5 Framework:** Use the SAPUI5 framework to develop the Fiori application, leveraging pre-built controls and components.
   - o **Testing:** Conduct thorough testing to ensure the application functions correctly and provides a seamless user experience.

Best Practices for Designing Fiori Applications

1. **User-Centric Design:** Focus on the needs and preferences of the end-users to create intuitive and efficient applications.
2. **Consistency:** Maintain consistency in design elements and interaction patterns to provide a coherent user experience.
3. **Accessibility:** Follow accessibility guidelines to ensure the application is accessible to all users, including those with disabilities.
4. **Performance:** Optimize the application's performance to ensure quick loading times and responsiveness.
5. **Feedback Loop:** Establish a feedback loop with users to gather insights and improve the application continuously.

Deploying SAP Fiori Applications

SAP Fiori Architecture

SAP Fiori applications are built using the SAPUI5 framework and run on the SAP Fiori front-end server, which connects to the SAP back-end systems via OData services. The architecture ensures that Fiori applications are scalable, secure, and easy to maintain.

Steps to Deploy Fiori Applications

1. **Set Up Fiori Front-End Server:**
   - o **Installation:** Install and configure the SAP Fiori front-end server.
   - o **Configuration:** Set up the Fiori launchpad and configure the necessary services and roles.

2. **Develop and Test Fiori Applications:**
    o **Development Environment:** Set up a development environment with SAP Web IDE or another suitable development tool.
    o **Coding:** Develop the Fiori application using SAPUI5 and test it thoroughly to ensure functionality and performance.
3. **Register OData Services:**
    o **Service Creation:** Create OData services in the SAP back-end system to provide the necessary data for the Fiori application.
    o **Service Registration:** Register the OData services in the SAP Gateway to make them available to the Fiori front-end server.
4. **Deploy the Application:**
    o **Transport Requests:** Create transport requests to move the Fiori application and related configurations from the development environment to the quality assurance (QA) and production environments.
    o **Deployment:** Deploy the Fiori application to the Fiori front-end server.
5. **Configure Roles and Permissions:**
    o **Role Definition:** Define roles and permissions for the Fiori application to ensure users have the appropriate access.
    o **Role Assignment:** Assign roles to users and test the access controls to ensure security.
6. **Go-Live and Support:**
    o **Go-Live Preparation:** Prepare for the go-live by conducting final testing, data validation, and user training.
    o **Support:** Provide ongoing support and maintenance for the Fiori application to address any issues and ensure optimal performance.

Best Practices for Deploying Fiori Applications

1. **Scalability:** Design the architecture to scale quickly with the growth of users and data.
2. **Security:** Implement robust security measures to protect data and ensure compliance with regulations.

3. **Testing:** Conduct extensive testing at each stage of the deployment process to identify and resolve issues.
4. **Documentation:** Maintain detailed documentation of the deployment process, including configurations, roles, and permissions.
5. **User Training:** Provide comprehensive training to users to ensure they understand how to use the Fiori application effectively.

Enhancing User Experience (UX) with SAP Fiori

Key UX Principles
1. **Empathy:** Understand users' needs, pain points, and preferences to create solutions that genuinely address their problems.
2. **Clarity:** Ensure the user interface is straightforward to understand, reducing cognitive load and making tasks straightforward.
3. **Feedback:** Provide immediate and clear feedback for user actions to keep them informed and in control.
4. **Consistency:** Maintain consistency across the application to ensure that users can predict and understand how to interact with it.
5. **Efficiency:** Optimize workflows and interfaces to help users complete tasks quickly and efficiently.

Techniques to Enhance UX
1. **User Research:**
   o **Interviews:** Conduct user interviews to gather insights into user needs, behaviors, and pain points.
   o **Surveys:** Use surveys to collect quantitative user preferences and satisfaction data.
   o **Observation:** Observe users in their work environment to understand their context and challenges.
2. **Persona Development:**
   o **Personas:** Develop personas representing different user types and guiding design decisions.
   o **Scenarios:** Create scenarios and use cases to illustrate how personas interact with the application.
3. **Journey Mapping:**

- o **User Journeys:** Map user journeys to visualize the steps users take to complete tasks and identify pain points and opportunities for improvement.
- o **Touchpoints:** Identify touchpoints where users interact with the application and ensure a seamless experience across them.

4. **Prototyping and Testing:**
   - o **Wireframes:** Create wireframes to visualize the layout and structure of the application.
   - o **Prototypes:** Develop interactive prototypes to test design concepts and gather user feedback.
   - o **Usability Testing:** Conduct usability testing with real users to identify issues and refine the design.
5. **Continuous Improvement:**
   - o **Feedback Mechanisms:** Implement feedback mechanisms, such as in-app surveys and feedback forms, to gather ongoing user feedback.
   - o **Iteration:** Use feedback and analytics to continuously improve the application, making iterative updates based on user needs and behaviors.

Best Practices for Enhancing UX

1. **User-Centered Design:** Focus on the needs and preferences of users throughout the design and development process.
2. **Agile Development:** Use agile methodologies to iterate quickly and incorporate user feedback.
3. **Collaborative Design:** Involve stakeholders, designers, and developers in the design process to ensure a holistic approach.
4. **Accessibility:** Follow accessibility guidelines to ensure the application is accessible to all users, including those with disabilities.
5. **Performance Optimization:** Optimize the application's performance to ensure quick loading times and responsiveness.

Conclusion
SAP Fiori represents a significant advancement in SAP's approach to user experience, providing a modern, intuitive, and responsive

interface for SAP applications. By adhering to Fiori design guidelines, effectively deploying Fiori applications, and continuously enhancing the user experience, organizations can achieve higher productivity, improved user satisfaction, and greater adoption of SAP solutions. Implementing best practices in each of these areas ensures that Fiori applications are user-friendly, efficient, and aligned with the needs of the business.

Chapter 17: Deployment Options

Selecting the right deployment strategy is crucial for the success of an SAP implementation. Each deployment option has unique advantages, challenges, and considerations. This chapter delves into three primary deployment options: Global Template, Big Bang, and Phased Rollout. It provides detailed guidance on each approach and best practices to ensure a smooth and successful deployment.

Global Template

Overview of Global Template

The Global Template approach involves designing a standardized SAP solution that can be implemented across multiple locations, business units, or subsidiaries within an organization. This template serves as a blueprint for local implementations, ensuring consistency and efficiency while allowing for necessary localizations.

Key Features of Global Template

1. **Standardization:** Establishes a standard set of processes, configurations, and data structures for all implementations.
2. **Flexibility:** It allows localization to meet the specific legal, regulatory, and business requirements of different regions or business units.
3. **Scalability:** Facilitates scalable deployments as the organization expands or acquires new entities.

Steps to Develop a Global Template

1. **Define Scope and Objectives:**
   - **Stakeholder Engagement:** Engage stakeholders from various regions and business units to define the scope and objectives of the global template.
   - **Requirements Gathering:** Collect requirements that are common across all locations as well as those that are unique to specific regions or business units.

2. **Standardize Processes:**
   - ○ **Process Mapping:** Identify and map business processes that can be standardized.
   - ○ **Best Practices:** Incorporate industry best practices and SAP standard processes into the template.
3. **Develop the Template:**
   - ○ **Configuration:** Configure the SAP system based on the standardized processes and requirements.
   - ○ **Documentation:** Document the global template, including configurations, process flows, and localization guidelines.
4. **Pilot Implementation:**
   - ○ **Pilot Site Selection:** To test the global template, select a pilot site.
   - ○ **Implementation:** Implement the template at the pilot site and gather feedback to refine the template.
5. **Rollout Plan:**
   - ○ **Deployment Strategy:** Develop a deployment strategy for rolling out the template to other locations.
   - ○ **Localization:** Define guidelines for localizing the template to meet the specific requirements of each region or business unit.
6. **Training and Support:**
   - ○ **Training Programs:** Develop training programs to educate users on the global template.
   - ○ **Support Structure:** Establish a support structure to assist local teams during and after the rollout.

Best Practices for Global Template Deployment

1. **Strong Governance:** Establish strong governance structures to manage the global template's development, approval, and maintenance.
2. **Stakeholder Involvement:** Engage stakeholders from different regions and business units throughout the process to ensure the template meets their needs.
3. **Flexibility:** Allow for necessary localizations while maintaining the integrity of the global template.
4. **Continuous Improvement:** Regularly review and update the template based on feedback and changing business requirements.

5. **Knowledge Sharing:** Promote sharing and collaboration between locations to leverage best practices and lessons learned.

Big Bang

Overview of Big Bang Deployment

The Big Bang deployment approach involves implementing the SAP system across the entire organization simultaneously. All modules and functionalities go live simultaneously, replacing the existing systems in one major transition.

Key Features of Big Bang Deployment

1. **Simultaneous Go-Live:** All locations, business units, and functions simultaneously switch to the new SAP system.
2. **Comprehensive Testing:** Extensive testing is required to ensure that all aspects of the system function correctly before the life.
3. **High Coordination:** Requires high levels of coordination and planning to manage the transition smoothly.

Steps to Execute a Big Bang Deployment
1. **Planning and Preparation:**
   o **Project Plan:** Develop a detailed project plan outlining the required deployment timeline, resources, and activities.
   o **Stakeholder Engagement:** Engage organizational stakeholders to ensure alignment and support.
2. **System Design and Configuration:**
   o **Requirements Gathering:** Collect and document business requirements for all modules and functions.
   o **System Configuration:** Configure the SAP system based on the gathered requirements.
3. **Data Migration:**
   o **Data Cleansing:** Cleanse and prepare data for migration to the new system.

- o **Data Migration Plan:** Develop a detailed data migration plan, including extraction, transformation, and loading (ETL) processes.
4. **Testing:**
   - o **Unit Testing:** Test individual components to ensure they function correctly.
   - o **Integration Testing:** Test interactions between different modules and systems.
   - o **User Acceptance Testing (UAT):** Involve end-users in testing to validate the system against business requirements.
5. **Training:**
   - o **Training Programs:** Develop and deliver training programs to prepare users for the new system.
   - o **Training Materials:** Create comprehensive training materials, including user manuals and quick reference guides.
6. **Go-Live Preparation:**
   - o **Cutover Plan:** Develop a detailed plan outlining the steps required to transition to the new system.
   - o **Communication:** Communicate the go-live plan to all stakeholders, including the schedule and support mechanisms.
7. **Go-Live and Support:**
   - o **Go-Live:** Execute the cutover plan and transition to the new system.
   - o **Support:** Provide immediate post-go-live support to address issues and assist users.

Best Practices for Big Bang Deployment

1. **Thorough Planning:** Develop a detailed and realistic project plan, accounting for all activities, dependencies, and risks.
2. **Extensive Testing:** Conduct comprehensive testing to ensure the system is fully functional and meets business requirements.
3. **Effective Communication:** Maintain open and transparent communication with all stakeholders throughout the project.
4. **Robust Training:** Provide thorough training to ensure users are well-prepared for the new system.

5. **Strong Support Structure:** Establish a robust support structure to address issues quickly and minimize disruption during the go-live.

Phased Rollout

Overview of Phased Rollout

The Phased Rollout approach involves implementing the SAP system in stages by business unit, location, or functionality. This incremental approach allows for a more manageable transition and reduces the risk associated with the deployment.

Key Features of Phased Rollout

1. **Incremental Implementation:** The system is deployed in phases, allowing for gradual adoption and adjustment.
2. **Risk Mitigation:** Reduces risk by limiting the scope of each phase and addressing issues as they arise.
3. **Flexibility:** Provides flexibility to adapt the deployment plan based on feedback and lessons learned from earlier phases.

Steps to Execute a Phased Rollout

1. **Planning and Strategy:**
   - **Phasing Strategy:** Define the phasing strategy, including the sequence and criteria for each phase.
   - **Detailed Plan:** Develop a detailed plan for each phase, outlining activities, resources, and timelines.
2. **Initial Phase Implementation:**
   - **Pilot Project:** Implement a pilot project in a selected business unit or location to validate the system and approach.
   - **Feedback and Adjustments:** Gather feedback from the pilot and make necessary adjustments to the system and plan.
3. **Subsequent Phases:**
   - **Rollout Plan:** Develop and execute a rollout plan for each subsequent phase based on the lessons learned from the pilot.
   - **Data Migration:** Conduct data migration for each phase, ensuring data integrity and consistency.

4. **Testing:**
    o   **Phase-Specific Testing:** Conduct unit, integration, and user acceptance testing for each phase to ensure functionality and performance.
    o   **End-to-end Testing:** Perform end-to-end testing to validate the entire process across multiple phases.
5. **Training:**
    o   **Tailored Training:** Develop and deliver training programs tailored to the specific needs of each phase.
    o   **Continuous Learning:** Provide continuous learning opportunities and resources to support users throughout the rollout.
6. **Go-Live and Support:**
    o   **Staggered Go-Live:** Execute go-live activities for each phase, ensuring a smooth transition.
    o   **Ongoing Support:** To address issues and support users in each phase, provide ongoing support and monitoring.

Best Practices for Phased Rollout

1. **Clear Phasing Strategy:** Define a clear and logical phasing strategy to ensure a smooth and manageable rollout.
2. **Pilot Testing:** Conduct a pilot project to validate the system and approach before full-scale deployment.
3. **Continuous Improvement:** Use feedback and lessons learned from each phase to improve the system and rollout process continuously.
4. **Effective Communication:** Maintain open communication with stakeholders to keep them informed and engaged throughout the rollout.
5. **Robust Training:** Provide tailored training programs to ensure users are prepared and supported in each phase.

Comparing Deployment Options

Factors to Consider
1. **Organizational Complexity:** Consider the organization's size, structure, and complexity when selecting a deployment strategy.

2. **Risk Tolerance:** When choosing between the Big Bang and Phased Rollout approaches, assess the organization's tolerance for risk and disruption.
3. **Resource Availability:** Evaluate the availability of resources, including time, budget, and personnel, to support the deployment.
4. **Business Priorities:** Align the deployment strategy with the organization's priorities.

Summary of Advantages and Challenges
1. **Global Template:**
   - **Advantages:** Standardization, consistency, scalability.
   - **Challenges:** Requires strong governance, stakeholder alignment, and flexibility for localization.
2. **Big Bang:**
   - **Advantages:** Faster transition, no need for long-term synchronization.
   - **Challenges:** High risk, extensive planning and testing, significant resource requirements.
3. **Phased Rollout:**
   - **Advantages:** Lower risk, manageable transition, flexibility to adapt.
   - **Challenges:** Longer deployment period, need for synchronization between phases, continuous resource commitment.

Deployment Isn't Just a Technical Decision—It's a Business Commitment

Choosing a deployment strategy for an SAP implementation is one of the most consequential decisions a program will make—and yet it's often treated as a binary choice made far too early or far too lightly. Whether an organization selects a Big Bang, Phased Rollout, or Global Template-led deployment, the decision should be grounded in operational reality, organizational maturity, and an honest assessment of the business's capacity to absorb change. No single approach is universally "right," but each comes with trade-offs that must be surfaced, debated, and agreed upon at the steering committee level—not just within the PMO or IT.

A Big Bang deployment, where all business units, geographies, and functions transition to SAP simultaneously, offers the benefit of a clean break from legacy systems and a shorter period of parallel operations. But the simplicity of the concept belies the complexity in execution. It demands complete readiness in every domain: data, testing, training, cutover, and business continuity planning. Any weakness becomes amplified under the pressure of a single go-live date. While it can work well for centralized organizations or businesses facing regulatory deadlines, the truth is that very few companies are structurally or culturally equipped to handle the level of orchestration Big Bang requires. I've witnessed teams stretch to deliver testing and training by year-end only to hit a wall during the first billing cycle because operational teams were too overloaded to absorb the change.

The Phased Rollout model, on the other hand, spreads the transition over time, reducing immediate risk and allowing for targeted learning and adjustments between waves. But this slower path introduces its own complications—such as prolonged reliance on legacy systems, complex interim interfaces, and change fatigue. A phased approach requires consistency in documentation, resources, and leadership over an extended timeline. Organizations often underestimate how hard it is to maintain focus and quality from the first phase to the last. The reality is that without strong change management and long-term sponsorship, these projects can lose momentum, leading to inconsistent adoption or scope erosion.

The Global Template strategy is not a deployment model by itself but a foundational decision that shapes how any rollout—Big Bang or phased—is executed. A well-governed template enables standardization, accelerates scale, and provides a single source of truth across the enterprise. But it must strike the right balance between harmonization and localization. Too rigid, and it becomes irrelevant to local users. Too loose, and you undermine the very benefits of having a template. The most successful programs I've seen build the template with deployment in mind: using pilots to validate design, maintaining strict governance to manage change, and embedding localization protocols from day one.

An often overlooked aspect of deployment strategy is *when* to go live. Many programs default to January 1 or the start of a new quarter, assuming that calendar alignment will simplify reporting and financial close. In theory, it makes sense. In practice, it often leads to burnout, errors, and poor adoption. When a project has been running for 18 to 24 months, and the go-live falls on January 1, what that really means is that critical cutover activities, business validation, and user training all happen during December—a month traditionally marked by holiday leave, year-end close, and minimal business availability. Finance teams are already stretched, operational leaders are focused on hitting targets, and project staff are expected to deliver one of the most complex transitions of their careers while skipping vacations. It's a perfect storm.

The better question to ask isn't "What date looks clean on a spreadsheet?" but "When is the business ready to own the system?" A go-live should be scheduled based on business cycle quiet periods—not just calendar start dates. For many, a late Q1 or early Q2 go-live offers a more stable footing. Others may benefit from aligning with seasonal lulls or post-audit windows. What matters is that go-live timing is driven by operational readiness and organizational availability, not symbolic symmetry. I've seen successful go-lives happen in April, July, and even September—not because they were ideal on paper, but because the business could breathe, focus, and support the transition.

Ultimately, deployment isn't a technical milestone—it's a behavioral shift across the enterprise. Success comes from matching the right strategy with the right timing, the right leadership, and the right level of readiness. Rushing a go-live to meet a symbolic date or choosing a model that doesn't reflect the company's operating structure invites disruption and dissatisfaction. A well-chosen deployment path, anchored in business reality and supported by disciplined execution, turns SAP from a project into a platform for transformation. That's the real win.

Conclusion

Choosing the right deployment option is critical to the success of an SAP implementation. Each approach—Global Template, Big Bang, and Phased Rollout—offers unique benefits and challenges. By carefully considering the organization's complexity, risk tolerance, resource availability, and business priorities and adhering to best practices for each deployment strategy, organizations can achieve a smooth and successful SAP implementation that meets their business needs and drives significant value.

Chapter 18: Localization Considerations

Localization is crucial to SAP implementation, especially for organizations operating in multiple countries or regions. It involves adapting the SAP system to meet local legal, regulatory, and business requirements. This chapter explores the critical considerations for localization, the steps involved in the process, and best practices to ensure a successful and compliant SAP implementation across different geographies.

Understanding Localization

Overview of Localization

Localization in the context of SAP implementation refers to adapting the SAP system to meet the specific needs of different countries or regions. This includes complying with local laws, regulations, business practices, language, and cultural preferences. Effective localization ensures the SAP system is functional, compliant, and efficient in each locale.

Key Components of Localization
1. **Legal and Regulatory Compliance:** Adhering to local laws and regulations related to finance, taxation, labor, data protection, etc.
2. **Language and Translation:** Support local languages and ensure that all user interfaces, documentation, and reports are accurately translated.
3. **Cultural Adaptation:** Adapting the system to align with local cultural norms and business practices.
4. **Currency and Fiscal Year Settings:** Configuring the system to handle local currencies, exchange rates, and fiscal year variations.
5. **Local Business Practices:** Customizing workflows, reports, and processes to align with local business practices and industry standards.

Steps in Localization

1. Conducting a Localization Assessment

Legal and Regulatory Requirements:
- **Compliance Research:** Conduct thorough research on local legal and regulatory requirements in each target country or region. This includes laws related to finance, taxation, labor, data protection, and industry-specific regulations.
- **Regulatory Bodies:** Identify the relevant regulatory bodies and standards that govern business operations in each locale.

Language and Cultural Needs:
- **Language Support:** Determine the languages spoken in each region and the need to translate user interfaces, documentation, and reports.
- **Cultural Preferences:** Understand local cultural norms, holidays, and business practices that may impact system configuration and user experience.

Local Business Practices:
- **Industry Standards:** Identify local industry standards and best practices that must be incorporated into the SAP system.
- **Business Processes:** Analyze local business processes to determine any unique requirements that differ from global processes.

2. Developing a Localization Strategy

Localization Plan:
- **Scope Definition:** Define the scope of localization for each region, including the specific requirements and customizations needed.
- **Resource Allocation:** Allocate resources, including budget, personnel, and tools, to support the localization efforts.

Stakeholder Engagement:
- **Local Experts:** Engage local experts and stakeholders to provide insights and guidance on localization requirements.

- **Cross-Functional Teams:** Form cross-functional teams with representatives from different regions to ensure comprehensive input and collaboration.

3. Implementing Localization

System Configuration:
- **Legal and Regulatory Compliance:** Configure the SAP system to comply with local legal and regulatory requirements, including tax codes, reporting standards, and data protection measures.
- **Language Settings:** Implement language support and translation for user interfaces, documentation, and reports.

Custom Development:
- **Local Customizations:** Develop custom solutions to address unique local business practices and requirements.
- **Interfaces and Integrations:** Ensure that the system integrates seamlessly with local systems and third-party applications.

Testing and Validation:
- **Localization Testing:** Conduct thorough testing to ensure the localized system functions correctly and meets local requirements.
- **User Acceptance Testing (UAT):** Involve local users in UAT to validate that the system meets their needs and expectations.

4. Training and Support

Localized Training Programs:
- **Training Materials:** Develop localized training materials, including user manuals, quick reference guides, and e-learning modules.
- **Training Sessions:** Conduct training sessions for local users to ensure they understand how to use the localized system.

Ongoing Support:
- **Local Support Teams:** Establish local support teams to provide assistance and resolve issues related to the localized system.

- **Continuous Improvement:** Gather feedback from local users and continuously improve the localized system based on their input.

Best Practices for Localization

1. Comprehensive Research and Planning

Thorough Research:
- **Local Regulations:** Stay up-to-date with local regulations and standards to ensure compliance.
- **Market Trends:** Understand each region's market trends and industry standards to align the system with local practices.

Detailed Planning:
- **Localization Roadmap:** Develop a detailed roadmap for localization, outlining the tasks, timelines, and resources needed.
- **Risk Management:** Identify potential risks and develop mitigation strategies.

2. Collaboration and Communication

Stakeholder Collaboration:
- **Local Experts:** Collaborate with local experts and stakeholders to gather insights and validate requirements.
- **Global Coordination:** Ensure effective communication and coordination between global and local teams to align efforts.

Regular Updates:
- **Progress Reports:** Provide regular updates on localization progress to all stakeholders.
- **Feedback Mechanisms:** Implement feedback mechanisms to gather input from local users and address their concerns.

3. Flexibility and Adaptability
Customizable Solutions:
- **Modular Design:** Design the system with modular components that can be easily customized to meet local requirements.

- **Scalable Architecture:** Ensure the system architecture is scalable to accommodate future localization needs.

Adaptability:
- **Continuous Improvement:** Monitor and adapt the system to address changing local requirements and regulations.
- **User Feedback:** Leverage user feedback to identify areas for improvement and implement changes promptly.

4. Robust Testing and Validation
Comprehensive Testing:
- **Localization Testing:** Conduct extensive testing to ensure the localized system meets all local requirements and functions correctly.
- **End-to-end Testing:** Perform end-to-end testing to validate the entire process flow and identify integration issues.

User Involvement:
- **UAT:** Involve local users in UAT to validate that the system meets their needs and expectations.
- **Beta Testing:** Consider conducting beta testing with a select group of users to gather feedback and make necessary adjustments.

5. Effective Training and Support
Localized Training:
- **Tailored Programs:** Develop training programs tailored to the specific needs of local users.
- **Interactive Learning:** Use interactive learning methods, such as workshops and hands-on practice, to enhance understanding.

Ongoing Support:
- **Local Support Teams:** Establish local support teams to provide timely assistance and resolve issues.
- **Knowledge Base:** To support users, create a knowledge base with localized documentation and FAQs.

Case Studies and Examples

Case Study 1: Global Manufacturing Company
Overview: A global manufacturing company implemented SAP in multiple countries. The localization efforts focused on ensuring

compliance with local tax regulations, supporting various languages, and adapting to local business practices.

Approach:

- **Localization Assessment:** Conducted a thorough assessment to identify local requirements for each region.
- **Custom Solutions:** Developed custom solutions for tax calculations, reporting, and integration with local systems.
- **Training and Support:** Provided localized training and established local support teams to assist users.

Outcome:

- **Compliance:** Achieved compliance with local regulations in all regions.
- **User Adoption:** Improved user adoption and satisfaction through tailored training and support.
- **Operational Efficiency:** Enhanced operational efficiency by standardizing processes while accommodating local variations.

Case Study 2: Retail Chain

Overview: A retail chain with stores in multiple countries implemented SAP to streamline its operations. The localization efforts included adapting the system for local currencies, fiscal years, and reporting requirements.

Approach:

- **Localization Strategy:** Developed a comprehensive localization strategy with input from local stakeholders.
- **Phased Rollout:** Implemented a phased rollout to manage the transition and gather feedback from each phase.
- **Continuous Improvement:** Continuously improved the system based on feedback and changing local requirements.

Outcome:

- **Seamless Transition:** Achieved a seamless transition with minimal disruption to operations.
- **Regulatory Compliance:** Ensured compliance with local financial and reporting regulations.
- **Improved Reporting:** Enhanced reporting capabilities with localized reports and dashboards.

Localization is More Than Compliance – It's Culture in Code

When organizations implement SAP across multiple countries, they often approach localization as a checklist of tax codes, legal structures, and language packs. But the reality is far more nuanced. True localization is about embedding each region's cultural identity, business expectations, and user behavior into the fabric of a global ERP. It's not just about translating labels or configuring currency – it's about earning trust and adoption at the local level while preserving strategic cohesion globally.

The cultural dimension of localization cannot be overstated. Business habits, communication norms, hierarchy in decision-making, and even how users interact with software vary dramatically across geographies. In Germany, users may expect rigorous auditability and system rigidity, while teams in Southeast Asia may place higher value on system flexibility and quick on-screen access. A copy-paste rollout of a U.S.-centric template may fail not because the config is wrong, but because it violates unwritten expectations about how work gets done. Localization, then, is not a set of technical requirements – it's a change management journey that must be rooted in deep cultural awareness.

Workshops play a pivotal role in this process, but they must be adapted accordingly. Global design workshops held in English with limited local participation may appear efficient but often overlook the subtleties of local processes, vendor relationships, and reporting requirements. To avoid this trap, successful programs run localized deep-dive workshops *in-region* and in the local language when possible, leveraging interpreters and cultural liaisons to bridge gaps. These workshops are not just about gathering requirements – they're critical for surfacing risks, aligning stakeholders, and building trust. The sooner regional users feel they have a voice in the solution, the stronger their buy-in will be during deployment.

Training strategies must follow the same localized path. A global training curriculum built in a shared services center may tick every box from a content standpoint but still fall flat with local users. Language is only part of the challenge – how people learn varies by region. Some users respond best to classroom-style instruction; others prefer hands-on labs or scenario-driven simulations.

Programs that invest in localized, role-based training – supported by local trainers and relevant scenarios – consistently see higher user confidence and fewer post-go-live issues. Interactive training, gamified exercises, and in-person walkthroughs of new business flows can go further than any reference guide ever will.

Deployment sequencing must also account for localization complexity. It's not just about system readiness – it's about cultural readiness. Some regions may require longer ramp-up periods to gain alignment with legal authorities, adapt business practices, or secure government approvals for system usage (such as in Latin America or China). Others may need longer testing cycles due to legacy system interdependencies or reporting reconciliation processes unique to their market. When sequencing deployments, it's wise to avoid overloading regions with high localization complexity in early waves unless they've been heavily involved in template design. Otherwise, the deployment becomes not just a system transition – but a diplomatic recovery effort.

Finally, localization doesn't end at go-live. Support models must be designed to reflect the language, working hours, and escalation paths unique to each country. A shared support queue in Europe may work well across the EU, but it won't serve a branch in Japan during their business day. Local support teams – ideally with SAP expertise and contextual business knowledge – are essential. So too is a robust feedback loop: what didn't work, what needs improvement, and what future updates must accommodate evolving local laws and regulations. This is especially true in regions with frequent regulatory changes, such as GST rules in India or e-invoicing mandates in South America.

Localization is not a "technical subproject." It's a full-fledged capability that demands cultural fluency, region-specific planning, and sustained investment. The most successful SAP programs treat localization as a strategic differentiator – not just a requirement to fulfill. They embed it into their governance model, resource it with bilingual experts, and elevate it to the same level of scrutiny as testing, data migration, and security. In doing so, they don't just achieve compliance – they earn adoption. And in a global deployment, that's what turns a system implementation into a business transformation.

Conclusion

Localization is critical to SAP implementation, particularly for organizations operating in multiple countries or regions. By understanding the essential components of localization, following a structured process, and adhering to best practices, organizations can ensure that their SAP system is compliant, efficient, and user-friendly across all locations. Effective localization enhances operational efficiency, improves user satisfaction, and supports the organization's global strategy.

Chapter 19: Performance Optimization

Performance optimization is a critical component of SAP implementation that ensures the system operates efficiently, effectively, and at peak performance. This chapter delves into monitoring system performance, identifying bottlenecks, and fostering continuous improvement to maintain and enhance SAP systems' performance.

Monitoring System Performance

Overview of System Performance Monitoring
System performance monitoring involves continuously tracking the SAP system's performance metrics to ensure it meets the required performance standards. Effective monitoring helps identify potential issues before they impact users and allows timely intervention to maintain system health.

Critical Aspects of System Performance Monitoring
1. **Real-Time Monitoring:**
   o **Definition:** Real-time monitoring involves continuously tracking system metrics to provide immediate insights into system performance.
   o **Tools:** Utilize tools such as SAP Solution Manager, SAP Cloud Platform, and third-party monitoring solutions to monitor system performance in real-time.
2. **Performance Metrics:**
   o **System Utilization:** Monitor CPU, memory, and disk usage to ensure optimal resource utilization.
   o **Response Times:** Track response times for various transactions and processes to ensure they meet performance standards.
   o **Throughput:** Measure the volume of data the system processes to ensure it can handle the workload.
   o **Error Rates:** Monitor error rates to identify and address issues that may impact system performance.

3. **User Experience:**
   o **End-User Monitoring:** Track the performance from an end-user perspective to ensure users are experiencing optimal performance.
   o **Synthetic Monitoring:** Synthetic transactions simulate user interactions and measure system performance.
4. **Alerts and Notifications:**
   o **Thresholds:** Set performance thresholds and configure alerts to notify administrators when metrics exceed acceptable limits.
   o **Automated Responses:** Implement automated responses to common issues to minimize downtime and maintain performance.

Steps to Implement System Performance Monitoring
   1. **Define Performance Metrics:**
      o **Key Metrics:** Identify the key performance metrics to be monitored based on business requirements and system architecture.
      o **Baseline Performance:** Establish baseline performance metrics to serve as a reference for normal system behavior.
   2. **Select Monitoring Tools:**
      o **Tool Selection:** Choose appropriate monitoring tools that provide comprehensive insights into system performance.
      o **Integration:** Ensure the selected tools integrate seamlessly with the SAP system and other IT infrastructure.
   3. **Configure Monitoring:**
      o **Metric Collection:** Configure the monitoring tools to collect the identified performance metrics.
      o **Alert Configuration:** Set up alerts and notifications for critical performance metrics to enable proactive management.
   4. **Regular Review:**
      o **Performance Reports:** Generate regular performance reports to review system performance trends and identify areas for improvement.

  o **Stakeholder Meetings:** Regularly meet with stakeholders to discuss performance insights and action plans.

Best Practices for System Performance Monitoring
1. **Comprehensive Coverage:** Ensure that all critical components and metrics of the SAP system are monitored.
2. **Proactive Monitoring:** Implement proactive monitoring to identify and address issues before they impact users.
3. **User-Centric Metrics:** Focus on metrics directly impacting the user experience to ensure optimal performance.
4. **Regular Updates:** Regularly update monitoring tools and configurations to keep pace with system changes and evolving requirements.
5. **Continuous Improvement:** Use performance insights to improve system performance and user satisfaction.

Identifying Bottlenecks

Overview of Bottlenecks in SAP Systems
Bottlenecks are points in the system that limit performance, causing delays and reducing overall efficiency. Identifying and addressing bottlenecks is crucial for maintaining optimal system performance.

Common Types of Bottlenecks
1. **Hardware Bottlenecks:**
   o **CPU Utilization:** High CPU utilization can slow processing and impact system performance.
   o **Memory Usage:** Insufficient memory can increase paging and slower response times.
   o **Disk I/O:** High disk I/O can cause delays in data retrieval and storage operations.
2. **Software Bottlenecks:**
   o **Database Performance:** Slow database queries and inefficient indexing can impact system performance.
   o **Application Code:** Inefficient application code can lead to slow transaction processing and high resource consumption.
   o **Integration Points:** Slow or inefficient integrations with other systems can create performance bottlenecks.

3. **Network Bottlenecks:**
   - o **Bandwidth:** Insufficient network bandwidth can cause delays in data transmission.
   - o **Latency:** High network latency can impact the performance of remote transactions and data access.

Steps to Identify Bottlenecks
1. **Performance Baseline:**
   - o **Establish Baselines:** Establish baseline performance metrics to understand normal system behavior.
   - o **Compare Metrics:** Compare current performance metrics against the baseline to identify deviations and potential bottlenecks.
2. **Detailed Analysis:**
   - o **System Logs:** Analyze system logs and performance data to identify patterns and anomalies.
   - o **Root Cause Analysis:** Conduct root cause analysis to determine the underlying causes of performance issues.
3. **Performance Testing:**
   - o **Load Testing:** Perform load testing to simulate high workloads and identify performance bottlenecks.
   - o **Stress Testing:** Conduct stress testing to determine the system's capacity limits and identify potential failure points.
4. **Tool Utilization:**
   - o **Monitoring Tools:** Monitoring tools identify bottlenecks by analyzing performance metrics and system behavior.
   - o **Profiling Tools:** Employ profiling tools to analyze application code and database queries for inefficiencies.

Best Practices for Identifying Bottlenecks
1. **Regular Monitoring:** Continuously monitor system performance to detect bottlenecks early.
2. **Comprehensive Analysis:** To identify bottlenecks, combine monitoring tools, logs, and performance testing.
3. **Proactive Approach:** Address potential bottlenecks proactively to prevent performance degradation.

4. **Collaborative Effort:** Involve cross-functional teams in identifying and resolving bottlenecks to leverage diverse expertise.
5. **Iterative Process:** Treat bottleneck identification and resolution as an iterative process, continuously refining and optimizing system performance.

Continuous Improvement

Overview of Continuous Improvement
Continuous improvement involves regularly evaluating and enhancing system performance to meet evolving business needs and user expectations. This process requires a proactive approach to performance management and a commitment to ongoing optimization.

Critical Components of Continuous Improvement
1. **Performance Reviews:**
   o **Regular Reviews:** Conduct regular performance reviews to evaluate system performance and identify areas for improvement.
   o **Stakeholder Involvement:** Involve stakeholders from different business units to gather diverse perspectives on performance and improvement opportunities.
2. **Performance Tuning:**
   o **System Tuning:** Regularly tune system configurations, including database settings, application parameters, and hardware resources, to optimize performance.
   o **Code Optimization:** Continuously review and optimize application code to improve efficiency and reduce resource consumption.
3. **Capacity Planning:**
   o **Usage Trends:** Monitor usage trends to anticipate future capacity needs and plan for system scalability.
   o **Resource Allocation:** Allocate resources based on current and projected workloads to ensure the system can handle increased demand.

4. **Process Optimization:**
    o   **Workflow Analysis:** Analyze business workflows to identify inefficiencies and opportunities for automation and optimization.
    o   **Best Practices:** Implement industry best practices to streamline processes and enhance system performance.
5. **User Feedback:**
    o   **Feedback Mechanisms:** Establish feedback mechanisms to gather user input on system performance and usability.
    o   **Actionable Insights:** Use feedback to identify performance issues and prioritize improvement efforts.

Steps for Continuous Improvement
1. **Establish a Framework:**
    o   **Improvement Plan:** Develop a continuous improvement plan outlining goals, activities, and responsibilities.
    o   **Performance Metrics:** Define key performance metrics to track progress and measure the impact of improvement efforts.
2. **Implement Improvement Initiatives:**
    o   **Quick Wins:** Identify and implement quick wins to achieve immediate performance gains.
    o   **Long-Term Projects:** Plan and execute long-term improvement projects to address more complex performance issues.
3. **Measure Impact:**
    o   **Performance Measurement:** Continuously measure system performance to assess the impact of improvement initiatives.
    o   **Adjust Strategies:** Adjust improvement strategies based on performance data and feedback to maximize impact.
4. **Foster a Culture of Improvement:**
    o   **Encourage Innovation:** Encourage team members to suggest innovative ideas for performance improvement.

    ○ **Recognize Contributions:** Recognize and reward contributions to performance improvement to motivate continuous efforts.

Best Practices for Continuous Improvement

1. **Data-Driven Decisions:** Use performance data and user feedback to drive improvement initiatives and prioritize efforts.
2. **Agile Approach:** Adopt an agile approach to continuous improvement, iteratively implementing and refining changes.
3. **Cross-functional collaboration:** To leverage diverse expertise and insights and foster collaboration between IT, business units, and end-users.
4. **Regular Training:** Provide training and development opportunities for team members to stay updated on best practices and new technologies.
5. **Scalability:** To accommodate future growth and evolving business needs, ensure scalable improvement initiatives.

Case Studies and Examples

Case Study 1: Financial Services Company

Overview: A financial services company implemented SAP to streamline its operations. Post-implementation, the focus was on performance optimization to ensure the system met the company's high transaction volumes and user demands.

Approach:
- **System Performance Monitoring:** Implemented real-time monitoring tools to track system performance metrics.
- **Identifying Bottlenecks:** Conducted detailed analysis and performance testing to identify bottlenecks in database queries and application code.
- **Continuous Improvement:** Established a continuous improvement framework involving regular performance reviews, system tuning, and code optimization.

Outcome:
- **Improved Performance:** Achieved significant improvements in system response times and throughput.
- **User Satisfaction:** Enhanced user satisfaction through proactive performance management and issue resolution.

- **Scalability:** Ensured the system could handle future growth and increased transaction volumes.

Case Study 2: Manufacturing Company

Overview: A manufacturing company implemented SAP to integrate its global operations. Performance optimization was a key focus to support complex manufacturing processes and real-time data access.

Approach:
- **Monitoring System Performance:** Deployed monitoring tools to track system performance and user activity continuously.
- **Identifying Bottlenecks:** Identified bottlenecks related to network latency and hardware resource utilization through detailed analysis and stress testing.
- **Continuous Improvement:** Implemented a continuous improvement process, focusing on system tuning, process optimization, and user feedback.

Outcome:
- **Optimized Performance:** Improved system performance, enabling real-time data access and efficient manufacturing processes.
- **Operational Efficiency:** Increased efficiency through streamlined workflows and optimized system configurations.
- **Proactive Management:** Established a proactive performance management approach, ensuring ongoing optimization and user satisfaction.

Conclusion

Performance optimization is essential for maintaining and enhancing the efficiency and effectiveness of SAP systems. By monitoring system performance, identifying bottlenecks, and fostering continuous improvement, organizations can ensure their SAP systems operate at peak performance, meet business needs, and deliver a superior user experience. Adhering to best practices in these areas helps drive ongoing optimization, scalability, and long-term success.

Chapter 20: Security and Compliance

Security and compliance are critical aspects of SAP implementation that protect sensitive data, maintain system integrity, and meet regulatory requirements. This chapter provides detailed guidance on SAP security best practices, user role and authorization management, and compliance and auditing. Adhering to these guidelines helps organizations safeguard their SAP systems and ensure regulatory compliance.

SAP Security Best Practices

Overview of SAP Security
SAP security encompasses various measures and practices to protect SAP systems from unauthorized access, data breaches, and other security threats. Adequate SAP security ensures data and systems' confidentiality, integrity, and availability.

Critical Components of SAP Security
1. **System Hardening:**
   o **Patch Management:** Regularly apply security patches and updates to SAP systems to protect against vulnerabilities.
   o **Configuration Management:** Ensure that SAP systems are configured securely, following industry best practices and SAP recommendations.
2. **Access Control:**
   o **Authentication:** Implement robust authentication mechanisms, such as multi-factor authentication (MFA), to verify user identities.
   o **Authorization:** Use role-based access control (RBAC) to ensure users have appropriate permissions based on their roles and responsibilities.
3. **Data Protection:**
   o **Encryption:** Encrypt sensitive data at rest and in transit to protect it from unauthorized access.
   o **Data Masking:** Data masking techniques anonymize sensitive data in non-production environments.

4. **Network Security:**
   o **Firewalls:** Deploy firewalls to protect SAP systems from unauthorized access and network-based attacks.
   o **VPNs:** Use Virtual Private Networks (VPNs) to secure remote access to SAP systems.
5. **Monitoring and Logging:**
   o **Activity Monitoring:** Continuously monitor user activities and system events to detect and respond to security incidents.
   o **Audit Logs:** Maintain detailed audit logs to track changes, access, and other critical actions in the SAP system.

Steps to Implement SAP Security Best Practices
1. **Security Assessment:**
   o **Risk Assessment:** Conduct a risk assessment to identify potential security threats and vulnerabilities in the SAP environment.
   o **Gap Analysis:** Perform a gap analysis to compare the current security posture against best practices and regulatory requirements.
2. **Security Planning:**
   o **Security Policies:** Develop and implement security policies that define the security controls and practices to be followed.
   o **Security Architecture:** Design a security architecture that includes network segmentation, access controls, and encryption.
3. **Implementation:**
   o **Patch Management:** Establish a patch management process to ensure timely application of security patches and updates.
   o **Access Controls:** Implement strong authentication and authorization mechanisms to control access to SAP systems.
4. **Training and Awareness:**
   o **User Training:** Provide security training to users to raise awareness about security threats and best practices.

o **Incident Response:** Train the security team on incident response procedures to ensure quick and effective handling of security incidents.

5. **Monitoring and Maintenance:**
    o **Continuous Monitoring:** Implement continuous monitoring tools and practices to detect and respond to security threats.
    o **Regular Audits:** Conduct regular security audits to verify compliance with security policies and identify areas for improvement.

Best Practices for SAP Security

1. **Layered Security:** Implement a multi-layered security approach to provide in-depth defense and protection against various threats.
2. **Least Privilege:** Follow the principle of least privilege, granting users the minimum access necessary to perform their roles.
3. **Segregation of Duties:** Implement segregation of duties (SoD) to prevent conflicts of interest and reduce the risk of fraud.
4. **Regular Updates:** Keep SAP systems and security tools up-to-date with the latest patches and updates.
5. **Incident Response:** Develop and regularly test incident response plans to ensure quick and effective handling of security incidents.

User Role and Authorization Management

Overview of User Role and Authorization Management
User role and authorization management involves defining and managing user roles, permissions, and access rights in SAP systems. Effective management ensures that users have the appropriate access to perform their tasks while minimizing the risk of unauthorized access and data breaches.

Critical Components of User Role and Authorization Management

1. **Role Design:**
    o **Role Definition:** Define roles based on job functions and responsibilities, ensuring each role has the necessary permissions.

- o **Role Hierarchies:** Create role hierarchies to simplify management and ensure consistent access controls.
2. **Authorization Management:**
   - o **Permission Assignment:** Assign permissions to roles based on the principle of least privilege.
   - o **Segregation of Duties:** Implement segregation of duties (SoD) controls to prevent conflicts of interest and reduce the risk of fraud.
3. **User Provisioning:**
   - o **User Creation:** Create user accounts and assign roles based on their job functions and responsibilities.
   - o **Access Requests:** Implement a standardized process for requesting and approving access to SAP systems.
4. **Access Reviews:**
   - o **Regular Reviews:** Regularly reviews user roles and permissions to ensure they remain appropriate and aligned with job functions.
   - o **Certification:** Implement a certification process to verify that users have the correct access rights.
5. **Role Maintenance:**
   - o **Role Updates:** Regularly update roles and permissions to reflect job functions, responsibilities, and organizational structure changes.
   - o **Role Cleanup:** Periodically clean up unused roles and permissions to reduce complexity and improve security.

Steps to Implement User Role and Authorization Management
1. **Role Definition:**
   - o **Job Functions:** Identify job functions and responsibilities within the organization.
   - o **Role Creation:** Create roles based on job functions, ensuring each role has the necessary permissions to perform tasks.
2. **Permission Assignment:**
   - o **Access Requirements:** Determine the access requirements for each role based on job functions and responsibilities.
   - o **Permission Allocation:** Assign permissions to roles following the principle of least privilege and segregation of duties.

3. **User Provisioning:**
    o **Access Requests:** Implement a standardized process for requesting and approving access to SAP systems.
    o **User Creation:** Create user accounts and assign roles based on approved access requests.
4. **Access Reviews:**
    o **Regular Reviews:** Regularly reviews user roles and permissions to ensure they remain appropriate and aligned with job functions.
    o **Certification:** Implement a certification process to verify that users have the correct access rights.
5. **Role Maintenance:**
    o **Role Updates:** Regularly update roles and permissions to reflect job functions, responsibilities, and organizational structure changes.
    o **Role Cleanup:** Periodically clean up unused roles and permissions to reduce complexity and improve security.

Best Practices for User Role and Authorization Management
1. **Principle of Least Privilege:** Grant users the minimum access necessary to perform their roles.
2. **Segregation of Duties:** Implement SoD controls to prevent conflicts of interest and reduce the risk of fraud.
3. **Regular Reviews:** Review user roles and permissions regularly to ensure they remain appropriate and aligned with job functions.
4. **Standardized Processes:** Implement standardized processes for requesting, approving, and provisioning access to SAP systems.
5. **Automation:** Use automation tools to streamline user provisioning, access reviews, and role maintenance.

Compliance and Auditing

Overview of Compliance and Auditing
Compliance and auditing ensure the SAP system adheres to relevant laws, regulations, and industry standards. Effective compliance and auditing practices help organizations avoid legal penalties, maintain data integrity, and build stakeholder trust.

Critical Components of Compliance and Auditing

1. **Regulatory Compliance:**
   - **Legal Requirements:** Identify and understand the legal and regulatory requirements applicable to the organization.
   - **Compliance Controls:** Implement controls to ensure compliance with relevant laws and regulations.
2. **Internal Policies:**
   - **Policy Development:** Develop internal policies and procedures to govern the use and management of the SAP system.
   - **Policy Enforcement:** Ensure that policies are enforced consistently across the organization.
3. **Audit Management:**
   - **Audit Planning:** Develop an audit plan that outlines the scope, objectives, and schedule of audits.
   - **Audit Execution:** Conduct audits to evaluate compliance with regulatory requirements and internal policies.
4. **Risk Management:**
   - **Risk Assessment:** Conduct risk assessments to identify potential compliance risks and vulnerabilities.
   - **Mitigation Strategies:** Develop and implement strategies to mitigate identified risks.
5. **Reporting and Documentation:**
   - **Audit Reports:** Generate audit reports documenting findings, recommendations, and corrective actions.
   - **Compliance Documentation:** Maintain comprehensive documentation to demonstrate compliance with regulatory requirements and internal policies.

Steps to Implement Compliance and Auditing
1. **Compliance Framework:**
   - **Regulatory Requirements:** Identify and understand the legal and regulatory requirements applicable to the organization.
   - **Internal Policies:** Develop internal policies and procedures to govern the use and management of the SAP system.

2. **Audit Planning:**
   o **Scope and Objectives:** Define the scope and objectives of audits to evaluate compliance with regulatory requirements and internal policies.
   o **Audit Schedule:** Develop an audit schedule that outlines the frequency and timing of audits.
3. **Audit Execution:**
   o **Audit Preparation:** Gather relevant documentation, access logs, and system configurations for audits.
   o **Audit Conduct:** Conduct audits to evaluate compliance, identify vulnerabilities, and recommend corrective actions.
4. **Risk Management:**
   o **Risk Assessment:** Conduct risk assessments to identify potential compliance risks and vulnerabilities.
   o **Mitigation Strategies:** Develop and implement strategies to mitigate identified risks.
5. **Reporting and Documentation:**
   o **Audit Reports:** Generate audit reports documenting findings, recommendations, and corrective actions.
   o **Compliance Documentation:** Maintain comprehensive documentation to demonstrate compliance with regulatory requirements and internal policies.

Best Practices for Compliance and Auditing
1. **Comprehensive Framework:** Develop a comprehensive compliance and auditing framework that covers all relevant laws, regulations, and internal policies.
2. **Regular Audits:** Conduct regular audits to evaluate compliance, identify vulnerabilities, and recommend corrective actions.
3. **Risk-Based Approach:** Adopt a risk-based approach to compliance and auditing, focusing on areas with the highest risk.
4. **Stakeholder Engagement:** Engage stakeholders in the compliance and auditing process to ensure alignment and support.
5. **Continuous Improvement:** Use audit findings and risk assessments to improve compliance and security practices continuously.

Case Studies and Examples

Case Study 1: Financial Services Company
Overview: A financial services company implemented SAP to streamline its operations. The focus was on ensuring security and compliance to protect sensitive data and meet regulatory requirements.

Approach:
- **SAP Security Best Practices:** Implemented strong authentication, encryption, and continuous monitoring to protect the SAP system.
- **User Role and Authorization Management:** Defined roles based on job functions, implemented SoD controls, and conducted regular access reviews.
- **Compliance and Auditing:** Developed a comprehensive compliance framework, conducted regular audits, and maintained detailed documentation.

Outcome:
- **Enhanced Security:** Achieved a high level of security, protecting sensitive data from unauthorized access and breaches.
- **Regulatory Compliance:** Ensured compliance with relevant financial regulations and avoided legal penalties.
- **Improved Trust:** Built trust with stakeholders through robust security and compliance practices.

Case Study 2: Manufacturing Company
Overview: A manufacturing company implemented SAP to integrate its global operations. The focus was securing the SAP system and ensuring compliance with industry standards.

Approach:
- **SAP Security Best Practices:** Implemented multi-layered security controls, including network segmentation, encryption, and regular patch management.
- **User Role and Authorization Management:** Created roles based on job functions, assigned permissions following the principle of least privilege, and conducted regular access reviews.
- **Compliance and Auditing:** Developed internal policies, conducted regular audits, and implemented risk mitigation strategies.

Outcome:

- **Robust Security:** Enhanced the security of the SAP system, protecting it from internal and external threats.
- **Industry Compliance:** Ensured compliance with industry standards and avoided legal and regulatory penalties.
- **Operational Efficiency:** Improved operational efficiency through secure and compliant SAP system management.

Client Data Security

When a system integrator works on client data, another aspect is to ensure proper data security and keep client data secure. The System Integrator should not store customer data on non-client environments, including laptops, servers, electronic devices, etc.

A security plan for Client Data Protection (CDP) should consist of:

1. **Risk Analysis**: During solution development, solution teams assess data protection risk based on the type and volume of data and the nature of access to the data to which the System Integrator is exposed. The results help identify areas of heightened risk and advance consistent application of control sets.

2. **Gap Analysis**: Client contractual requirements, relevant regulatory requirements, System Integrator policies, and CDP control standards are used to help identify gaps. Action plans and solutions are determined and planned.

3. **Implementation**: The engagement team completes a formalized CDP plan, implements it in System Integrator's proprietary hosted CDP tool, and approves it with appropriate System Integrator data protection subject matter experts from the CDP team. All controls and action plans are validated as fully implemented.

4. **Compliance Monitoring**: The Information Security Risk and Compliance team or the System Integrator's internal audit team may select engagements for a compliance review. The team assesses the engagement's compliance with its CDP plan.

Security Starts on Day One—Not at Cutover

Security and compliance are often mistakenly treated as post-implementation activities—issues to be resolved during go-live prep or left for audit cycles. In reality, they should be embedded from the first day of project planning. Organizations that fail to engage their security, risk, and compliance teams early in an SAP program often find themselves scrambling to retrofit controls, rework role designs, or defend untracked access by the time auditors arrive. These aren't just governance oversights—they're business risks that can jeopardize the entire implementation.

A major misconception in SAP programs is that security begins with user role design or system patching. In truth, it begins with program governance. From the start, your SAP program must include representation from the enterprise security office, compliance leaders, internal audit, and—where applicable—legal and privacy counsel. These stakeholders should not only be consulted but embedded into key workstreams such as business process design, data migration, and interface architecture. Their early involvement helps identify red flags, such as segregation of duties violations or potential data exposure in outbound interfaces, long before they become expensive issues to remediate.

The security strategy must go beyond traditional access control. One of the most underestimated risks is how *development environments*, *test environments*, and *partner access* can become vectors for data leakage or internal misuse. Many system integrators and business users request access to full production data sets in non-production environments, often to "help with testing realism." Without proper masking, tokenization, or anonymization protocols in place, this opens the door to privacy violations—particularly in industries governed by HIPAA, GDPR, or PCI-DSS. In healthcare, defense, or financial services, even inadvertent access to unmasked personal or client data can trigger investigations or regulatory penalties. For these industries, data minimization and client data protection must be built into every phase of the SAP lifecycle.

Role design, provisioning, and auditing are essential controls—but they can't succeed without context. Many security issues don't arise from malicious insiders but from poorly defined responsibilities, inherited access from role duplications, or misalignment between security models and evolving org structures. That's why best-in-class SAP programs invest early in a Role Governance Council and leverage security architects who understand the nuances of both SAP authorization concepts (like composite vs. derived roles) and organizational change.

Segregation of duties (SoD) is particularly complex in SAP implementations because processes span modules—and business users often wear multiple hats. Without automated tools to model SoD violations during the role design phase, most projects either over-restrict access (crippling productivity) or allow toxic combinations (exposing the company to fraud). Automation tools, such as SAP GRC Access Control or third-party platforms like SailPoint or Saviynt, are not optional in regulated environments—they are strategic enablers. They should be implemented *during* the program, not after go-live.

Audit readiness also needs early planning. Waiting until a pre-go-live audit is too late. Instead, programs should define "auditable moments" during each phase—especially during data migration, cutover planning, and configuration freezes. Everything from system settings to interface controls and data retention logic should be reviewable. Establish a documentation repository where configuration decisions, control designs, and risk assessments are versioned, traceable, and review-ready. Doing so helps not only pass audits but also builds institutional memory for future upgrades and rollouts.

Equally important is industry context. Companies in financial services, pharmaceuticals, energy, healthcare, and defense face significantly higher scrutiny—not just from regulators, but from customers and shareholders. These industries often require compliance with specialized frameworks such as SOX, FDA 21 CFR

Part 11, ITAR, or NIST. For these organizations, the SAP security model must integrate with broader enterprise controls and monitoring systems. Logging must be real-time, role changes auditable, and exception handling documented. External auditors will ask not just *if* you have controls, but *how* you monitor them — and *what happens when they fail.*

Finally, don't overlook the human factor. Security is not only technical — it's behavioral. That means training should extend beyond password policies and phishing awareness. SAP users, functional consultants, and even developers need to be trained on *why security matters, how to handle data responsibly,* and *what to do in case of a suspected breach or access issue.* Consider integrating security principles into onboarding, project workshops, and role testing scenarios. A secure system is only as strong as the habits of those using it.

In short, SAP security and compliance aren't tasks to check off — they are dimensions of program excellence that must be planned, funded, staffed, and governed from the top. When treated as a core workstream — with leadership visibility, early stakeholder involvement, automation support, and cultural training — security becomes more than a defensive mechanism. It becomes an enabler of trust, operational resilience, and regulatory assurance. And in a world where data is currency, that might be your most valuable implementation outcome.

Conclusion

Security and compliance are critical components of SAP implementation, ensuring the protection of sensitive data, maintaining system integrity, and meeting regulatory requirements. Organizations can safeguard their SAP systems and ensure long-term success by following SAP security best practices, managing user roles and authorizations effectively, and implementing a comprehensive compliance and auditing framework. Adhering to these guidelines helps organizations achieve a high level of security, maintain regulatory compliance, and build trust with stakeholders.

Chapter 21: Project Management Methodologies

Effective project management is crucial for the successful implementation of SAP systems. The proper methodology, tools, and techniques can significantly impact the project's success, ensuring it is delivered on time, within budget, and meets the business objectives. This chapter explores different project management methodologies, specifically Agile vs. Waterfall in SAP projects, the SAP Activate methodology, project management tools and techniques, and risk management.

Overview of Agile and Waterfall Methodologies
Agile and Waterfall are two distinct project management methodologies with different approaches to planning, execution, and delivery. Understanding their differences and how they apply to SAP projects is essential for selecting the right approach.

Waterfall Methodology

The Waterfall methodology is a linear and sequential approach to project management. It involves distinct phases that must be completed before moving on to the next one. These phases typically include requirements gathering, design, implementation, testing, deployment, and maintenance.

Critical Characteristics of Waterfall:
1. **Linear Progression:** Each phase must be completed before the next one begins, creating a structured and predictable project flow.
2. **Detailed Planning:** Requires comprehensive planning and documentation before project execution.
3. **Clear Milestones:** Defined milestones and deliverables for each phase.

Advantages of Waterfall:
1. **Structured Approach:** Provides a straightforward, structured approach with well-defined phases and deliverables.

2. **Documentation:** Emphasizes comprehensive documentation, which can be helpful for compliance and future reference.
3. **Predictability:** The detailed upfront planning makes it easier to predict timelines and costs.

Disadvantages of Waterfall:
1. **Inflexibility:** It is difficult to accommodate changes once the project is in the later phases.
2. **Late Testing:** Testing is typically done at the end, leading to late discovery of issues.
3. **Risk of Misalignment:** Risk of delivering a solution that does not fully meet user needs if requirements change during the project.

Agile Methodology

The Agile methodology is an iterative and incremental approach to project management. It focuses on delivering small, workable increments of the project through continuous collaboration, flexibility, and customer feedback.

Key Characteristics of Agile:
1. **Iterative Process:** Projects are divided into small iterations or sprints, each delivering a potentially shippable product increment.
2. **Collaboration:** Emphasizes collaboration between cross-functional teams and stakeholders.
3. **Flexibility:** Adaptable to changes in requirements throughout the project lifecycle.

Advantages of Agile:
1. **Flexibility:** Can quickly adapt to requirements or market conditions changes.
2. **Continuous Improvement:** Regular feedback loops and retrospectives lead to continuous improvement.
3. **Early Delivery:** Delivers functional components early and frequently, providing value to users sooner.

Disadvantages of Agile:
1. **Less Predictability:** It can be harder to predict timelines and costs due to its iterative nature.
2. **Requires Discipline:** Requires strong discipline and commitment from all team members to follow Agile practices.
3. **Documentation:** This may result in less comprehensive documentation than Waterfall.

Agile vs. Waterfall in SAP Projects

Applicability in SAP Projects:
1. **Waterfall:**
   o **Best for** Projects with well-defined requirements, minimal changes expected, and where comprehensive documentation is critical.
   o **Examples:** Large-scale ERP implementations with extensive regulatory requirements.
2. **Agile:**
   o **Best for:** Projects with dynamic requirements, a need for rapid delivery, and where user feedback is crucial.
   o **Examples:** Implementations of specific SAP modules or functionalities that need frequent adjustments based on user feedback.

Choosing the Right Methodology:
1. **Project Scope and Complexity:** Consider the project's scope and complexity. Waterfall may suit large, complex projects with precise requirements, while Agile is better for smaller, flexible projects.
2. **Stakeholder Engagement:** Evaluate the level of stakeholder engagement required. Agile requires active participation from stakeholders throughout the project.
3. **Regulatory Requirements:** Assess regulatory and compliance requirements. Waterfall's emphasis on documentation can be beneficial for regulatory compliance.

Activate Methodology

Overview of SAP Activate Methodology
The SAP Activate methodology is a modular and agile framework designed specifically for SAP projects. It combines best practices from Agile and Waterfall methodologies, offering a structured yet flexible approach to SAP implementation.

Critical Phases of SAP Activate Methodology:
1. **Discover:**
   - **Objectives:** Identify the project scope, objectives, and initial requirements.
   - **Activities:** Conduct initial planning, create a project charter, and define high-level requirements.
2. **Prepare:**
   - **Objectives:** Set up the project infrastructure, finalize the project plan, and prepare the project team.
   - **Activities:** Establish the project governance framework, conduct kickoff meetings, and finalize the project schedule.
3. **Explore:**
   - **Objectives:** Validate the project scope and requirements through workshops and prototyping.
   - **Activities:** Conduct fit-gap analysis, create initial prototypes, and refine requirements based on feedback.
4. **Realize:**
   - **Objectives:** Build and configure the SAP system based on the refined requirements.
   - **Activities:** Develop and test the system in iterations, conduct integration testing, and finalize configurations.
5. **Deploy:**
   - **Objectives:** Transition the SAP system to the production environment and prepare for go-live.
   - **Activities:** Conduct user acceptance testing (UAT), finalize data migration, and execute the cutover plan.
6. **Run:**
   - **Objectives:** Ensure the system is running smoothly and provide ongoing support.
   - **Activities:** Monitor system performance, provide user support, and conduct post-go-live reviews.

Best Practices for SAP Activate Methodology:
1. **Early Involvement:** Engage stakeholders throughout the project to ensure alignment and gather continuous feedback.
2. **Iterative Approach:** Build and test the system using an iterative approach, allowing continuous refinement and improvement.
3. **Comprehensive Planning:** Develop a detailed project plan, including risk management and contingency plans.
4. **Clear Governance:** Establish a framework with defined roles, responsibilities, and decision-making processes.
5. **Continuous Improvement:** Conduct regular retrospectives to identify areas for improvement and implement changes accordingly.

Project Management Tools and Techniques

Overview of Project Management Tools and Techniques
Effective project management relies on various tools and techniques to plan, execute, and monitor projects. These tools help project managers and teams stay organized, communicate effectively, and track progress.

Essential Project Management Tools:
1. **Project Planning Tools:**
   o **Microsoft Project:** A comprehensive project management tool that allows for detailed planning, scheduling, and tracking of project activities.
   o **Smartsheet:** A flexible tool for project planning and collaboration, offering customizable templates and real-time updates.
2. **Collaboration Tools:**
   o **Microsoft Teams:** A collaboration platform that integrates with other Microsoft Office tools, facilitating communication and document sharing.
   o **Slack:** A messaging app for teams that supports real-time communication and integrates with various project management tools.

3. **Issue Tracking Tools:**
   - o **Jira:** A popular tool for issue and project tracking, widely used in Agile projects for managing backlogs, sprints, and tasks.
   - o **Trello:** A visual project management tool that uses boards, lists, and cards to organize tasks and track progress.
4. **Documentation Tools:**
   - o **Confluence:** A collaborative documentation tool that integrates with Jira, allowing teams to create, share, and manage project documentation.
   - o **Google Docs:** A cloud-based documentation tool that supports real-time collaboration and document sharing.

Essential Project Management Techniques:
1. **Work Breakdown Structure (WBS):**
   - o **Definition:** A hierarchical project decomposition into smaller, manageable components or tasks.
   - o **Benefits:** Helps organize and define the total scope of the project, making it easier to assign responsibilities and track progress.

2. **Gantt Charts:**
   - o **Definition:** A visual representation of the project schedule, showing tasks' start and end dates and their dependencies.
   - o **Benefits:** It provides a clear timeline of project activities, helps track progress, and identifies potential delays.
3. **Critical Path Method (CPM):**
   - o **Definition:** A technique to identify the most extended sequence of dependent tasks and determine the minimum project duration.
   - o **Benefits:** Helps identify critical tasks that must be completed on time to avoid delays in the project.
4. **Kanban Boards:**
   - o **Definition:** A visual tool used in Agile projects to manage workflows, showing tasks in different stages of completion.

- ○ **Benefits:** Enhances visibility of the project status, allowing teams to manage and prioritize tasks effectively.

Best Practices for Using Project Management Tools and Techniques:
1. **Tool Selection:** Choose tools that align with the project's needs and the team's preferences to ensure adequate usage.
2. **Integration:** Integrate project management tools with other systems and platforms used by the team to streamline workflows.
3. **Training:** Train team members to use the selected tools and techniques effectively.
4. **Regular Updates:** Keep project plans, schedules, and documentation up-to-date to reflect the current status.
5. **Collaboration:** Foster a collaborative environment where team members can communicate, share updates, and work together effectively.

Risk Management

Overview of Risk Management
Risk management involves identifying, assessing, and mitigating risks that could impact a project's success. Effective risk management ensures that potential issues are addressed proactively, minimizing their impact on the project.

Critical Components of Risk Management:
1. **Risk Identification:**
   - ○ **Techniques:** Identify potential risks using brainstorming, SWOT analysis, and checklists.
   - ○ **Categories:** Categorize risks based on their sources, such as technical risks, financial risks, operational risks, and external risks.
2. **Risk Assessment:**
   - ○ **Probability and Impact:** Assess the probability and impact of each identified risk to prioritize them based on their potential effect on the project.
   - ○ **Risk Matrix:** Use a risk matrix to plot risks based on their probability and impact, helping to visualize and prioritize them.

3. **Risk Mitigation:**
   - **Mitigation Strategies:** Develop strategies to mitigate high-priority risks, such as implementing additional controls, contingency plans, or risk avoidance measures.
   - **Resource Allocation:** Allocate resources and budget to implement risk mitigation strategies effectively.

4. **Risk Monitoring:**
   - **Tracking:** Continuously monitor identified risks and their status throughout the project lifecycle.
   - **Reporting:** Regularly report on the status of risks to stakeholders, ensuring they are informed and engaged in risk management activities.

Steps to Implement Risk Management in SAP Projects:

1. **Risk Management Plan:**
   - **Development:** Develop a comprehensive risk management plan that outlines the process for identifying, assessing, mitigating, and monitoring risks.
   - **Communication:** Communicate the risk management plan to all stakeholders to ensure understanding and buy-in.

2. **Risk Identification:**
   - **Workshops:** Conduct risk identification workshops with project team members and stakeholders to gather diverse perspectives on potential risks.
   - **Documentation:** Document identified risks in a risk register, including details such as risk description, category, and potential impact.

3. **Risk Assessment:**
   - **Assessment Criteria:** Define criteria for assessing the probability and impact of risks, ensuring consistency in evaluation.
   - **Prioritization:** Prioritize risks based on their assessment to focus on those with the highest potential impact.

4. **Risk Mitigation:**
   - **Mitigation Plans:** Develop detailed mitigation plans for high-priority risks, including specific actions, responsible parties, and timelines.

- Implementation: Implement mitigation plans and allocate necessary resources to address identified risks.

5. **Risk Monitoring and Reporting:**
   - **Regular Reviews:** Conduct regular risk reviews to assess the status of identified risks and the effectiveness of mitigation strategies.
   - **Updates:** Update the risk register and management plan as new risks are identified or existing risks change.
   - **Reporting:** Provide regular risk status reports to stakeholders, ensuring they are informed and engaged in risk management activities.

Best Practices for Risk Management:

1. **Proactive Approach:** Adopt a proactive approach to risk management, identifying and addressing risks early in the project lifecycle.
2. **Stakeholder Involvement:** Engage stakeholders in risk management activities to gather diverse perspectives and ensure buy-in.
3. **Continuous Monitoring:** Continuously monitor risks and the effectiveness of mitigation strategies to ensure they remain relevant and practical.
4. **Documentation:** To ensure transparency and accountability, maintain comprehensive documentation of risks, assessments, and mitigation plans.
5. **Adaptability:** Adapt risk management strategies as new risks emerge or existing risks evolve.

Case Studies and Examples

Case Study 1: Financial Services Company

Overview: A financial services company implemented SAP to streamline its operations. The project management methodology selected was a hybrid of Agile and Waterfall to balance flexibility and structure.

Approach:

- **Agile Iterations:** Agile iterations are used for early development and testing key functionalities, allowing continuous feedback and refinement.

- **Waterfall Phases:** Applied Waterfall phases for detailed planning, compliance documentation, and final integration.
- **Activate Methodology:** Followed SAP Activate methodology to structure the project and ensure alignment with best practices.
- **Risk Management:** Developed a comprehensive risk management plan, conducted regular risk reviews, and implemented mitigation strategies.

Outcome:
- **Successful Implementation:** Achieved a successful implementation on time and within budget, meeting business requirements.
- **Enhanced Flexibility:** Balanced flexibility and structure to accommodate changes while ensuring comprehensive planning and documentation.
- **Risk Mitigation:** Effectively mitigated risks, minimizing their impact on the project and ensuring a smooth transition to the new system.

Case Study 2: Manufacturing Company

Overview: A manufacturing company implemented SAP to integrate its global operations. The project management approach focused on the SAP Activate methodology and comprehensive risk management.

Approach:
- **Activate Methodology:** I followed the SAP Activate methodology, including the Discover, Prepare, Explore, Realize, Deploy, and Run phases.
- **Project Management Tools:** Used Microsoft Project for detailed planning and Smartsheet for real-time updates and collaboration.
- **Risk Management:** Identified potential risks early, developed mitigation strategies, and continuously monitored risks throughout the project.

Outcome:
- **Streamlined Operations:** Successfully integrated global operations, enhancing efficiency and data visibility.
- **Effective Collaboration:** Facilitated effective collaboration and communication among global teams using project management tools.

- **Proactive Risk Management:** Proactively managed risks, ensuring the project stayed on track and met business objectives.

Challenges of Using Pure Agile in SAP Deployments

Applying a pure Agile approach to SAP deployments presents several practical challenges. While Agile works well in software development environments that support iterative delivery and continuous user feedback, SAP implementations involve deeply integrated systems, complex business processes, and strict regulatory and data dependencies that do not easily align with a purely Agile structure.

SAP solutions, particularly in an S/4HANA transformation, include interconnected modules where changes in one area often affect others. Finance, procurement, manufacturing, and HR share data structures and process flows. This makes it difficult to deliver discrete, independent increments every sprint, as Agile would typically prescribe. Most business processes in SAP require end-to-end integration and are not easily compartmentalized into short cycles of standalone value.

Another issue is the lack of early deliverables that can be considered "done" from an end-user perspective. Unlike web applications or digital products, where functionality can be released and tested incrementally, SAP functions are typically not viable until configuration, data, interfaces, and security are all aligned. This delays feedback and value realization, which undermines one of the core promises of Agile.

Governance and compliance expectations also pose limitations. Senior stakeholders, auditors, and finance teams require structured reporting, milestone tracking, and deliverable sign-offs. Pure Agile ceremonies such as sprint reviews and daily standups do not fulfill the detailed documentation and reporting standards expected in enterprise-scale ERP projects. This creates a mismatch between team-level Agile activity and executive-level program governance.

Agile frameworks also assume a level of cultural maturity that may not exist across all stakeholders. SAP projects often include third-party consultants, global business units, and offshore development teams, many of whom are more familiar with traditional delivery models. Expecting all parties to adopt Agile behaviors without extensive enablement can lead to miscommunication, unclear responsibilities, and inconsistent delivery standards.

As a result, most SAP programs that start with Agile principles evolve into hybrid models. These combine sprint-based development and backlog management with structured planning, stage gates, and formal integration and cutover schedules. This blend tends to balance flexibility with control, allowing teams to remain responsive while still meeting program constraints and stakeholder expectations.

Lessons Learned from Using Jira and Other Project Management Tools

Many SAP teams that adopt Agile or hybrid delivery frameworks introduce tools like Jira to manage backlogs, track tasks, and facilitate collaboration. Jira excels at managing user stories and sprint execution, but significant configuration is required before it can support enterprise reporting and governance.

In practice, teams often start using Jira with minimal setup, assuming it will evolve organically. But without a clear structure from the beginning—such as consistent naming conventions, field configurations, issue types, workflows, and linking between stories and features—reporting quickly becomes fragmented. By the time the program reaches the Realize phase, PMOs are unable to extract consolidated views of progress, deliverables, or risk across workstreams.

To avoid this, it is critical to establish a tool governance model during the Prepare phase. This includes defining how Jira will support not only sprint tracking, but also deliverable ownership, milestone alignment, cross-team dependencies, and reporting. Templates should be agreed upon across teams, and reporting dashboards should be prototyped early—well before leadership demands status views. Without this foundation, sprint data becomes difficult to consolidate or interpret at the program level.

The same holds true for tools like Microsoft Project, which may be used to track milestones, critical paths, and resource allocations. If MS Project is not aligned with Jira or other tools used by technical teams, reporting becomes disconnected. This disconnect creates unnecessary manual work and erodes confidence in program tracking. To resolve this, program management offices should define how each tool is used, ensure data consistency between them, and appoint owners responsible for updates and quality control.

Tool integration and training are also often overlooked. Team members need to understand not just how to use the tools, but how their data contributes to reporting, governance, and decision-making. When tools like Jira or Smartsheet are used inconsistently, they become noise rather than insight. SAP programs that succeed in this area treat tools as part of the governance structure, not just as trackers for tasks.

Ultimately, tools should be selected based on the needs of the program, configured with enterprise reporting in mind, and supported with clear standards. Agile can work in SAP if supported by tools that connect sprint activity to program outcomes. Without this foundation, even the best-intentioned Agile practices will fail to deliver the clarity and control required by large-scale ERP deployments.

Conclusion

Effective project management is crucial for the successful implementation of SAP systems. By understanding and applying the proper methodologies, tools, and techniques, organizations can ensure their SAP projects are delivered on time, within budget, and meet business objectives. Whether using Agile, Waterfall, or the SAP Activate methodology, it is essential to tailor the approach to the project's needs and continuously manage risks to achieve long-term success.

Chapter 22: Surviving SAP Project

Implementing SAP systems can be complex and challenging, requiring significant time, resources, and expertise. Success hinges on robust project management, strategic planning, effective communication, and adept change management. This chapter explores key strategies and best practices for surviving SAP projects, focusing on preparation, stakeholder engagement, change management, effective communication, and dealing with challenges.

Preparation and Planning

Thorough Preparation

1. **Needs Assessment:**

    o   **Objective:** Conduct a detailed needs assessment to understand the specific requirements and goals of the organization.

    o   **Activities:** Interview critical stakeholders, review existing processes, and identify gaps and areas for improvement.

2. **Project Scope Definition:**

    o   **Objective:** Clearly define the project's scope, including the modules to be implemented, the timeline, and the resources required.

    o   **Activities:** Develop a detailed project charter outlining objectives, deliverables, and success criteria.

3. **Resource Allocation:**

    o   **Objective:** Ensure that the necessary resources, including personnel, budget, and technology, are allocated to the project.

- o **Activities:** Create a resource management plan, identifying key team members, their roles, and the budget required for the project.

4. **Risk Assessment:**

   - o **Objective:** Identify potential risks and develop mitigation strategies to address them proactively.

   - o **Activities:** Conduct a risk assessment workshop, document identified risks, and develop a risk management plan.

Best Practices for Preparation and Planning

1. **Comprehensive Needs Assessment:** Engage various stakeholders to understand and document all needs and expectations.

2. **Clear Scope Definition:** Avoid scope creep by clearly defining and agreeing upon the project scope early in the planning phase.

3. **Adequate Resource Allocation:** Ensure sufficient resources are allocated, including skilled personnel and a realistic budget.

4. **Proactive Risk Management:** Identify risks early and develop mitigation plans to address potential issues before they arise.

Stakeholder Engagement

Engaging Key Stakeholders

1. **Stakeholder Identification:**

   - o **Objective:** Identify all stakeholders to whom the SAP implementation will impact.

- o **Activities:** Create a stakeholder map, categorizing stakeholders by their influence and interest in the project.

2. **Stakeholder Analysis:**

   - o **Objective:** Understand each stakeholder group's needs, concerns, and expectations.

   - o **Activities:** Conduct stakeholder interviews and surveys to gather insights and feedback.

3. **Stakeholder Communication Plan:**

   - o **Objective:** Develop a communication plan to keep stakeholders informed and engaged throughout the project.

   - o **Activities:** Define communication channels, frequency, and content for stakeholder updates.

4. **Stakeholder Involvement:**

   - o **Objective:** Actively involve stakeholders to ensure their needs are addressed, and they feel invested in the project's success.

   - o **Activities:** Create stakeholder committees, hold regular review meetings, and involve stakeholders in decision-making.

Best Practices for Stakeholder Engagement

1. **Early and Continuous Engagement:** Engage stakeholders early and maintain regular communication throughout the project.

2. **Transparent Communication:** Keep stakeholders informed of project progress, challenges, and changes.

3. **Active Involvement:** Involve stakeholders in critical decisions and ensure their feedback is considered.

4. **Address Concerns:** Proactively address stakeholder concerns and demonstrate how their input is being used to shape the project.

Change Management

Implementing Effective Change Management

1. **Change Management Strategy:**

   o **Objective:** Develop a comprehensive change management strategy to address the impact of the SAP implementation on the organization.

   o **Activities:** Define change management objectives, identify change agents, and develop a plan.

2. **Change Impact Assessment:**

   o **Objective:** Assess the impact of the SAP implementation on existing processes, systems, and personnel.

   o **Activities:** Conduct change impact assessments, identify resistance areas, and develop mitigation strategies.

3. **Communication and Training:**

   o **Objective:** Ensure all employees are informed about the changes and have the necessary skills to use the new system effectively.

   o **Activities:** Develop a communication plan, create training programs, and provide ongoing support and resources.

4. **Change Readiness Assessment:**

   o **Objective:** Assess the organization's readiness for change and identify barriers to successful implementation.

- o **Activities:** Conduct readiness assessments, identify additional support areas, and develop action plans.

Best Practices for Change Management

1. **Clear Change Management Strategy:** Develop a comprehensive strategy addressing all change process aspects.

2. **Assess Impact and Readiness:** Regularly assess the impact of changes and the organization's readiness to adopt them.

3. **Effective Communication:** Communicate changes clearly and frequently to ensure all employees are informed and engaged.

4. **Comprehensive Training:** Provide thorough training and support to help employees adapt to the new system.

Effective Communication

Ensuring Effective Communication

1. **Communication Plan:**

   - o **Objective:** Develop a communication plan that outlines how information will be shared throughout the project.

   - o **Activities:** Identify critical messages, define communication channels, and establish a schedule.

2. **Regular Updates:**

   - o **Objective:** Keep all project stakeholders informed of progress, challenges, and changes.

   - o **Activities:** Hold regular project status meetings, send periodic updates, and maintain an up-to-date project dashboard.

3. **Feedback Mechanisms:**

   o **Objective:** Provide opportunities for stakeholders to give feedback and voice concerns.

   o **Activities:** Implement surveys, suggestion boxes, and open forums for feedback.

4. **Crisis Communication:**

   o **Objective:** Develop a crisis communication plan to address any issues during the project.

   o **Activities:** Define crisis communication protocols, identify key contacts, and develop template messages for various scenarios.

Best Practices for Effective Communication

1. **Consistent Messaging:** Ensure all communications align with the project objectives.

2. **Transparent Updates:** Provide honest and transparent updates on project progress and challenges.

3. **Active Listening:** Encourage and actively listen to feedback from stakeholders to address concerns promptly.

4. **Preparedness for Crisis:** Have a crisis communication plan to handle any issues that arise effectively.

Dealing with Challenges

Managing Challenges and Issues

1. **Issue Tracking and Resolution:**

   o **Objective:** Implement a system for tracking and resolving project issues.

o **Activities:** Use an issue tracking tool, document issues, assign responsibility, and monitor resolution progress.

2. **Conflict Management:**

   o **Objective:** Address conflicts that arise during the project promptly and effectively.

   o **Activities:** Implement conflict resolution strategies, hold mediation sessions, and involve neutral third parties if necessary.

3. **Managing Scope Changes:**

   o **Objective:** Control scope changes to prevent scope creep and ensure the project stays on track.

   o **Activities:** Implement a change control process, assess the impact of scope changes, and obtain necessary approvals.

4. **Resource Management:**

   o **Objective:** Ensure resources are managed effectively to avoid bottlenecks and delays.

   o **Activities:** Monitor resource allocation, adjust resource plans as needed, and address resource constraints promptly.

Best Practices for Dealing with Challenges

1. **Proactive Issue Tracking:** Implement a robust system for tracking and resolving issues as they arise.

2. **Effective Conflict Resolution:** Address conflicts promptly and effectively to maintain a positive project environment.

3. **Control Scope Changes:** Implement a change control process to manage scope changes and prevent scope creep.

4. **Monitor Resources:** Monitor resource allocation and address constraints to avoid delays.

Building a Strong Project Team

Assembling and Managing the Project Team

1. **Team Selection:**

   o **Objective:** To ensure project success, select a team with the right skills, experience, and attitude.

   o **Activities:** Define team roles, conduct interviews, and select team members based on their qualifications and fit with the project culture.

2. **Team Building:**

   o **Objective:** Build a cohesive and motivated project team.

   o **Activities:** Conduct team-building activities, foster open communication, and create a supportive team environment.

3. **Role Clarity:**

   o **Objective:** Ensure that all team members understand their roles and responsibilities.

   o **Activities:** Develop clear role descriptions, hold regular team meetings, and provide role-specific training.

4. **Performance Management:**

   o **Objective:** Monitor and manage team performance to ensure project success.

   o **Activities:** Implement performance metrics, provide regular feedback, and recognize and reward high performance.

Best Practices for Building a Strong Project Team

1. **Right Team Composition:** Select team members with the right skills and experience for the project.

2. **Foster Team Cohesion:** Build a cohesive team through regular team-building activities and open communication.

3. **Clear Roles and Responsibilities:** Ensure all team members understand their roles and responsibilities.

4. **Monitor Performance:** Continuously monitor and manage team performance to maintain high standards.

Endurance Tactics for Multi-Year SAP Projects

SAP programs that span two or more years test more than budgets and timelines — they test patience, morale, and organizational stamina. Unlike short-term IT projects, long SAP implementations can stretch across multiple fiscal cycles, leadership changes, and shifting business priorities. Surviving and succeeding in these long-haul projects requires a fundamentally different mindset — one built on endurance, adaptability, and strategic pacing.

One of the most significant challenges is maintaining team energy and engagement over time. Project fatigue sets in when key contributors are pulled from their day jobs for extended periods or when timelines slip and deliverables feel endlessly deferred. Burnout becomes a serious risk, especially when combined with the high-pressure nature of ERP work. Organizations must plan not just for initial staffing but for long-term support, including rotations, backup resources, and mechanisms for re-engagement. Celebrating milestones, even small ones, and recognizing contributions publicly can help sustain momentum.

Another point of failure in multi-year SAP projects is the misalignment between the project timeline and the natural rhythms of the business. Planning go-live for January 1st or quarter-end dates often seems appealing for financial reasons, but it can backfire. These periods are when business users are already stretched thin with audits, reporting, and performance reviews. Cutting into holiday leave or demanding peak effort during critical business cycles undermines both adoption and morale. It's essential to decouple go-live from arbitrary calendar milestones and instead align it with periods of operational stability. In some cases, going live in late February or mid-May — after year-end closing and before peak vacation months — proves far more successful.

Over time, even the strongest governance frameworks begin to fray. Leadership changes, shifting priorities, and accumulated delays often lead to unclear accountability or blurred decision-making. A common pattern is to let steering committees become ceremonial rather than directional. To counter this, governance structures must be reinforced periodically. That means revisiting RACI models, redefining escalation protocols, and ensuring that decision-making bodies remain empowered and responsive. Long projects should expect and plan for executive turnover and have succession strategies in place for both sponsors and critical team members.

Another key to survival is recalibrating expectations and messaging throughout the journey. What stakeholders were excited about in year one may feel stale or irrelevant by year two. Business priorities evolve, and new technologies or acquisitions can alter the landscape. Leadership must continuously reframe the narrative — reminding teams why the project matters, how it aligns to new goals, and what tangible progress has been made. Without this narrative refresh, projects risk becoming background noise rather than a strategic priority.

Finally, tools and processes established at the start of the project often become obsolete or inadequate as scale increases. Reporting tools like Jira, Microsoft Project, or Smartsheet need to evolve with the program. A configuration that worked for five teams and 100 tasks may not scale to 40 workstreams and thousands of backlog items. Teams must revisit tool configurations, integrate data sources, and establish reporting standards that serve not just day-to-day operations but also executive dashboards. Waiting until go-live to realize reporting gaps is a critical failure point. Ensuring tools are scalable, interoperable, and owned by designated roles is fundamental to surviving long programs.

In the end, surviving multi-year SAP programs is as much about endurance and culture as it is about planning and delivery. Teams must be led with empathy and strategy, governance must remain active and evolving, and the organization must continuously re-engage with the "why" behind the program. Long projects are marathons, not sprints—and they must be run with discipline, resilience, and a plan to finish strong.

Conclusion

Surviving SAP projects requires thorough preparation, effective stakeholder engagement, robust change management, clear communication, and adept handling of challenges. By following these best practices, organizations can navigate the complexities of SAP implementations, ensuring they are completed successfully and deliver the expected business benefits. The key to surviving and thriving in SAP projects lies in strategic planning, proactive management, and continuous improvement.

Chapter 23: Types of SAP Projects

SAP implementation projects can be broadly categorized into Brownfield, Bluefield (lift & shift), and Greenfield. Each type has its own set of characteristics, advantages, and challenges. This chapter thoroughly explores these different types of SAP projects, providing insights into their unique aspects and best practices to ensure successful implementation.

Brownfield Implementation

Overview of Brownfield Implementation

A Brownfield implementation refers to upgrading or migrating an existing SAP system to a new version or platform while retaining the existing processes, customizations, and data. This approach is typically used when an organization wants to take advantage of the latest SAP technologies and features without completely overhauling its current system.

Critical Characteristics of Brownfield Implementation

1. **Retention of Existing Processes:** Retains the existing business processes and configurations, minimizing disruption to ongoing operations.

2. **Data Migration:** This involves migrating historical and current data to the new system.

3. **Customization Preservation:** Preserves existing customizations and enhancements, reducing the need for extensive redevelopment.

4. **Incremental Changes:** Focuses on making incremental changes to improve the system's performance and capabilities.

Steps in Brownfield Implementation

1. **Assessment and Planning:**

   o **System Assessment:** Conduct a thorough assessment of the current SAP system to identify areas for improvement and potential challenges.

   o **Planning:** Develop a detailed project plan that outlines the scope, timeline, resources, and milestones for the implementation.

2. **System Preparation:**

   o **Backup and Cleanup:** Perform a full backup of the existing system and clean up obsolete data and configurations.

   o **Hardware and Software Preparation:** Ensure that the necessary hardware and software infrastructure is in place to support the upgraded system.

3. **Migration and Upgrade:**

   o **Data Migration:** Migrate historical and current data to the new system, ensuring data integrity and consistency.

   o **System Upgrade:** Upgrade the existing system to the new SAP version or platform, preserving customizations and configurations.

4. **Testing and Validation:**

   o **Functional Testing:** Conduct functional testing to ensure that all business processes and customizations work as expected.

   o **Performance Testing:** Perform performance testing to ensure the system operates efficiently under expected workloads.

   o **User Acceptance Testing (UAT):** Involve end-users in testing to validate the system's functionality and usability.

5. **Go-Live and Support:**

   o **Go-Live Preparation:** Prepare for the go-live by conducting final testing, data validation, and user training.

   o **Go-Live:** Execute the go-live plan, transitioning the system to the new version or platform.

   o **Post-Go-Live Support:** To address issues and ensure system stability, provide ongoing support and monitoring.

Best Practices for Brownfield Implementation

1. **Thorough Assessment:** Conduct a detailed assessment of the existing system to identify areas for improvement and potential challenges.

2. **Comprehensive Planning:** Develop a comprehensive project plan that outlines the scope, timeline, resources, and milestones.

3. **Effective Data Migration:** Ensure data migration is carefully planned and executed to maintain data integrity and consistency.

4. **Extensive Testing:** Conduct extensive testing to validate the system's functionality, performance, and usability.

5. **User Training:** Provide thorough training to end-users to ensure they are comfortable with the upgraded system.

Lift & Shift (also known as Bluefield Implementation)

Overview of Lift & Shift Implementation

Bluefield implementation, the lift & shift approach, involves migrating an existing SAP system to a new infrastructure or platform without significantly changing the existing processes or configurations. This approach is often used when an organization wants to move its SAP system to the cloud or a new data center.

Critical Characteristics of Bluefield Implementation

1. **Minimal Changes:** Focuses on migrating the system as-is, with minimal changes to processes and configurations.

2. **Infrastructure Migration:** Moving the SAP system to a new infrastructure like a cloud platform or a new data center.

3. **Quick Transition:** The goal is to quickly and efficiently transition to the new environment with minimal disruption to business operations.

4. **Scalability and Flexibility:** Leverages the new infrastructure's scalability and flexibility to improve system performance and efficiency.

Steps in Bluefield Implementation

1. **Assessment and Planning:**

   o **Infrastructure Assessment:** Assess the current infrastructure and identify the requirements for the new environment.

   o **Planning:** Develop a detailed migration plan that outlines the scope, timeline, resources, and milestones for the implementation.

2. **System Preparation:**

   o **Backup and Cleanup:** Perform a full backup of the existing system and clean up obsolete data and configurations.

   o **Infrastructure Setup:** Set up the new infrastructure, ensuring it meets the requirements for the SAP system.

3. **Migration:**

   o **Data Migration:** Migrate historical and current data to the new infrastructure, ensuring data integrity and consistency.

   o **System Migration:** Migrate the existing SAP system to the new infrastructure, preserving customizations and configurations.

4. **Testing and Validation:**

   o **Infrastructure Testing:** Conduct infrastructure testing to ensure the new environment is stable and performs as expected.

   o **Functional Testing:** Perform functional testing to ensure that all business processes and customizations work as expected.

   o **User Acceptance Testing (UAT):** Involve end-users in testing to validate the system's functionality and usability in the new environment.

5. **Go-Live and Support:**

   o **Go-Live Preparation:** Prepare for the go-live by conducting final testing, data validation, and user training.

   o **Go-Live:** Execute the go-live plan, transitioning the system to the new infrastructure.

   o **Post-Go-Live Support:** To address issues and ensure system stability, provide ongoing support and monitoring.

Best Practices for Bluefield Implementation

1. **Infrastructure Assessment:** Conduct a thorough assessment of the current and new infrastructure to ensure compatibility and performance.

2. **Detailed Planning:** Develop a detailed migration plan that outlines the scope, timeline, resources, and milestones.

3. **Effective Data Migration:** Ensure data migration is carefully planned and executed to maintain data integrity and consistency.

4. **Thorough Testing:** Conduct thorough testing to validate the system's functionality, performance, and usability in the new environment.

5. **User Training:** Provide thorough training to end-users to ensure they are comfortable with the system in the new infrastructure.

Greenfield Implementation

Overview of Greenfield Implementation

A Greenfield implementation involves implementing a new SAP system from scratch without considering the existing system. This approach is typically used when an organization wants to completely redesign its business processes and fully take advantage of the latest SAP technologies and best practices.

Critical Characteristics of Greenfield Implementation

1. **Fresh Start:** Implementing a new SAP system from scratch, allowing for complete process redesign and optimization.

2. **Best Practices:** Leverages SAP's latest best practices and standard processes to optimize business operations.

3. **Customization Reduction:** Aim to minimize customizations and align with standard SAP functionalities.

4. **Comprehensive Change:** Significant business processes, systems, and organizational structure changes are required.

Steps in Greenfield Implementation

1. **Discovery and Planning:**

   o **Business Assessment:** Conduct a thorough assessment of the current business processes and identify areas for improvement.

   o **Planning:** Develop a detailed project plan that outlines the scope, timeline, resources, and milestones for the implementation.

2. **Design:**

   o **Process Redesign:** Redesign business processes to align with SAP's best practices and standard functionalities.

   o **System Design:** Design the new SAP system, including configurations, customizations, and integrations.

3. **Build:**

   o **System Configuration:** Configure the new SAP system based on the redesigned business processes and system design.

   o **Development:** Develop necessary customizations and integrations to meet specific business requirements.

4. **Testing and Validation:**

   o **Unit Testing:** To ensure individual components and functionalities work as expected.

   o **Integration Testing:** Perform integration testing to validate that all system components and integrations work together seamlessly.

   o **User Acceptance Testing (UAT):** Involve end-users in testing to validate the system's functionality and usability.

5. **Data Migration:**

   o **Data Mapping:** Map data from the legacy system to the new SAP system.

   o **Data Cleansing:** Cleanse data to ensure accuracy and consistency.

   o **Data Migration:** Migrate data to the new system, ensuring data integrity and consistency.

6. **Go-Live and Support:**

   o **Go-Live Preparation:** Prepare for the go-live by conducting final testing, data validation, and user training.

   o **Go-Live:** Execute the go-live plan, transitioning to the new SAP system.

   o **Post-Go-Live Support:** To address issues and ensure system stability, provide ongoing support and monitoring.

Best Practices for Greenfield Implementation

1. **Thorough Assessment:** Conduct a comprehensive assessment of current business processes to identify areas for improvement.

2. **Detailed Planning:** Develop a detailed project plan that outlines the scope, timeline, resources, and milestones.

3. **Process Optimization:** Redesign business processes to align with SAP's best practices and standard functionalities.

4. **Comprehensive Testing:** Conduct extensive testing to validate the system's functionality, performance, and usability.

5. **Effective Data Migration:** Ensure data migration is carefully planned and executed to maintain data integrity and consistency.

6. **User Training:** Provide thorough training to end-users to ensure their comfort with the new system and processes.

Comparing Brownfield, Bluefield, and Greenfield Implementations

Advantages and Challenges

1. **Brownfield:**

   o **Advantages:** Minimizes disruption to ongoing operations, retains existing customizations and data, and is typically quicker and less expensive than a complete overhaul.

   o **Challenges:** Limited opportunities for process optimization and innovation, potential complexity in maintaining legacy customizations.

2. **Bluefield:**

   o **Advantages:** Quick transition to new infrastructure, minimal changes to existing processes and configurations, leverages new infrastructure benefits.

   o **Challenges:** Potential compatibility issues with new infrastructure and limited opportunities for process improvement.

3. **Greenfield:**

   o **Advantages:** Complete process redesign and optimization, leverages latest SAP technologies and best practices, minimal legacy constraints.

   o **Challenges:** Significant changes to business processes and systems, typically more time-consuming and expensive, require extensive change management.

Choosing the Right Approach

1. **Business Objectives:** Align the chosen approach with the organization's business objectives and strategic goals.

2. **Current System State:** Assess the current state of the existing SAP system and the need for process optimization and innovation.

3. **Budget and Timeline:** Consider the available budget and timeline for the implementation project.

4. **Risk Tolerance:** Evaluate the organization's tolerance for risk and disruption during the implementation process.

5. **Stakeholder Engagement:** Engage key stakeholders in decision-making to ensure alignment and buy-in.

Aligning Implementation Type with Business and Technology Strategy

The decision between Brownfield, Bluefield, and Greenfield implementations should never be made in isolation. It must be grounded in the broader business transformation strategy and long-range technology roadmap. These project types represent not just technical delivery models, but philosophical orientations toward change, innovation, and operational agility.

A Brownfield implementation often signals a strategic decision to preserve the core of what already works—leveraging existing investments while modernizing incrementally. This approach is typically aligned with organizations that prioritize operational continuity and cost efficiency, and have mature processes that don't require full redesign. It supports a business strategy focused on evolutionary improvement, especially in environments where regulatory complexity or legacy dependencies make full reinvention high risk.

Bluefield, or lift-and-shift, serves organizations that are more focused on technical modernization than business transformation. It's frequently adopted when the primary goal is to move SAP into the cloud or another scalable environment without disrupting existing workflows. This aligns with technology strategies focused on infrastructure modernization, data center exits, or mergers and acquisitions where time and platform flexibility are more important than business process redesign. While it doesn't deliver radical change to the business model, it lays foundational infrastructure for future transformation.

Greenfield, on the other hand, reflects a bold strategic posture. It aligns with organizations undergoing significant transformation — entering new markets, restructuring operations, or radically changing business models. Greenfield implementations allow companies to break away from legacy constraints and design processes around industry standards and SAP best practices. This approach requires strong executive sponsorship, cross-functional alignment, and a roadmap that recognizes the disruption and opportunity embedded in starting fresh.

Ultimately, the type of SAP project should be a natural extension of the organization's strategic intent. Is the company optimizing what it has? Replatforming for agility? Or reinventing itself for the future? The answer shapes everything — from governance models and funding cycles to change management strategies and success metrics. A misalignment between implementation approach and business trajectory is one of the leading causes of SAP program failure. The most successful programs are those where technology execution reinforces strategic ambition and where the implementation plan reflects not just how the system will be delivered — but why.

Conclusion

Choosing the correct type of SAP implementation project is crucial for the initiative's success. Brownfield, Bluefield, and Greenfield implementations each offer unique advantages and challenges, and the choice should be based on the organization's specific needs, objectives, and constraints. By understanding the characteristics of each approach and following best practices, organizations can ensure a successful SAP implementation that delivers the expected business benefits and supports long-term growth and innovation.

Chapter 24: Key Success Factors

Implementing SAP systems is a complex process that requires meticulous planning, coordination, and execution. The success of an SAP implementation project depends on several key factors that must be managed effectively throughout the project lifecycle. This chapter explores the critical success factors in SAP implementation, including strategic alignment, executive sponsorship, project management, change management, stakeholder engagement, data management, and post-implementation support. Each section provides detailed insights and best practices to ensure a successful SAP implementation.

Strategic Alignment

Overview of Strategic Alignment

Strategic alignment ensures that the SAP implementation project closely aligns with the organization's strategic goals and objectives. It involves understanding the business drivers behind the implementation and ensuring that the project supports the organization's long-term vision.

Critical Components of Strategic Alignment

1. **Understanding Business Drivers:**

   o **Objective:** Identify the critical business drivers and objectives behind the SAP implementation.

   o **Activities:** Conduct interviews with senior management, review strategic plans, and analyze current business challenges.

2. **Setting Clear Objectives:**

   o **Objective:** Define clear and measurable objectives for the SAP implementation project.

   o **Activities:** Develop a project charter that outlines the project's goals, deliverables, and success criteria.

3. **Aligning with Business Strategy:**

   ○ **Objective:** Ensure the SAP implementation aligns with the organization's business strategy.

   ○ **Activities:** Regularly review the project's progress against strategic goals and adjust the plan as needed.

4. **Continuous Alignment:**

   ○ **Objective:** Maintain continuous alignment between the project and business strategy throughout the project lifecycle.

   ○ **Activities:** Regular strategic alignment meetings with key stakeholders to ensure ongoing alignment.

Best Practices for Strategic Alignment

1. **Engage Senior Management:** Involve senior management early in the project to ensure their support and alignment with strategic goals.

2. **Define Clear Objectives:** Set clear, measurable objectives for the project that align with the organization's strategic goals.

3. **Regular Reviews:** Conduct regular reviews to ensure the project remains aligned with business strategy and adjust plans as necessary.

4. **Communicate Vision:** Communicate the project's strategic vision and objectives to all team members and stakeholders.

Executive Sponsorship

Overview of Executive Sponsorship

Executive sponsorship is crucial for the success of SAP implementation projects. It involves senior executives actively supporting and championing the project, providing the necessary resources and authority to drive it forward.

Critical Components of Executive Sponsorship

1. **Selecting the Right Sponsor:**

   o **Objective:** Identify a senior executive with the authority and influence to act as the project sponsor.

   o **Activities:** Select an executive who understands the strategic importance of the project and is committed to its success.

2. **Defining Sponsor Responsibilities:**

   o **Objective:** Clearly define the responsibilities and expectations of the project sponsor.

   o **Activities:** Develop a sponsor role description that outlines their responsibilities, including decision-making, resource allocation, and stakeholder communication.

3. **Active Involvement:**

   o **Objective:** Ensure that the project sponsor is actively involved.

   o **Activities:** Schedule regular meetings between the sponsor and project team and involve the sponsor in critical decisions and milestones.

4. **Providing Support and Resources:**

   o **Objective:** Ensure the project sponsor provides the necessary support and resources.

   o **Activities:** Facilitate open communication between the project sponsor and team and escalate issues promptly for resolution.

Best Practices for Executive Sponsorship

1. **Select a Committed Sponsor:** Choose a sponsor who is genuinely committed to the project's success and has the authority to make critical decisions.

2. **Define Clear Responsibilities:** Clearly define the responsibilities and expectations of the project sponsor.

3. **Ensure Active Involvement:** Encourage the sponsor to participate actively in the project, attending meetings and supporting the team.

4. **Facilitate Open Communication:** Maintain open lines of communication between the sponsor and project team to ensure issues are addressed promptly.

Project Management

Overview of Project Management

Effective project management is essential for the successful implementation of SAP systems. It involves planning, executing, and monitoring the project to ensure it is completed on time, within budget, and meets the defined objectives.

Key Components of Project Management

1. **Project Planning:**

   o **Objective:** Develop a detailed project plan that outlines the scope, timeline, resources, and milestones.

   o **Activities:** Create a project charter, define project deliverables, develop a work breakdown structure (WBS), and establish a project schedule.

2. **Resource Management:**

   o **Objective:** Ensure the necessary resources are available and utilized throughout the project.

   o **Activities:** Identify resource requirements, allocate resources, and monitor resource utilization.

3. **Risk Management:**

   o **Objective:** Identify, assess, and mitigate risks that could impact the project.

- o **Activities:** Conduct a risk assessment, develop a risk management plan, and monitor risks throughout the project.

4. **Communication Management:**

   - o **Objective:** Ensure effective communication among project team members, stakeholders, and sponsors.

   - o **Activities:** Develop a communication plan, schedule regular project meetings, and provide status updates.

5. **Quality Management:**

   - o **Objective:** Ensure that the project deliverables meet the required quality standards.

   - o **Activities:** Develop a quality management plan, conduct quality reviews, and implement quality control measures.

6. **Monitoring and Control:**

   - o **Objective:** Monitor project progress and adjust to ensure successful completion.

   - o **Activities:** Track project milestones, monitor project performance and implement corrective actions as needed.

Best Practices for Project Management

1. **Comprehensive Planning:** Develop a detailed project plan that outlines the scope, timeline, resources, and milestones.

2. **Effective Resource Management:** Ensure the necessary resources are available and utilized throughout the project.

3. **Proactive Risk Management:** Identify, assess, and mitigate risks that could impact the project.

4. **Clear Communication:** Ensure effective communication among project team members, stakeholders, and sponsors.

5. **Quality Assurance:** Implement quality control measures to ensure the project deliverables meet the required standards.

Change Management

Overview of Change Management

Change management is a critical component of SAP implementation projects. It involves preparing, supporting, and guiding individuals and organizations through the changes brought about by the new system.

Critical Components of Change Management

1. **Change Management Strategy:**

    o **Objective:** Develop a comprehensive change management strategy that addresses the impact of the SAP implementation on the organization.

    o **Activities:** Define change management objectives, identify change agents, and develop a plan.

2. **Change Impact Assessment:**

    o **Objective:** Assess the impact of the SAP implementation on existing processes, systems, and personnel.

    o **Activities:** Conduct change impact assessments, identify resistance areas, and develop mitigation strategies.

3. **Communication and Training:**

    o **Objective:** Ensure all employees are informed about the changes and have the necessary skills to use the new system effectively.

    o **Activities:** Develop a communication plan, create training programs, and provide ongoing support and resources.

4. **Change Readiness Assessment:**

    o **Objective:** Assess the organization's readiness for change and identify barriers to successful implementation.

    o **Activities:** Conduct readiness assessments, identify additional support areas, and develop action plans.

Best Practices for Change Management

1. **Comprehensive Strategy:** Develop a comprehensive change management strategy that addresses all aspects of the change process.

2. **Impact Assessment:** Regularly assess the impact of changes and the organization's readiness to adopt them.

3. **Effective Communication:** Communicate changes clearly and frequently to ensure all employees are informed and engaged.

4. **Comprehensive Training:** Provide thorough training and support to help employees adapt to the new system.

Stakeholder Engagement

Overview of Stakeholder Engagement

Effective stakeholder engagement is crucial for the success of SAP implementation projects. It involves identifying, understanding, and managing the needs and expectations of all stakeholders impacted by the project.

Critical Components of Stakeholder Engagement

1. **Stakeholder Identification:**

    o **Objective:** Identify all stakeholders to whom the SAP implementation will impact.

    o **Activities:** Create a stakeholder map, categorizing stakeholders by their influence and interest in the project.

2. **Stakeholder Analysis:**

    o **Objective:** Understand each stakeholder group's needs, concerns, and expectations.

    o **Activities:** Conduct stakeholder interviews and surveys to gather insights and feedback.

3. **Stakeholder Communication Plan:**

   o **Objective:** Develop a communication plan to keep stakeholders informed and engaged throughout the project.

   o **Activities:** Define communication channels, frequency, and content for stakeholder updates.

4. **Stakeholder Involvement:**

   o **Objective:** Actively involve stakeholders to ensure their needs are addressed, and they feel invested in the project's success.

   o **Activities:** Create stakeholder committees, hold regular review meetings, and involve stakeholders in decision-making.

Best Practices for Stakeholder Engagement

1. **Early and Continuous Engagement:** Engage stakeholders early and maintain regular communication throughout the project.

2. **Transparent Communication:** Keep stakeholders informed of project progress, challenges, and changes.

3. **Active Involvement:** Involve stakeholders in critical decisions and ensure their feedback is considered.

4. **Address Concerns:** Proactively address stakeholder concerns and demonstrate how their input is being used to shape the project.

Data Management

Overview of Data Management

Effective data management is crucial for the success of SAP implementation projects. It ensures data is accurately migrated, managed, and maintained in the new SAP system.

Key Components of Data Management

1. **Data Assessment:**

    o **Objective:** Assess the quality and structure of the existing data to identify any issues that need to be addressed before migration.

    o **Activities:** Conduct data quality assessments, identify data cleansing requirements, and develop a data migration plan.

2. **Data Migration:**

    o **Objective:** Ensure data is accurately migrated from the legacy system to the new SAP system.

    o **Activities:** Develop a data migration strategy, map data from the legacy system to the new system, and conduct data migration tests.

3. **Data Cleansing:**

    o **Objective:** Ensure that data is accurate, complete, and consistent before it is migrated to the new system.

    o **Activities:** Identify and correct data errors, remove duplicate records, and standardize data formats.

4. **Data Validation:**

    o **Objective:** Validate that data has been accurately migrated and functions correctly in the new system.

    o **Activities:** Conduct data validation tests, compare migrated data to the legacy system, and address discrepancies.

Best Practices for Data Management

1. **Thorough Assessment:** Conduct a comprehensive assessment of the existing data to identify any issues that must be addressed before migration.

2. **Effective Data Migration:** Ensure data migration is carefully planned and executed to maintain data integrity and consistency.

3. **Data Cleansing:** Cleanse data to ensure accuracy, completeness, and consistency before migration.

4. **Rigorous Validation:** Conduct rigorous data validation tests to ensure the new system's migrated data is accurate and functional.

Post-Implementation Support

Overview of Post-Implementation Support

Post-implementation support is critical for ensuring the long-term success of the SAP system. It involves providing ongoing support, monitoring system performance, and making necessary adjustments to ensure the system continues to meet business needs.

Critical Components of Post-Implementation Support

1. **Support Structure:**

    o **Objective:** Establish a support structure to provide ongoing assistance and address any issues that arise after going live.

    o **Activities:** Set up a help desk, define support processes, and allocate support resources.

2. **System Monitoring:**

    o **Objective:** Continuously monitor system performance to identify and address any issues.

    o **Activities:** Implement monitoring tools, track system performance metrics, and conduct regular health checks.

3. **User Training and Support:**

    o **Objective:** Provide ongoing training and support to ensure users are comfortable and proficient with the new system.

- o **Activities:** Develop training programs, create user guides, and offer ongoing support resources.

4. **Continuous Improvement:**

   - o **Objective:** Continuously improve the system based on user feedback and changing business needs.

   - o **Activities:** Gather user feedback, identify areas for improvement, and implement system enhancements.

Best Practices for Post-Implementation Support

1. **Robust Support Structure:** Establish a robust support structure to provide ongoing assistance and address any issues promptly.

2. **Continuous Monitoring:** Monitor system performance to identify and address issues.

3. **Ongoing Training:** Provide ongoing training and support to ensure users are comfortable and proficient with the new system.

4. **Continuous Improvement:** Use user feedback and changing business needs to improve the system continuously.

Conclusion

The success of an SAP implementation project depends on several critical factors, including strategic alignment, executive sponsorship, project management, change management, stakeholder engagement, data management, and post-implementation support. By understanding and effectively managing these factors, organizations can ensure a successful SAP implementation that delivers the expected business benefits and supports long-term growth and innovation. Adhering to best practices in these areas will help organizations navigate the complexities of SAP implementation and achieve their strategic goals.

Chapter 25: Project Governance

Project governance is a critical component of SAP implementation that ensures the project is managed effectively, aligns with organizational goals, and delivers the expected outcomes. Effective governance provides a framework for decision-making, risk management, and accountability throughout the project lifecycle. This chapter explores the critical aspects of project governance, including establishing a governance structure, defining roles and responsibilities, setting up governance processes, and ensuring continuous improvement. It also provides best practices to ensure successful project governance in SAP implementations.

Establishing a Governance Structure

Overview of Governance Structure
A robust governance structure is essential for overseeing the SAP implementation project, ensuring alignment with organizational goals, and facilitating effective decision-making. It involves setting up a governing body hierarchy that provides strategic direction, oversight, and support throughout the project.

Critical Components of Governance Structure
1. **Steering Committee:**
   o **Objective:** Provide strategic direction and oversight for the SAP implementation project.
   o **Composition:** Senior executives and key stakeholders from various business units.
   o **Responsibilities:** Approve project objectives, allocate resources, make high-level decisions, and resolve escalated issues.
2. **Project Management Office (PMO):**
   o **Objective:** Provide administrative support, standardize project management practices, and ensure project alignment with organizational goals.
   o **Composition:** Project management professionals with expertise in SAP implementations.
   o **Responsibilities:** Develop project management standards, monitor progress, and guide teams.

3. **Project Team:**
   o **Objective:** Execute the SAP implementation project according to the approved plan.
   o **Composition:** Project managers, functional and technical consultants, business analysts, and key personnel.
   o **Responsibilities:** Perform project tasks, manage day-to-day activities, and ensure deliverables meet quality standards.
4. **Business Process Owners:**
   o **Objective:** Represent business units and ensure the SAP system meets their needs.
   o **Composition:** Key representatives from various business units.
   o **Responsibilities:** Provide input on business requirements, validate system configurations, and support user acceptance testing.

Best Practices for Establishing a Governance Structure
1. **Inclusive Composition:** Ensure that the governance structure includes representatives from all relevant business units and levels of the organization.
2. **Clear Hierarchy:** Establish a governing body hierarchy to facilitate effective decision-making and accountability.
3. **Defined Responsibilities:** Clearly define the roles and responsibilities of each governing body to avoid overlaps and ensure accountability.
4. **Regular Meetings:** Schedule meetings for each governing body to review progress, address issues, and make decisions.

Defining Roles and Responsibilities

Overview of Roles and Responsibilities
Defining clear roles and responsibilities is crucial for effective project governance. It ensures that all team members and stakeholders understand their duties, fosters accountability, and facilitates efficient project execution.

Key Roles and Responsibilities

1. **Project Sponsor:**
   - **Objective:** Provide overall leadership and support for the SAP implementation project.
   - **Responsibilities:** Approve project objectives, allocate resources, resolve high-level issues, and ensure alignment with organizational goals.

2. **Project Manager:**
   - **Objective:** Plan, execute, and monitor the SAP implementation project.
   - **Responsibilities:** Develop project plans, manage project resources, track progress, and ensure deliverables meet quality standards.

3. **Functional Consultants:**
   - **Objective:** Design and configure the SAP system to meet business requirements.
   - **Responsibilities:** Gather business requirements, configure SAP modules, perform system testing, and provide user training.

4. **Technical Consultants:**
   - **Objective:** Provide technical expertise for the SAP implementation project.
   - **Responsibilities:** Develop custom enhancements, integrate SAP with other systems, perform data migration, and ensure system performance.

5. **Business Process Owners:**
   - **Objective:** Ensure that the SAP system meets the needs of their respective business units.
   - **Responsibilities:** Provide input on business requirements, validate system configurations, support user acceptance testing, and champion the project within their units.

6. **Change Management Lead:**
   - **Objective:** Manage the organizational change associated with the SAP implementation.
   - **Responsibilities:** Develop change management strategies, conduct impact assessments, plan and execute communication and training programs, and monitor change readiness.

Best Practices for Defining Roles and Responsibilities
1. **Detailed Role Descriptions:** Develop detailed descriptions that outline the responsibilities, skills, and qualifications required for each role.
2. **Clear Accountability:** Ensure each role is accountable for specific tasks and deliverables.
3. **Role Alignment:** Align roles and responsibilities with the project's objectives and the organization's strategic goals.
4. **Regular Updates:** Review and update role descriptions regularly to reflect changes in project scope, priorities, or team composition.

Setting Up Governance Processes

Key Governance Processes
1. **Decision-Making Process:**
   - **Objective:** Ensure timely and effective decision-making throughout the project.
   - **Activities:** Establish decision-making criteria, define decision-making authority at different levels, and set up escalation procedures for unresolved issues.
2. **Issue Resolution Process:**
   - **Objective:** Identify, track, and resolve issues promptly to minimize their impact on the project.
   - **Activities:** Implement an issue tracking system, assign responsibility for issue resolution, and establish regular review meetings to address open issues.
3. **Risk Management Process:**
   - **Objective:** Identify, assess, and mitigate risks impacting the project's success.
   - **Activities:** Conduct risk assessments, develop risk mitigation plans, monitor risks throughout the project, and update risk management strategies as needed.
4. **Performance Monitoring Process:**
   - **Objective:** Track project progress and performance against predefined metrics and milestones.
   - **Activities:** Define key performance indicators (KPIs), establish a performance monitoring system, conduct regular performance reviews, and adjust project plans based on performance data.

Best Practices for Setting Up Governance Processes
1. **Clear Criteria:** Establish clear criteria for decision-making, issue resolution, and risk management to ensure consistency and transparency.
2. **Effective Tracking:** Implement robust tracking systems for issues, risks, and performance metrics to facilitate monitoring and reporting.
3. **Regular Reviews:** Review project performance, risks, and issues to ensure timely intervention and corrective actions.
4. **Continuous Improvement:** Improve governance processes based on lessons learned and stakeholder feedback.

Below is a typical Program Governance structure

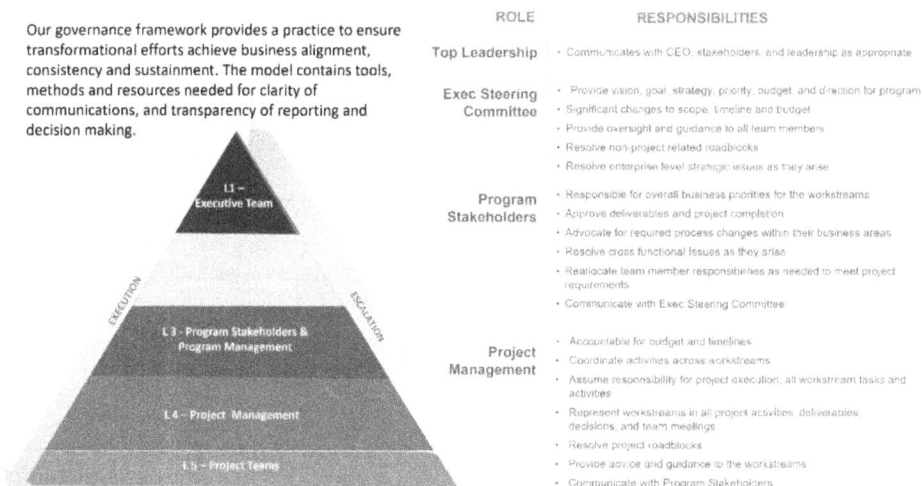

Our governance framework provides a practice to ensure transformational efforts achieve business alignment, consistency and sustainment. The model contains tools, methods and resources needed for clarity of communications, and transparency of reporting and decision making.

L1 – Executive Team

EXECUTION

ESCALATION

L3 - Program Stakeholders & Program Management

L4 – Project Management

L5 – Project Teams

ROLE

Top Leadership

Exec Steering Committee

Program Stakeholders

Project Management

RESPONSIBILITIES

- Communicates with CEO, stakeholders, and leadership as appropriate

- Provide vision, goal, strategy, priority, budget, and direction for program
- Significant changes to scope, timeline and budget
- Provide oversight and guidance to all team members
- Resolve non-project related roadblocks
- Resolve enterprise level strategic issues as they arise

- Responsible for overall business priorities for the workstreams
- Approve deliverables and project completion
- Advocate for required process changes within their business areas
- Resolve cross functional issues as they arise
- Reallocate team member responsibilities as needed to meet project requirements
- Communicate with Exec Steering Committee

- Accountable for budget and timelines
- Coordinate activities across workstreams
- Assume responsibility for project execution, all workstream tasks and activities
- Represent workstreams in all project activities, deliverables, decisions, and team meetings
- Resolve project roadblocks
- Provide advice and guidance to the workstreams
- Communicate with Program Stakeholders

Ensuring Continuous Improvement

Overview of Continuous Improvement
Continuous improvement involves regularly evaluating and enhancing project governance practices to ensure they remain effective and aligned with organizational goals. It focuses on learning from experience, incorporating feedback, and adapting to changing project needs.

Critical Components of Continuous Improvement

1. **Lessons Learned:**
   - o **Objective:** Capture and apply lessons from previous projects and ongoing activities.
   - o **Activities:** Conduct post-project reviews, document lessons learned, and integrate them into future project plans and governance practices.
2. **Stakeholder Feedback:**
   - o **Objective:** Gather and incorporate feedback from stakeholders to improve governance practices.
   - o **Activities:** Implement feedback mechanisms, such as surveys and focus groups, to collect stakeholder input and use this feedback to refine governance processes.
3. **Performance Reviews:**
   - o **Objective:** Regularly review project performance and governance effectiveness.
   - o **Activities:** Conduct performance reviews, analyze performance data, identify areas for improvement, and implement changes to governance practices.
4. **Adaptability:**
   - o **Objective:** Ensure that governance practices can adapt to changing project needs and external factors.
   - o **Activities:** Monitor project environment, assess the impact of changes, and adjust governance practices as needed.

Best Practices for Ensuring Continuous Improvement

1. **Document Lessons Learned:** Capture and document lessons learned from each project phase and use them to improve future projects.
2. **Incorporate Feedback:** Regularly gather and incorporate stakeholder feedback to enhance governance practices.
3. **Conduct Regular Reviews:** Perform regular reviews of project performance and governance effectiveness to identify and address areas for improvement.
4. **Maintain Flexibility:** Ensure that governance practices can adapt to changing project needs and external factors.

Case Studies and Examples

Case Study 1: Financial Services Company

Overview: A financial services company implemented SAP to streamline its operations. The project governance structure included a steering committee, PMO, and project team with clearly defined roles and responsibilities.

Approach:

- **Governance Structure:** Established a steering committee for strategic oversight, a PMO for administrative support, and a project team for execution.
- **Decision-Making Process:** Implemented a transparent decision-making process with defined criteria and escalation procedures.
- **Performance Monitoring:** Set up performance monitoring processes with key performance indicators and regular reviews.

Outcome:

- **Successful Implementation:** Achieved a successful SAP implementation on time and within budget.
- **Effective Decision-Making:** Facilitated timely and effective decision-making, minimizing project delays.
- **Continuous Improvement:** Continuously improved governance practices based on lessons learned and stakeholder feedback.

Case Study 2: Manufacturing Company

Overview: A manufacturing company implemented SAP to integrate its global operations. The project governance framework included a robust risk management process and regular performance reviews.

Approach:

- **Risk Management:** Conducted regular risk assessments, developed mitigation plans, and monitored risks throughout the project.
- **Stakeholder Engagement:** Actively engaged stakeholders through regular communication and involvement in decision-making.
- **Continuous Improvement:** Implemented continuous improvement practices, incorporating lessons learned and stakeholder feedback.

Outcome:

- **Proactive Risk Management:** Effectively managed risks, preventing significant issues and ensuring project success.
- **Enhanced Stakeholder Engagement:** Fostered strong stakeholder engagement, ensuring alignment and support.
- **Ongoing Improvement:** Continuously improved governance practices, leading to enhanced project performance and outcomes.

Conclusion

Effective project governance is crucial for the successful implementation of SAP systems. It provides a structured framework for decision-making, risk management, and accountability, ensuring that the project is managed efficiently and aligned with organizational goals. Organizations can navigate the complexities of SAP implementation and achieve their strategic objectives by establishing a robust governance structure, defining clear roles and responsibilities, setting up effective governance processes, and ensuring continuous improvement. Adhering to best practices in project governance will help organizations ensure successful SAP implementations and deliver the expected business benefits.

Chapter 26: Building the Right Team

The success of an SAP implementation project largely depends on assembling the right team with the necessary skills, experience, and commitment. Building a well-rounded team involves selecting individuals who possess technical expertise, understand the business processes, and can effectively manage change. This chapter delves into the critical aspects of building the right team for SAP implementation, including team structure, roles and responsibilities, recruitment and selection, training and development, and fostering a collaborative team environment. Best practices are provided to ensure the team is well-equipped to handle the complexities of SAP implementation.

Team Structure

Overview of Team Structure

An effective team structure for SAP implementation ensures that all necessary roles are filled and responsibilities are clearly defined. This structure typically includes project management, functional and technical expertise, business process knowledge, and change management capabilities.

Critical Components of Team Structure

1. **Project Steering Committee:**

   o **Objective:** Provide strategic direction and oversight for the SAP implementation project.

   o **Composition:** Senior executives and key stakeholders from various business units.

   o **Responsibilities:** Approve project objectives, allocate resources, make high-level decisions, and resolve escalated issues.

2. **Project Management Office (PMO):**

   o **Objective:** Ensure that project management standards are maintained and the project is aligned with organizational goals.

   o **Composition:** Project managers and administrative support staff.

   o **Responsibilities:** Develop project plans, track progress, manage risks, and coordinate communication.

3. **Functional Team:**

   o **Objective:** Ensure the SAP system meets the business's needs.

   o **Composition:** Functional consultants with expertise in different SAP modules (e.g., FI, CO, MM, SD).

- o **Responsibilities:** Gather business requirements, configure SAP modules, and validate system functionality.

4. **Technical Team:**

- o **Objective:** Provide technical expertise for the SAP implementation project.

- o **Composition:** Technical consultants, ABAP developers, basis administrators, and integration specialists.

- o **Responsibilities:** Develop custom enhancements, migrate data, integrate SAP with other systems, and ensure system performance.

5. **Business Process Owners:**

- o **Objective:** Represent the interests of their respective business units and ensure that the SAP system supports their processes.

- o **Composition:** Key representatives from various business units.

- o **Responsibilities:** Provide input on business requirements, validate system configurations, and support user acceptance testing.

6. **Change Management Team:**

- o **Objective:** Manage the organizational change associated with the SAP implementation.

- o **Composition:** Change management specialists, communication experts, and training coordinators.

- o **Responsibilities:** Develop change management strategies, conduct impact assessments, plan and execute communication and training programs, and monitor change readiness.

Best Practices for Team Structure

1. **Inclusive Structure:** Ensure that the team structure includes representatives from all relevant business units and levels of the organization.

2. **Clear Hierarchy:** Establish a clear hierarchy and reporting lines to facilitate effective decision-making and accountability.

3. **Balanced Composition:** Maintain a balanced team composition with a mix of technical and functional expertise, business process knowledge, and change management capabilities.

4. **Defined Responsibilities:** Clearly define each team member's roles and responsibilities to avoid overlaps and ensure accountability.

Roles and Responsibilities

Overview of Roles and Responsibilities

Defining clear roles and responsibilities is essential for ensuring all team members understand their duties and contribute effectively to the project. This section outlines the key roles in an SAP implementation project and their responsibilities.

Key Roles and Responsibilities

1. **Project Sponsor:**

   o **Objective:** Provide overall leadership and support for the SAP implementation project.

   o **Responsibilities:** Approve project objectives, allocate resources, resolve high-level issues, and ensure alignment with organizational goals.

2. **Project Manager:**

   o **Objective:** Plan, execute, and monitor the SAP implementation project.

- o **Responsibilities:** Develop project plans, manage project resources, track progress, and ensure deliverables meet quality standards.

3. **Functional Consultants:**

   - o **Objective:** Design and configure the SAP system to meet business requirements.

   - o **Responsibilities:** Gather business requirements, configure SAP modules, perform system testing, and provide user training.

4. **Technical Consultants:**

   - o **Objective:** Provide technical expertise for the SAP implementation project.

   - o **Responsibilities:** Develop custom enhancements, integrate SAP with other systems, perform data migration, and ensure system performance.

5. **Business Process Owners:**

   - o **Objective:** Ensure that the SAP system meets the needs of their respective business units.

   - o **Responsibilities:** Provide input on business requirements, validate system configurations, support user acceptance testing, and champion the project within their units.

6. **Change Management Lead:**

   - o **Objective:** Manage the organizational change associated with the SAP implementation.

   - o **Responsibilities:** Develop change management strategies, conduct impact assessments, plan and execute communication and training programs, and monitor change readiness.

7. **Data Migration Specialist:**

   o **Objective:** Ensure accurate and effective data migration from legacy systems to the new SAP system.

   o **Responsibilities:** Develop data migration plans, map data from legacy systems, perform data cleansing, and validate migrated data.

8. **Integration Specialist:**

   o **Objective:** Ensure seamless integration between SAP and other systems.

   o **Responsibilities:** Design integration solutions, develop and test integration interfaces, and monitor integration performance.

Best Practices for Defining Roles and Responsibilities

1. **Detailed Role Descriptions:** Develop detailed descriptions that outline the responsibilities, skills, and qualifications required for each role.

2. **Clear Accountability:** Ensure each role is accountable for specific tasks and deliverables.

3. **Role Alignment:** Align roles and responsibilities with the project's objectives and the organization's strategic goals.

4. **Regular Updates:** Review and update role descriptions regularly to reflect changes in project scope, priorities, or team composition.

Recruitment and Selection

Overview of Recruitment and Selection

Recruiting and selecting the right individuals for the SAP implementation team is crucial for the project's success. This involves identifying the necessary skills and experience, sourcing candidates, and selecting the best fit for each role.

Critical Steps in Recruitment and Selection

1. **Identify Skills and Experience:**

   o **Objective:** Determine the skills and experience required for each role on the SAP implementation team.

   o **Activities:** Develop a skills matrix, define role-specific qualifications, and identify gaps in existing team capabilities.

2. **Source Candidates:**

   o **Objective:** Identify potential candidates for the SAP implementation team.

   o **Activities:** Use various sourcing methods, such as internal postings, external job boards, recruitment agencies, and professional networks.

3. **Screen and Shortlist:**

   o **Objective:** Screen candidates to identify the best fit for each role.

   o **Activities:** Review resumes, conduct initial interviews, and shortlist candidates based on their skills, experience, and cultural fit.

4. **Conduct Interviews:**

   o **Objective:** Evaluate shortlisted candidates through in-depth interviews.

   o **Activities:** Conduct technical and behavioral interviews, assess candidates' problem-solving abilities, and evaluate their fit with the team and organizational culture.

5. **Select and Onboard:**

   o **Objective:** Select the best candidates and onboard them effectively.

- Activities: Make final selection decisions, extend job offers, and provide a comprehensive onboarding program to integrate new team members into the project.

Best Practices for Recruitment and Selection

1. **Comprehensive Skills Assessment:** Develop a detailed skills matrix to identify the specific skills and experience required for each role.

2. **Diverse Sourcing Methods:** Use various sourcing methods to identify a diverse pool of candidates.

3. **Structured Interviews:** Conduct structured interviews with standardized questions to ensure a fair and consistent evaluation process.

4. **Effective Onboarding:** Provide a comprehensive onboarding program to help new team members integrate into the project and understand their roles and responsibilities.

Training and Development

Overview of Training and Development

Providing continuous training and development opportunities ensures the SAP implementation team has the necessary skills and knowledge to succeed. This involves identifying training needs, developing training programs, and fostering a culture of continuous learning.

Critical Components of Training and Development

1. **Training Needs Assessment:**

    - **Objective:** Identify the training needs of the SAP implementation team.

    - **Activities:** Conduct skills assessments, gather input from team members and stakeholders, and analyze project requirements.

2. **Develop Training Programs:**

   o **Objective:** Develop training programs to address identified training needs.

   o **Activities:** Create training materials, schedule sessions, and select appropriate training methods (e.g., classroom training, online courses, workshops).

3. **Deliver Training:**

   o **Objective:** Provide training to the SAP implementation team.

   o **Activities:** Conduct training sessions, monitor attendance and participation, and provide hands-on practice and real-world application opportunities.

4. **Evaluate Training Effectiveness:**

   o **Objective:** Assess the effectiveness of training programs and make improvements as needed.

   o **Activities:** Gather participant feedback, measure skills and knowledge changes, and adjust training programs based on evaluation results.

5. **Foster Continuous Learning:**

   o **Objective:** Encourage continuous learning and development within the SAP implementation team.

   o **Activities:** Provide access to ongoing training resources, encourage participation in professional development activities, and create a culture of continuous improvement.

Best Practices for Training and Development

1. **Regular Needs Assessment:** Conduct regular training needs assessments to identify gaps in skills and knowledge.

2. **Comprehensive Training Programs:** Develop comprehensive training programs that address identified needs and provide opportunities for hands-on practice.

3. **Ongoing Evaluation:** Continuously evaluate the effectiveness of training programs and make improvements based on feedback and performance data.

4. **Encourage Continuous Learning:** Foster a culture of continuous learning by providing access to ongoing training resources and encouraging professional development.

Fostering a Collaborative Team Environment

Overview of Collaborative Team Environment

A collaborative team environment is essential for the success of the SAP implementation project. It promotes open communication, teamwork, and a shared commitment to achieving project goals.

Critical Components of a Collaborative Team Environment

1. **Open Communication:**

   o **Objective:** Foster open communication among team members and stakeholders.

   o **Activities:** Encourage regular team meetings, create open channels for communication, and promote transparency in project updates and decision-making.

2. **Team Building:**

   o **Objective:** Build a cohesive and motivated project team.

   o **Activities:** Conduct team-building activities, create opportunities for social interaction, and foster a sense of camaraderie and trust among team members.

3. **Shared Goals and Vision:**

   o **Objective:** Ensure all team members align with the project's goals and vision.

- Activities: Communicate the project's strategic objectives, involve team members in goal-setting, and reinforce the shared vision regularly.

4. **Recognition and Rewards:**

   - **Objective:** Recognize and reward team members for their contributions and achievements.

   - **Activities:** Implement a recognition program, celebrate project milestones, and provide incentives for outstanding performance.

5. **Conflict Resolution:**

   - **Objective:** Address conflicts promptly and effectively to maintain a positive team environment.

   - **Activities:** Implement conflict resolution strategies, hold mediation sessions, and involve neutral third parties if necessary.

Best Practices for Fostering a Collaborative Team Environment

1. **Promote Open Communication:** Encourage open and transparent communication among team members and stakeholders.

2. **Invest in Team Building:** Conduct regular team-building activities to foster a sense of camaraderie and trust.

3. **Align with Shared Goals:** Ensure all team members align with the project's goals and vision.

4. **Recognize Contributions:** Implement a recognition program to celebrate achievements and motivate team members.

5. **Resolve Conflicts Promptly:** Address conflicts promptly and effectively to maintain a positive team environment.

Case Studies and Examples

Case Study 1: Pharmaceutical Company

Overview: A pharmaceutical company implemented SAP to streamline its operations. The project team comprised functional and technical consultants, business process owners, and a dedicated change management team.

Approach:

- **Team Structure:** Established a clear team structure with defined roles and responsibilities for each member.

- **Recruitment and Selection:** Used a combination of internal postings and external recruitment to build a diverse and skilled team.

- **Training and Development:** Conducted comprehensive training programs to ensure team members were proficient in their respective areas.

- **Collaborative Environment:** Fostered a collaborative team environment through regular team meetings, team-building activities, and open communication channels.

Outcome:

- **Successful Implementation:** Achieved a successful SAP implementation on time and within budget.

- **Effective Collaboration:** Promoted effective collaboration and teamwork, improving problem-solving and innovation.

- **Continuous Improvement:** Fostered a continuous learning and development culture, enhancing team capabilities.

Case Study 2: Manufacturing Company

Overview: A manufacturing company implemented SAP to integrate its global operations. The project team included managers, functional and technical consultants, business process owners, and change management specialists.

Approach:

- **Roles and Responsibilities:** Clearly define each team member's roles and responsibilities to ensure accountability and practical contribution.

- **Recruitment and Selection:** Conducted a thorough recruitment process to select individuals with the necessary skills and experience.

- **Training and Development:** Provided continuous training and development opportunities to enhance team capabilities.

- **Collaborative Environment:** Fostered a collaborative team environment through open communication, shared goals, and recognition of achievements.

Outcome:

- **Proactive Risk Management:** Effectively managed risks, preventing significant issues and ensuring project success.

- **Enhanced Stakeholder Engagement:** Fostered strong stakeholder engagement, ensuring alignment and support.

- **Ongoing Improvement:** Continuously improved governance practices, leading to enhanced project performance and outcomes.

Conclusion

Building the right team for SAP implementation is crucial for the project's success. By establishing a robust team structure, clearly defining roles and responsibilities, recruiting and selecting the right individuals, providing continuous training and development, and fostering a collaborative team environment, organizations can ensure their SAP implementation projects are successful and deliver the expected business benefits. Adhering to best practices in these areas will help organizations navigate the complexities of SAP implementation and achieve their strategic goals.

Chapter 27: Should SAP Implementation be led by Business or IT within Organizations?

SAP implementation is a complex, strategic initiative that requires meticulous planning, coordination, and execution. Organizations' critical decision is whether the business or IT departments should lead the implementation. This chapter explores the pros and cons of each approach, provides detailed insights into the roles and responsibilities of business and IT leaders, and offers best practices for achieving a successful SAP implementation regardless of the leadership model chosen.

The Case for Business-Led SAP Implementation

Overview
A business-led SAP implementation emphasizes the organization's strategic goals and operational needs. This approach ensures that the implementation aligns closely with business objectives, enhances user adoption, and delivers tangible business value.

Advantages of Business-Led Implementation
1. **Strategic Alignment:**
   - o **Objective:** Ensure the SAP implementation aligns with the organization's strategic goals and objectives.
   - o **Impact:** Increased likelihood of achieving desired business outcomes and competitive advantage.
2. **Operational Focus:**
   - o **Objective:** Prioritize business process optimization and operational efficiency.
   - o **Impact:** Improved business processes, streamlined operations, and enhanced productivity.
3. **User Adoption:**
   - o **Objective:** Enhance user adoption by involving business users in the implementation process.
   - o **Impact:** Higher user satisfaction, reduced resistance to change, and more effective use of the SAP system.
4. **Customization to Business Needs:**
   - o **Objective:** Ensure the SAP system is tailored to the business's needs.

- o **Impact:** Increased relevance and utility of the system for end-users, leading to better business performance.

Challenges of Business-Led Implementation
1. **Technical Oversight:**
   - o **Issue:** Potential lack of technical oversight and expertise.
   - o **Impact:** Increased risk of technical issues, integration challenges, and suboptimal system performance.
2. **Resource Constraints:**
   - o **Issue:** Business leaders may not have sufficient resources to manage the technical aspects of the implementation.
   - o **Impact:** Potential delays and cost overruns due to inadequate technical support.
3. **Change Management:**
   - o **Issue:** Managing change and ensuring effective communication across technical and business teams.
   - o **Impact:** Potential misalignment and resistance if change management is not effectively handled.

Best Practices for Business-Led Implementation
1. **Strong Collaboration with IT:**
   - o Ensure close collaboration between business leaders and IT to address technical challenges and ensure seamless integration.
   - o Establish joint governance structures and regular communication channels.
2. **Clear Business Objectives:**
   - o Define clear business objectives and success criteria for the SAP implementation.
   - o Align project goals with the organization's strategic priorities.
3. **User Involvement:**
   - o Involve end-users in the planning, design, and testing phases to ensure the system meets their needs.
   - o Provide comprehensive training and support to facilitate user adoption.
4. **Balanced Resource Allocation:**
   - o Allocate sufficient resources for both business and technical aspects of the implementation.

o Ensure that business leaders have access to necessary technical expertise and support.

o

The Case for IT-Led SAP Implementation

Overview

An IT-led SAP implementation focuses on leveraging technical expertise to ensure the system is implemented efficiently, integrated seamlessly, and maintained effectively. This approach emphasizes technical rigor, system performance, and integration with existing IT infrastructure.

Advantages of IT-Led Implementation

1. **Technical Expertise:**
   o **Objective:** Leverage the technical expertise of the IT team to manage the implementation.
   o **Impact:** Reduced risk of technical issues, efficient system integration, and optimal performance.

2. **Efficient Project Management:**
   o **Objective:** Utilize IT project management methodologies to ensure efficient execution.
   o **Impact:** Timely completion of the project, adherence to budget, and effective risk management.

3. **System Integration:**
   o **Objective:** Ensure seamless integration of SAP with existing IT systems and infrastructure.
   o **Impact:** Improved data consistency, streamlined workflows, and enhanced system performance.

4. **Security and Compliance:**
   o **Objective:** Ensure the SAP system meets security and compliance requirements.
   o **Impact:** Reduced risk of data breaches, improved compliance with regulatory requirements, and enhanced data integrity.

Challenges of IT-Led Implementation

1. **Business Alignment:**
   o **Issue:** Potential misalignment with business goals and priorities.
   o **Impact:** Reduced relevance and utility of the system for end-users, leading to lower user adoption.

2. **User Engagement:**
   - o **Issue:** Limited involvement of business users in the implementation process.
   - o **Impact:** Increased resistance to change, lower user satisfaction, and suboptimal system use.
3. **Process Optimization:**
   - o **Issue:** Potential lack of focus on business process optimization and operational efficiency.
   - o **Impact:** Missed opportunities for process improvements and enhanced productivity.

Best Practices for IT-Led Implementation
1. **Close Collaboration with Business:**
   - o Ensure close collaboration between IT and business leaders to align the implementation with business objectives.
   - o Establish joint governance structures and regular communication channels.
2. **Business Involvement:**
   - o Involve business users in critical implementation phases, including planning, design, and testing.
   - o Provide comprehensive training and support to facilitate user adoption.
3. **Clear Technical Objectives:**
   - o Define clear technical objectives and success criteria for the SAP implementation.
   - o Align project goals with the organization's IT strategy and infrastructure requirements.
4. **Comprehensive Change Management:**
   - o Implement a robust change management strategy to address potential resistance and ensure effective communication.
   - o Engage change champions to drive user adoption and support.

The Balanced Approach: Collaborative Leadership

Overview
A balanced approach that combines the strengths of both business and IT leadership can maximize the benefits of SAP implementation.

Collaborative leadership ensures the project aligns with business goals while leveraging technical expertise for efficient execution.

Advantages of Collaborative Leadership

1. **Holistic View:**
   - **Objective:** Combine business and technical perspectives to achieve a holistic view of the implementation.
   - **Impact:** Balanced focus on strategic alignment, technical efficiency, and user adoption.

2. **Enhanced Decision-Making:**
   - **Objective:** Leverage the combined expertise of business and IT leaders for better decision-making.
   - **Impact:** Improved project outcomes through informed and balanced decisions.

3. **Improved Communication:**
   - **Objective:** Foster open communication and collaboration between business and IT teams.
   - **Impact:** Reduced misalignment, improved stakeholder engagement, and enhanced project coordination.

4. **Comprehensive Change Management:**
   - **Objective:** Address both business and technical aspects of change management.
   - **Impact:** Increased user adoption, reduced resistance to change, and smoother transition to the new system.

Best Practices for Collaborative Leadership

1. **Joint Governance Structures:**
   - Establish joint governance structures that include representatives from both business and IT.
   - Define clear roles and responsibilities for each governance body.

2. **Regular Communication:**
   - Schedule regular communication and collaboration sessions between business and IT teams.
   - Use multiple communication channels to ensure all stakeholders are informed and engaged.

3. **Integrated Planning:**
   - Develop integrated project plans that consider both business and technical objectives.
   - Align project goals with the organization's strategic priorities and IT strategy.
4. **Unified Change Management:**
   - Implement a unified change management strategy that addresses business and technical aspects.
   - Engage change champions from both business and IT to drive user adoption and support.

Case Studies: Business-Led, IT-Led, and Collaborative Leadership

Case Study 1: Business-Led Implementation at a Consumer Goods Company
Background: A leading consumer goods company decided to implement SAP S/4HANA to streamline its supply chain and enhance customer experience. The business team led the project to ensure alignment with strategic goals.

Approach:
- **Stakeholder Engagement:** Engaged key stakeholders from supply chain, sales, and marketing to define project objectives.
- **User-Centric Design:** Focused on designing the system to meet the specific needs of end-users.
- **Change Management:** Implemented a robust change management strategy, including comprehensive training and support.

Results:
- **Improved Supply Chain Efficiency:** Achieved significant improvements in supply chain efficiency and customer satisfaction.
- **High User Adoption:** High user adoption rates due to user-centric design and effective change management.

Lessons Learned:
- **Strategic Alignment:** Ensuring alignment with business goals is crucial for achieving desired outcomes.

- **User Involvement:** Involving end-users in the design and testing phases enhances adoption and satisfaction.

Case Study 2: IT-Led Implementation at a Financial Services Firm

Background: A financial services firm implemented SAP S/4HANA to improve its financial reporting and regulatory compliance. The IT department led the project to ensure technical rigor and integration with existing systems.

Approach:
- **Technical Expertise:** Leveraged the technical expertise of the IT team to manage the implementation.
- **System Integration:** Focused on seamlessly integrating existing financial systems and infrastructure.
- **Security and Compliance:** Ensured the system met all security and compliance requirements.

Results:
- **Enhanced Reporting:** Improved financial reporting capabilities and regulatory compliance.
- **Efficient Integration:** Achieved seamless integration with existing systems, enhancing data consistency and accuracy.

Lessons Learned:
- **Technical Rigor:** Leveraging technical expertise is essential for managing complex integrations and ensuring system performance.
- **Security Focus:** Ensuring security and compliance is critical for financial systems.

Case Study 3: Collaborative Leadership at a Manufacturing Company

Background: A global manufacturing company implemented SAP S/4HANA to standardize its operations and improve data visibility. The project was led collaboratively by business and IT leaders.

Approach:
- **Joint Governance:** Established a joint governance structure with representatives from business and IT.
- **Integrated Planning:** Developed an integrated project plan that aligned business and technical objectives.
- **Unified Change Management:** Implemented a unified change management strategy to address business and technical aspects.

Results:

- **Standardized Operations:** Achieved standardized operations and improved data visibility across the organization.
- **Balanced Focus:** Balanced focus on strategic alignment, technical efficiency, and user adoption.

Lessons Learned:

- **Collaborative Leadership:** Combining business and IT leadership enhances decision-making and project outcomes.
- **Unified Approach:** A unified approach to change management increases user adoption and reduces resistance to change.

Conclusion

Whether SAP implementation should be led by business or IT depends on the organization's specific needs, goals, and context. Both approaches have their advantages and challenges. A business-led implementation ensures strategic alignment and user adoption, while an IT-led implementation leverages technical expertise and ensures efficient system integration. However, a balanced, collaborative leadership model that combines the strengths of both business and IT is often the most effective approach. Organizations can achieve successful SAP implementations that deliver tangible business value and support their strategic objectives by adopting best practices for collaboration, communication, and change management.

Chapter 28: Inhouse or Outsource - How to Choose the Right System Integrator

Choosing the right system integrator (SI) is critical in the SAP implementation. This decision can significantly impact the project's success, cost, timeline, and overall outcome. Organizations must carefully evaluate whether to handle the SAP implementation in-house or to outsource it to an external SI. This chapter explores the factors involved in making this decision, the advantages and disadvantages of each approach, and best practices for selecting the suitable SI for your SAP implementation project.

Inhouse vs. Outsource: Key Considerations

Overview of Inhouse vs. Outsource

Deciding between in-house and outsourcing for SAP implementation involves assessing various factors such as internal capabilities, project complexity, cost, and strategic goals. Each approach has benefits and challenges; the choice depends on the organization's specific needs and circumstances.

Factors to Consider

1. **Internal Capabilities:**

    o   **Skills and Expertise:** Assess the availability of internal resources with the necessary skills and expertise for SAP implementation.

    o   **Capacity:** Evaluate whether the internal team can manage the project alongside their regular responsibilities.

2. **Project Complexity:**

    o   **Scope and Scale:** Consider the complexity and scale of the SAP implementation project. Larger, more complex projects may require specialized skills and experience.

- o **Integration Needs:** Assess the need to integrate SAP with other systems and the potential challenges involved.

3. **Cost:**

   - o **Budget:** Compare the costs of in-house implementation versus outsourcing, including salaries, training, consulting fees, and potential overheads.

   - o **Value for Money:** Evaluate the cost-benefit ratio of each approach, considering factors such as expertise, efficiency, and risk mitigation.

4. **Strategic Goals:**

   - o **Long-term Objectives:** Align the decision with the organization's long-term strategic goals, such as developing internal capabilities or leveraging external expertise for faster implementation.

   - o **Risk Management:** Consider the risks associated with each approach and the organization's risk tolerance.

Best Practices for Inhouse vs. Outsource Decision

1. **Conduct a Comprehensive Assessment:** Evaluate internal capabilities, project complexity, cost, and strategic goals to make an informed decision.

2. **Engage Key Stakeholders:** Involve key stakeholders in decision-making to ensure alignment and buy-in.

3. **Consider Hybrid Approaches:** Explore hybrid approaches that combine in-house and outsourced resources to leverage both strengths.

4. **Align with Strategic Goals:** Ensure the decision aligns with the organization's long-term strategic objectives and risk management strategies.

Inhouse Implementation

Overview of Inhouse Implementation

Inhouse implementation involves managing the SAP implementation project using internal resources. This approach allows the organization to maintain control over the project and leverage existing internal knowledge and expertise.

Advantages of Inhouse Implementation

1. **Control and Ownership:**

   o **Direct Control:** Retain direct control over the project's scope, timeline, and deliverables.

   o **Ownership:** Maintain ownership of the project and the knowledge gained during implementation.

2. **Internal Knowledge:**

   o **Business Processes:** Leverage internal knowledge of existing business processes and systems.

   o **Cultural Fit:** Ensure the implementation team understands the organizational culture and specific business needs.

3. **Cost Efficiency:**

   o **Cost Savings:** Lower costs by utilizing existing internal resources and avoiding high consulting fees.

   o **Long-term Value:** Invest in developing internal capabilities that can be leveraged for future projects.

4. **Alignment with Strategic Goals:**

   o **Capability Development:** Develop internal capabilities and expertise for long-term strategic benefits.

   o **Organizational Alignment:** Ensure alignment with the organization's strategic goals and objectives.

Challenges of Inhouse Implementation

1. **Resource Constraints:**

   o **Capacity:** Limited internal capacity to manage the project alongside regular responsibilities.

   o **Skill Gaps:** Potential skill gaps that require additional training or hiring.

2. **Risk of Delays:**

   o **Learning Curve:** Longer learning curve for internal resources, potentially leading to project delays.

   o **Limited Expertise:** Risk of delays and issues due to limited expertise in specialized areas.

3. **Potential Overhead:**

   o **Overhead Costs:** Increased overhead costs associated with training, hiring, and project management.

Best Practices for Inhouse Implementation

1. **Assess Internal Capabilities:** Conduct a thorough assessment of internal capabilities and identify any skill gaps.

2. **Invest in Training:** Provide comprehensive training and development opportunities to ensure the internal team has the necessary skills and expertise.

3. **Manage Capacity:** Ensure that the internal team can manage the project alongside their regular responsibilities.

4. **Leverage Internal Knowledge:** Utilize internal knowledge of business processes and systems to ensure a smooth implementation.

Outsource Implementation

Overview of Outsource Implementation

Outsourcing the SAP implementation project involves engaging an external system integrator (SI) with specialized expertise and experience. This approach can provide access to specialized skills, reduce project risks, and accelerate implementation timelines, instilling confidence in the project's success.

Advantages of Outsource Implementation

1. **Access to Expertise:**

   o **Specialized Skills:** Access specialized skills and expertise that may not be available internally.

   o **Industry Knowledge:** Leverage the SI's industry knowledge and best practices.

2. **Efficiency and Speed:**

   o **Accelerated Timeline:** Potentially faster implementation due to the SI's experience and efficiency.

   o **Focus:** Allow internal resources to focus on their core responsibilities while the SI manages the implementation.

3. **Risk Mitigation:**

   o **Proven Methodologies:** Benefit from the SI's proven methodologies and frameworks for managing SAP implementations.

   o **Reduced Risk:** Mitigate risks associated with skill gaps and resource constraints.

4. **Cost Management:**

- **Cost Predictability:** Potentially more predictable costs with a fixed-price or time-and-materials contract.

- **Value for Money:** Leverage the SI's expertise for better value.

Challenges of Outsource Implementation

1. **Dependency on External Partner:**

- **Control:** Reduced control over the project and reliance on the external partner for critical decisions.

- **Dependency:** Potential dependency on the SI for ongoing support and maintenance.

2. **Alignment with Business Needs:**

- **Knowledge Transfer:** Risk of inadequate knowledge transfer and alignment with internal business needs.

- **Cultural Fit:** Potential challenges with aligning the SI's approach and culture with the organizations.

3. **Cost Considerations:**

- **High Fees:** Potentially high consulting fees and costs associated with engaging a reputable SI.

- **Scope Creep:** Risk of scope creep and additional costs if the project scope is not clearly defined.

Best Practices for Outsource Implementation

1. **Select the Right SI:** Conduct a thorough evaluation of potential SIs, considering their expertise, experience, and cultural fit.

2. **Define Clear Objectives:** Define project objectives, scope, and deliverables to ensure alignment with the SI.

3. **Establish Strong Governance:** Implement a robust governance framework to oversee the SI's activities and ensure accountability.

4. **Facilitate Knowledge Transfer:** Through regular communication and collaboration, ensure effective knowledge transfer and alignment with internal business needs.

Choosing the Right System Integrator (SI)

Overview of Choosing the Right SI

Selecting a suitable SI is a critical decision that can significantly impact the success of the SAP implementation project. This section outlines the key steps and considerations for choosing the suitable SI, ensuring a secure decision-making process.

Key Steps in Choosing the Right SI

1. **Define Requirements:**

    o **Objective:** Clearly define the project's requirements, scope, and objectives.

    o **Activities:** Develop a detailed request for proposal (RFP) that outlines the project's requirements, deliverables, and evaluation criteria.

2. **Identify Potential SIs:**

    o **Objective:** Identify potential SIs with the necessary expertise and experience.

    o **Activities:** Conduct market research, seek recommendations, and review industry reports to identify potential SIs.

3. **Evaluate Proposals:**

- o **Objective:** Evaluate proposals from potential SIs based on predefined criteria.

- o **Activities:** Review proposals, conduct interviews, and assess the SI's experience, capabilities, and cultural fit.

4. **Conduct Due Diligence:**

- o **Objective:** Conduct thorough due diligence to verify the SI's credentials and capabilities.

- o **Activities:** Check references, review case studies, and assess the SI's financial stability and track record.

5. **Select the SI:**

- o **Objective:** Select the SI that best meets the project's requirements and aligns with the organization's goals.

- o **Activities:** Conduct final negotiations, agree on terms and conditions, and sign the contract.

Best Practices for Choosing the Right SI

1. **Comprehensive RFP:** Develop a comprehensive RFP that clearly defines the project's requirements, scope, and evaluation criteria.

2. **Thorough Evaluation:** Conduct a thorough evaluation of proposals, considering the SI's expertise, experience, and cultural fit.

3. **Due Diligence:** Conduct thorough due diligence to verify the SI's credentials and capabilities.

4. **Clear Contract:** Ensure that the contract clearly defines the project's scope, deliverables, timeline, and cost and includes provisions for risk management and performance monitoring.

Hybrid Approaches

Overview of Hybrid Approaches

A hybrid approach combines in-house resources with external SI expertise to leverage both strengths. This approach can provide a balanced solution addressing the organization's needs and constraints.

Advantages of Hybrid Approaches

1. **Leverage Internal Knowledge:**

   o **Business Processes:** Utilize internal knowledge of existing business processes and systems.

   o **Cultural Fit:** Ensure the implementation team understands the organizational culture and specific business needs.

2. **Access to Expertise:**

   o **Specialized Skills:** Access specialized skills and expertise from the external SI.

   o **Industry Knowledge:** Leverage the SI's industry knowledge and best practices.

3. **Flexibility and Control:**

   o **Balanced Control:** Maintain control over critical aspects of the project while benefiting from the SI's expertise.

   o **Adaptability:** Adapt the approach to changing project needs and constraints.

4. **Cost Management:**

   o **Cost Efficiency:** Potentially lower costs by utilizing internal and external resources.

- o **Value for Money:** Achieve better value for money by leveraging the strengths of both in-house and external resources.

Challenges of Hybrid Approaches

1. **Coordination:**

   - o **Integration:** Effective coordination and integration between in-house and external resources are needed.

   - o **Communication:** Potential communication challenges between internal and external team members.

2. **Governance:**

   - o **Complexity:** Increased complexity in governance and oversight due to the involvement of multiple parties.

   - o **Accountability:** Clear accountability and roles are needed to ensure effective project management.

Best Practices for Hybrid Approaches

1. **Define Roles and Responsibilities:** Clearly define the roles and responsibilities of internal and external resources to ensure effective coordination and accountability, making the audience feel organized and in control.

2. **Foster Collaboration:** Foster a collaborative team environment through regular communication and team-building activities.

3. **Implement Strong Governance:** Implement a robust governance framework to oversee the activities of both internal and external resources.

4. **Monitor Performance:** Continuously monitor the performance of internal and external resources to ensure alignment with project objectives and timely issue resolution.

Case Studies and Examples

Case Study 1: Healthcare Organization

Overview: A healthcare organization implemented SAP to streamline operations and improve patient care. The organization chose a hybrid approach, combining internal resources with an external SI.

Approach:

- **Hybrid Team:** Formed a project team comprising internal business process owners, functional consultants, and external technical consultants from the SI.

- **Role Definition:** Clearly define the roles and responsibilities of internal and external team members.

- **Collaboration:** Fostered a collaborative team environment through regular communication and team-building activities.

- **Governance:** Implemented a robust governance framework to oversee the activities of both internal and external resources.

Outcome:

- **Successful Implementation:** Achieved a successful SAP implementation that streamlined operations and improved patient care.

- **Effective Coordination:** Ensured effective coordination and integration between internal and external resources.

- **Value for Money:** Achieved better value for money by leveraging the strengths of both in-house and external resources.

Case Study 2: Manufacturing Company

Overview: A manufacturing company must implement SAP to integrate its global operations. The company opted to outsource the implementation to a reputable SI with extensive experience in the manufacturing sector.

Approach:

- **SI Selection:** Conducted a thorough evaluation of potential SIs, considering their expertise, experience, and cultural fit.

- **Clear Objectives:** Clearly defined project objectives, scope, and deliverables to ensure alignment with the SI.

- **Strong Governance:** Implemented a robust governance framework to oversee the SI's activities and ensure accountability.

- **Knowledge Transfer:** Facilitated effective knowledge transfer through regular communication and collaboration between the SI and internal stakeholders.

Outcome:

- **Accelerated Implementation:** Achieved a faster implementation timeline due to the SI's experience and efficiency.

- **Risk Mitigation:** Mitigated risks associated with skill gaps and resource constraints.

- **Successful Integration:** Successfully integrated global operations, enhancing efficiency and data visibility.

Practitioner's Insight: What Experience Teaches About SI Success

Having spent over two decades leading major SAP programs for system integrators—and another five years doing the same on behalf of clients—I've seen firsthand what separates a successful SI engagement from one that derails. The decision to outsource isn't just about capabilities or rates—it's about trust, alignment, and execution at scale. Too often, clients focus solely on technical expertise or commercial terms, while neglecting the deeper signals that determine whether an SI will be a true partner or just a contractor.

The most successful SI engagements I've led always start with mutual respect and shared goals. No matter how reputable the firm, the real differentiator is the individual team they assign to your program. A strong bench on paper doesn't mean much if your project gets a revolving door of resources or offshore teams you've never met. During SI selection, ask to interview key personnel. Push for continuity. Contracts can't deliver your project—people do.

One recurring mistake I've observed is clients assuming the SI will "just handle it." That mindset creates a vacuum in leadership and governance. Even in a full outsource model, clients must appoint strong internal leaders who are engaged daily, drive decisions, and escalate risks before they become issues. SAP isn't a set-and-forget system—you cannot abdicate accountability.

Another overlooked success factor is cultural alignment. Global SIs bring scale, but that scale sometimes comes with rigidity or "template tyranny"—forcing delivery approaches that don't reflect the client's operating model. Tailoring methodologies like SAP Activate requires nuance, especially in highly regulated or unique industries. You need an SI that listens first, configures second.

Finally, success lies in how well the business and technical teams converge. Many SIs excel at technical delivery but falter when it comes to change management or business engagement. An SI that doesn't prioritize organizational change is setting you up for resistance post-go-live, no matter how clean the code is.

After 30 years in the field, the truth is clear: choosing an SI is more than a procurement exercise. It's a strategic decision with cultural, operational, and leadership implications. Pick a partner who acts like an extension of your business—not just your IT department. Invest in building a relationship based on transparency, accountability, and joint ownership. That's the foundation of every SAP project that actually delivers on its promise.

Conclusion

Choosing between in-house and outsourcing for SAP implementation is a critical decision that depends on internal capabilities, project complexity, cost, and strategic goals. Both approaches have advantages and challenges, and the right choice depends on the organization's specific needs and circumstances. Organizations can make informed decisions that align with their strategic objectives by conducting a comprehensive assessment, engaging key stakeholders, and considering hybrid approaches. Adhering to best practices in selecting and managing the SI will help ensure a successful SAP implementation that delivers the expected business benefits.

Chapter 29: Things No System Integrator will tell you and what questions to ask

Selecting the right System Integrator (SI) is crucial for success when embarking on an SAP implementation project. However, there are certain aspects of the process that SIs may not openly discuss, which can significantly impact the project's outcome. This chapter delves into the hidden aspects of SAP implementation that no SI will tell you and provides essential questions to ask to uncover these truths. By being aware of these potential pitfalls and asking the right questions, organizations can make more informed decisions and manage their SAP implementation projects more effectively.

Hidden Costs and Budget Overruns

Overview of Hidden Costs

One of the most significant concerns in any SAP implementation project is the potential for hidden costs and budget overruns. These costs can arise from various sources, such as unexpected customizations, additional training needs, or underestimated data migration efforts.

Familiar Sources of Hidden Costs

1. **Customization:**

   o **Issue:** SIs may downplay the extent of customization required, leading to higher-than-expected costs.

   o **Impact:** Extensive customization can significantly increase project costs and timelines.

2. **Training:**

   o **Issue:** The need for additional training for end-users and IT staff is often underestimated.

   o **Impact:** Inadequate training can lead to lower user adoption and additional costs for supplementary training sessions.

3. **Data Migration:**

   o **Issue:** The complexity of data migration from legacy systems to SAP is often underestimated.

   o **Impact:** Unexpected challenges in data migration can lead to increased costs and delays.

4. **Change Requests:**

   o **Issue:** SIs may not fully disclose the potential for change requests and their impact on the budget.

   o **Impact:** Frequent change requests can lead to significant budget overruns.

Questions to Ask About Hidden Costs

1. **Customization:**

   o How much customization do you anticipate for our specific needs?

   o Can you provide examples of similar projects and the extent of customization required?

   o What is your process for managing and controlling customization costs?

2. **Training:**

   o What is your training plan, and how will it be delivered?

   o How do you assess training needs and ensure all users are adequately trained?

   o What additional training costs should we anticipate post-go-live?

3. **Data Migration:**

   o What is your approach to data migration, and how do you manage potential risks?

   o Can you provide case studies of similar data migration projects you have handled?

- What additional costs should we anticipate for data cleansing and validation?

4. **Change Requests:**

   - How do you manage change requests during the project?

   - What is the process for estimating and approving the costs associated with change requests?

   - Can you provide examples of how change requests have impacted project budgets in the past?

Project Timeline Realities

Overview of Project Timeline Realities

SIs often present optimistic timelines for SAP implementation projects to win contracts. However, these timelines may not always be realistic, leading to delays and unmet expectations.

Common Timeline Issues

1. **Underestimated Complexity:**

   - **Issue:** The project's complexity is often underestimated, leading to unrealistic timelines.

   - **Impact:** Delays and increased costs as the project scope expands.

2. **Resource Availability:**

   - **Issue:** The availability of critical resources from the SI and the client is often overestimated.

   - **Impact:** Resource constraints can lead to project delays and increased costs.

3. **Integration Challenges:**

- o **Issue:** The challenges of integrating SAP with existing systems are often underestimated.

- o **Impact:** Integration issues can cause significant delays and require additional resources.

4. **Testing Phases:**

- o **Issue:** The time required for thorough testing phases is often underestimated.

- o **Impact:** Inadequate testing can lead to post-go-live issues, requiring additional time and resources to fix.

Questions to Ask About Project Timelines

1. **Complexity:**

- o How do you assess the complexity of our project, and what factors could impact the timeline?

- o Can you provide examples of similar projects and their actual timelines compared to initial estimates?

2. **Resource Availability:**

- o How do you ensure the availability of critical resources throughout the project?

- o What contingency plans do you have in place for resource constraints?

3. **Integration Challenges:**

- o How do you approach system integration, and what challenges do you anticipate for our project?

- o Can you provide examples of integration issues from past projects and how you resolved them?

4. **Testing Phases:**

- o What is your approach to testing, and how do you ensure comprehensive coverage?

o How do you manage the risk of delays during the testing phases?

Post-Implementation Support and Hypercare

Overview of Post-Implementation Support

Post-implementation support, also known as hypercare, is critical for the success of the SAP system after it goes live. SIs may not fully disclose the extent and duration of the support required, leading to inadequate planning and budget allocation.

Common Post-Implementation Issues

1. **Inadequate Support:**

   o **Issue:** The support provided post-go-live is often insufficient to address user issues and system bugs.

   o **Impact:** Users may struggle with the new system, leading to lower adoption rates and operational disruptions.

2. **Duration of Hypercare:**

   o **Issue:** The duration of the Hypercare period is often underestimated.

   o **Impact:** Insufficient support duration can leave the organization unprepared to manage the system independently.

3. **Knowledge Transfer:**

   o **Issue:** Inadequate knowledge transfer from the SI to the internal team can hinder the organization's ability to manage the system post-go-live.

   o **Impact:** Dependence on the SI for ongoing support increases costs.

4. **Cost of Ongoing Support:**

   o **Issue:** The costs associated with ongoing support and maintenance are often not fully disclosed.

   o **Impact:** Unexpected expenses for ongoing support can strain the organization's budget.

Questions to Ask About Post-Implementation Support

1. **Support Level:**

   o What level of support will you provide during the Hypercare period?

   o How do you handle post-go-live issues and ensure timely resolution?

2. **Hypercare Duration:**

   o What is the duration of the Hypercare period, and what factors determine its length?

   o Can you provide examples of Hypercare periods from similar projects?

3. **Knowledge Transfer:**

   o What is your approach to knowledge transfer, and how do you ensure our internal team is prepared to manage the system?

   o How do you handle training and documentation for knowledge transfer?

4. **Ongoing Support Costs:**

   o What are the costs associated with ongoing support and maintenance post-go-live?

   o How do you structure your support agreements, and what options are available for long-term support?

Quality of Deliverables

Overview of Quality of Deliverables

The quality of deliverables, including system configurations, customizations, and documentation, is critical for the success of the SAP implementation. SIs may not always be transparent about their quality assurance processes, leading to potential issues post-go-live.

Common Quality Issues

1. **Inconsistent Documentation:**

   o **Issue:** Inadequate or inconsistent documentation can hinder system maintenance and user training.

   o **Impact:** Difficulty in troubleshooting issues and onboarding new users.

2. **Customization Quality:**

   o **Issue:** Customizations may not always meet the required quality standards, leading to system performance issues.

   o **Impact:** Increased maintenance costs and potential system downtime.

3. **Testing Coverage:**

   o **Issue:** Insufficient testing can lead to undetected bugs and issues post-go-live.

   o **Impact:** Operational disruptions and increased support costs.

4. **User Training Materials:**

   o **Issue:** Inadequate training materials can lead to lower user adoption and increased support requests.

   o **Impact:** Reduced productivity and higher training costs.

Questions to Ask About Quality of Deliverables

1. **Documentation:**

    o   How do you ensure the quality and consistency of documentation throughout the project?

    o   Can you provide examples of documentation from similar projects?

2. **Customization Quality:**

    o   What processes do you have in place to ensure the quality of customizations?

    o   How do you handle issues related to customizations post-go-live?

3. **Testing Coverage:**

    o   What is your approach to testing, and how do you ensure comprehensive coverage?

    o   Can you provide examples of testing plans and results from similar projects?

4. **User Training Materials:**

    o   How do you develop user training materials, and what is included in your training plan?

    o   How do you ensure that training materials are effective and meet user needs?

SI's Track Record and References

Overview of SI's Track Record

Understanding the SI's track record and past performance is essential for assessing their reliability and expertise. SIs may present an overly optimistic view of their capabilities, making it crucial to conduct thorough due diligence.

Common Issues with SI's Track Record

1. **Selective References:**

   o **Issue:** SIs may provide selective references that present only their best projects.

   o **Impact:** Incomplete picture of the SI's capabilities and potential issues.

2. **Lack of Transparency:**

   o **Issue:** SIs may not disclose issues or challenges faced in past projects.

   o **Impact:** Underestimation of potential risks and challenges.

3. **Performance Metrics:**

   o **Issue:** SIs may not provide detailed performance metrics from past projects.

   o **Impact:** Difficulty in assessing the SI's actual performance and reliability.

Questions to Ask About SI's Track Record

1. **References:**

   o Can you provide references from similar projects, and can we speak directly with these clients?

   o How do you handle challenges and issues in your projects, and can you provide examples?

2. **Transparency:**

   o What were your biggest challenges in similar projects, and how did you address them?

   o Can you provide examples of projects where you encountered significant issues and how they were resolved?

3. **Performance Metrics:**

   o What metrics do you use to measure the success of your projects, and can you provide examples?

   o How do you track and report on project performance throughout the project lifecycle?

Flexibility and Scalability

Overview of Flexibility and Scalability

The flexibility and scalability of the SAP system and the SI's approach are critical for accommodating future growth and changes. SIs may not fully disclose limitations in their proposed solutions, leading to potential challenges.

Common Issues with Flexibility and Scalability

1. **Rigid Solutions:**

   o **Issue:** SIs may propose solutions that are not flexible enough to accommodate future changes.

   o **Impact:** Difficulty in adapting the system to evolving business needs.

2. **Scalability Challenges:**

   o **Issue:** The proposed solution may not be scalable enough for future growth.

   o **Impact:** Increased costs and complexity when scaling the system.

3. **Customization Limitations:**

   o **Issue:** Limitations in the SI's ability to customize the solution to meet specific business needs.

   o **Impact:** Reduced system effectiveness and increased reliance on workarounds.

Questions to Ask About Flexibility and Scalability

1. **Solution Flexibility:**

- How flexible is your proposed solution in accommodating future changes and business needs?

- Can you provide examples of how you have adapted solutions for evolving business requirements?

2. **Scalability:**

- How scalable is your proposed solution, and what are the limitations?

- Can you provide examples of similar projects where the solution was successfully scaled?

3. **Customization:**

- What are the limitations of your proposed solution in terms of customization?

- How do you handle customization requests and ensure they meet our business needs?

Vendor Lock-In and Independence

Overview of Vendor Lock-In

Vendor lock-in occurs when an organization becomes overly dependent on a single SI for support and maintenance, limiting its ability to switch vendors or manage the system independently. SIs may not fully disclose the risks of vendor lock-in.

Common Issues with Vendor Lock-In

1. **Dependence on SI:**

- **Issue:** Over-reliance on the SI for ongoing support and maintenance.

- **Impact:** Limited flexibility in managing the system and potential for increased costs.

2. **Proprietary Solutions:**

- **Issue:** Use proprietary solutions or customizations that are difficult to transfer to another vendor.

- o **Impact:** Increased difficulty and cost in switching vendors or managing the system independently.

3. **Lack of Knowledge Transfer:**

   - o **Issue:** Inadequate knowledge transfer from the SI to the internal team.

   - o **Impact:** Dependence on the SI for ongoing support and reduced internal capability.

Questions to Ask About Vendor Lock-In

1. **Dependence on SI:**

   - o How do you ensure we do not become overly dependent on your ongoing support and maintenance services?

   - o What measures do you take to promote self-sufficiency in your clients?

2. **Proprietary Solutions:**

   - o Do you use any proprietary solutions or customizations that could limit our ability to switch vendors or manage the system independently?

   - o How do you ensure that the solutions you implement are transferable and maintainable by other vendors or our internal team?

3. **Knowledge Transfer:**

   - o What is your approach to knowledge transfer, and how do you ensure our internal team is prepared to manage the system independently?

   - o How do you handle training and documentation for knowledge transfer?

What They Don't Say Will Cost You: The Hidden Realities of Working with System Integrators

The most important truths about SAP programs are rarely found in glossy proposals or polished RFP responses. After years delivering both as the system integrator and on the client side, I can tell you that the biggest risks to success are not the things you see—but the ones no one talks about. System Integrators will often present a sanitized view of effort, risk, and ownership. They rarely disclose how many of their projects go over budget, underdeliver on scope, or require heroic recovery efforts behind the scenes. That's why this chapter matters. You're not just buying services—you're investing in trust, transparency, and control.

One of the first questions I always ask when evaluating an SI is: "What didn't go well in your last few programs?" If they can't answer that candidly, it's a red flag. Every complex SAP program has setbacks—it's how the SI responds that reveals their true value. Most SIs won't tell you that their margin depends on change requests. They'll come in with a lean estimate, knowing full well that they'll recover revenue once the client realizes the initial assumptions were overly optimistic. You need to get ahead of that— ask about their average change request volume per project and how they proactively prevent scope creep.

Another truth that rarely surfaces is the role of business readiness. SIs love to talk about cutover and go-live, but few emphasize what happens the day after. They'll commit to a hypercare window, but unless you press, they won't explain how much of that support is offshore, what their triage model looks like, or how they'll handle spikes in volume during financial close or order fulfillment. In some programs I've led, we've had more issues in the second month post-go-live than the first, because business stress increased while SI support tapered off. You need to plan for that gap—or your users will suffer.

Then there's the topic of go-live timing, which is almost always framed around calendar logic, not business logic. Many SIs push for January 1st or a quarter boundary, claiming it simplifies financial reporting. But after two years of intense delivery work, those periods are often when internal teams are exhausted, key staff are on holiday, and the business is laser-focused on year-end targets. It's the worst possible time to cut over unless your team is staffed for dual workloads. I've seen better success going live in quieter operational months — even mid-quarter — when business pressure is lower and focus is higher. Go-live should align with your business rhythm, not your SI's contract milestone.

Ultimately, the best defense against these hidden pitfalls is to ask the questions most clients don't. Push your SI beyond the slide deck. Demand transparency on risk, margin, accountability, and what they learned from their last failed implementation. You're not being difficult — you're being responsible. And the right SI will welcome that. The wrong one will try to sell you a fantasy.

Conclusion

Selecting the right System Integrator (SI) for SAP implementation is a critical decision that can significantly impact the project's success. By understanding the hidden aspects of SAP implementation that no SI will tell you and asking the right questions, organizations can make more informed decisions and manage their projects more effectively. Key areas to focus on include hidden costs, project timelines, post-implementation support, quality of deliverables, the SI's track record, flexibility and scalability, and the risks of vendor lock-in. Adhering to best practices in these areas will help organizations navigate the complexities of SAP implementation and achieve their strategic goals.

Chapter 30: RFP Process of SAP Implementation

The Request for Proposal (RFP) process is critical to the SAP implementation journey. It involves soliciting detailed proposals from potential vendors or system integrators (SIs), evaluating their responses, and selecting the best partner for your project. This chapter provides a thorough overview of the RFP process for SAP implementation, including the key components, steps involved, evaluation criteria, and best practices to ensure a successful selection.

Overview of the RFP Process

What is an RFP?

An RFP is a document that outlines the requirements and specifications for a project and invites vendors to submit proposals explaining how they would meet those needs. For SAP implementation, an RFP provides a comprehensive framework for vendors to understand the project scope, deliverables, and expectations.

Objectives of the RFP Process

1. **Identify the Right Partner:** Select the most suitable vendor or SI with the expertise, experience, and capabilities to implement SAP successfully.
2. **Clarify Requirements:** Communicate the project requirements, scope, and expectations to potential vendors.
3. **Compare Proposals:** Obtain detailed proposals to compare offerings, methodologies, costs, and timelines.
4. **Ensure Transparency:** Promote transparency and fairness in the vendor selection process.

Critical Components of an SAP Implementation RFP

1. Executive Summary
- **Purpose:** Provide an overview of the project and its strategic importance to the organization.
- **Content:** Brief organization description, project objectives, expected outcomes, and high-level requirements.

2. Project Scope and Objectives

- **Purpose:** Define the scope of the SAP implementation project and outline the specific objectives.
- **Content:** Detailed description of the project scope, including implementation modules, business processes to be covered, and key deliverables.

3. Functional and Technical Requirements

- **Purpose:** Specify the functional and technical requirements for the SAP system.
- **Content:** Detailed functional requirements for each module, technical specifications, integration needs, data migration requirements, and performance criteria.

4. Vendor Qualifications and Experience

- **Purpose:** Request information about the vendor's qualifications, experience, and past performance.
- **Content:** Vendor's company profile, relevant experience with SAP implementations, case studies, references, and team qualifications.

5. Implementation Approach and Methodology

- **Purpose:** Understand the vendor's approach and methodology for implementing SAP.
- **Content:** Description of the implementation methodology, project management approach, timeline, milestones, and deliverables.

6. Project Management and Governance

- **Purpose:** Outline the project management and governance structure.
- **Content:** Proposed project governance model, roles and responsibilities, risk management plan, and communication plan.

7. Training and Change Management

- **Purpose:** Ensure the vendor has a robust training and change management plan.
- **Content:** Training strategy, change management approach, user support plan, and post-go-live support.

8. Pricing and Commercial Terms

- **Purpose:** Obtain detailed pricing information and commercial terms.
- **Content:** Breakdown of costs (software, implementation, training, support), payment terms, and any additional costs.

9. Evaluation Criteria
- **Purpose:** Communicate the criteria that will be used to evaluate proposals.
- **Content:** List of evaluation criteria, weighting, and scoring methodology.

10. Submission Instructions
- **Purpose:** Provide clear instructions for proposal submission.
- **Content:** Submission deadline, format, contact information, and any specific requirements for submission.

Steps in the RFP Process

1. Preparation
- **Activities:**
  - o Define the project scope and objectives.
  - o Develop detailed functional and technical requirements.
  - o Identify potential vendors or SIs to invite.
  - o Draft the RFP document.
- **Best Practices:**
  - o Engage key stakeholders in defining requirements and objectives.
  - o Ensure that the RFP document is comprehensive and precise.
  - o Research potential vendors to ensure they have the necessary expertise.

2. Issuance of RFP
- **Activities:**
  - o Issue the RFP to selected vendors.
  - o Provide a timeline for proposal submission.
  - o Offer a briefing session or Q&A period for vendors.
- **Best Practices:**
  - o Communicate clearly with vendors about the RFP process and timelines.
  - o Be available to answer any questions or provide clarifications.
  - o Ensure that all vendors receive the same information to maintain fairness.

3. Proposal Submission
- **Activities:**
  - o Receive and acknowledge receipt of proposals from vendors.

- o Review proposals for completeness and adherence to submission guidelines.
- **Best Practices:**
  - o Set a firm deadline for proposal submission.
  - o Ensure that proposals are reviewed promptly upon receipt.
  - o Maintain confidentiality of vendor proposals.

4. Evaluation of Proposals

- **Activities:**
  - o Form an evaluation committee with representatives from relevant departments.
  - o Evaluate proposals based on predefined criteria.
  - o Score and rank proposals.
- **Best Practices:**
  - o Use a standardized evaluation framework to ensure consistency.
  - o Consider both qualitative and quantitative factors.
  - o Conducted reference checks and validated vendor claims.

5. Vendor Presentations and Demos

- **Activities:**
  - o Invite shortlisted vendors to present their proposals and conduct demos.
  - o Provide a structured format for presentations and demos.
- **Best Practices:**
  - o Prepare a standardized set of questions and scenarios for demos.
  - o Evaluate the presentations and demos based on specific criteria.
  - o Engage end-users in the evaluation process.

6. Final Selection and Negotiation

- **Activities:**
  - o Select the preferred vendor based on evaluation scores and fit with organizational needs.
  - o Negotiate terms and conditions, including pricing, deliverables, and timelines.
- **Best Practices:**
  - o Ensure that negotiations are conducted transparently and fairly.
  - o Address any concerns or issues raised during the evaluation process.

       o Formalize the agreement with a clear and comprehensive contract.

7. Contract Award and Kickoff

- **Activities:**
  - o Award the contract to the selected vendor.
  - o Conduct a project kickoff meeting to align all stakeholders.
- **Best Practices:**
  - o Communicate the decision to all stakeholders and vendors.
  - o Develop a detailed project plan and schedule.
  - o Establish a governance structure for project oversight.

Evaluation Criteria for SAP Implementation Proposals

1. Technical Expertise and Experience

- **Criteria:** Vendor's experience with SAP implementations, technical expertise, and track record.
- **Weighting:** High
- **Considerations:** Number of successful SAP implementations, industry-specific experience, and technical certifications.

2. Implementation Approach and Methodology

- **Criteria:** Quality and feasibility of the proposed implementation approach and methodology.
- **Weighting:** High
- **Considerations:** The implementation plan should be clear, aligned with best practices, and adaptable to the organization's needs.

3. Project Management and Governance

- **Criteria:** Effectiveness of the project management and governance model.
- **Weighting:** Medium
- **Considerations:** Roles and responsibilities, risk management plan, communication strategy, and governance structure.

4. Functional and Technical Fit

- **Criteria:** Alignment of the proposed solution with functional and technical requirements.

- **Weighting:** High
- **Considerations:** Extent to which the solution meets specified requirements, scalability, and integration capabilities.

5. Training and Change Management
- **Criteria:** Robustness of the training and change management plan.
- **Weighting:** Medium
- **Considerations:** Training strategy, change management approach, user support, and post-go-live support.

6. Cost and Value for Money
- **Criteria:** Overall cost and value for money.
- **Weighting:** High
- **Considerations:** Total cost of ownership, payment terms, and cost transparency.

7. Vendor's Capability and Resources
- **Criteria:** Vendor's capability to deliver the project, including resources and team qualifications.
- **Weighting:** Medium
- **Considerations:** Availability of qualified resources, team structure, and resource allocation.

8. Innovation and Added Value
- **Criteria:** Innovative solutions and added value offered by the vendor.
- **Weighting:** Medium
- **Considerations:** Advanced technologies, unique features, and additional benefits.

Best Practices for a Successful RFP Process

1. Engage Key Stakeholders
- **Objective:** Ensure that the RFP reflects the needs and expectations of all relevant stakeholders.
- **Activities:** Involve representatives from business units, IT, procurement, and finance in the RFP development and evaluation process.
- **Best Practices:** Conduct workshops and meetings to gather input and build consensus on requirements and evaluation criteria.

2. Develop a Comprehensive RFP Document
- **Objective:** Provide clear and detailed information to vendors to ensure accurate and relevant proposals.

- **Activities:** Include all necessary components, including project scope, requirements, evaluation criteria, and submission instructions.
- **Best Practices:** Use templates and checklists to ensure completeness and consistency. Seek feedback from stakeholders to refine the RFP document.

3. Maintain Transparency and Fairness
- **Objective:** Promote a transparent and fair selection process.
- **Activities:** Communicate clearly with vendors, provide equal access to information, and use standardized evaluation criteria.
- **Best Practices:** Document all communications and decisions. Ensure that the evaluation committee adheres to predefined processes and criteria.

4. Focus on Detailed Evaluation
- **Objective:** Conduct a thorough and objective evaluation of proposals.
- **Activities:** Use a standardized scoring framework, conduct reference checks, and validate vendor claims through demos and presentations.
- **Best Practices:** Engage subject matter experts in the evaluation process. Use a combination of qualitative and quantitative assessments.

5. Negotiate for Best Value
- **Objective:** Ensure that the final contract delivers the best value for the organization.
- **Activities:** Negotiate terms and conditions, including pricing, deliverables, timelines, and support.
- **Best Practices:** Prepare a negotiation strategy, identify non-negotiable terms, and aim for a win-win outcome. Involve legal and procurement experts in the negotiation process.

6. Establish Clear Governance
- **Objective:** Ensure effective project oversight and management.
- **Activities:** Establish a governance structure with defined roles and responsibilities, regular reporting, and issue escalation procedures.
- **Best Practices:** Develop a detailed project plan, conduct regular governance meetings, and use project management tools to track progress and manage risks.

Conclusion

The RFP process for SAP implementation is critical in selecting the right vendor or SI partner. Organizations can ensure a transparent and effective selection process by following a structured approach, engaging key stakeholders, and adhering to best practices. Developing a comprehensive RFP document, maintaining transparency and fairness, conducting detailed evaluations, and negotiating for best value are essential for selecting a partner that meets the organization's needs and expectations. Establishing clear governance structures further ensures the successful execution of the SAP implementation project, leading to improved business outcomes and operational efficiency.

Chapter 31: Case Studies and Best Practices

SAP implementation projects vary widely across industries and organizations, presenting unique challenges and opportunities. This chapter focuses on real-world case studies of SAP implementations, extracting lessons learned and best practices from these experiences. Additionally, it explores future trends in SAP implementation to provide a comprehensive understanding of the evolving landscape.

Real-World SAP Implementation Case Studies

Case Study 1: Global Manufacturing Company

Background: A global manufacturing company must integrate disparate systems across multiple countries to improve operational efficiency and data visibility. The company implemented SAP S/4HANA to standardize its processes and leverage advanced analytics.

Challenges:

- **Complex Integration:** Integrating multiple legacy systems with SAP S/4HANA.

- **Change Management:** Ensuring user adoption across different cultural and operational contexts.

- **Data Migration:** Migrating a large volume of historical data accurately and efficiently.

Approach:

1. **Assessment and Planning:**

   o Conducted a comprehensive assessment of existing systems and processes.

   o Developed a detailed project plan with clear milestones and deliverables.

2. **Stakeholder Engagement:**

   o Engaged critical stakeholders from each region to ensure alignment and buy-in.

   o Established a communication plan to keep stakeholders informed and involved.

3. **Data Migration:**

   o Developed a data migration strategy, including data cleansing and validation.

   o Utilized automated tools to streamline the migration process.

4. **Change Management:**

   o Implemented a robust change management strategy, including training programs and user support.

   o Established a network of change champions to drive user adoption.

Results:

- Successfully integrated multiple systems into a unified SAP S/4HANA platform.

- Improved operational efficiency and data visibility across the organization.

- Achieved high user adoption rates through effective change management.

Lessons Learned:

- **Comprehensive Planning:** Thorough planning and assessment are crucial for identifying potential challenges and mitigating risks.

- **Stakeholder Engagement:** Active engagement of stakeholders ensures alignment and support throughout the project.

- **Effective Data Migration:** A well-defined data migration strategy is essential for maintaining data integrity and minimizing disruptions.

- **Change Management:** Robust change management practices are crucial to achieving high user adoption and project success.

Best Practices:

- Conduct detailed assessments of existing systems and processes to inform planning.

- Develop clear communication and engagement plans for stakeholders.

- Utilize automated tools for efficient data migration.

- Implement comprehensive training and support programs to facilitate change management.

Case Study 2: Retail Chain

Background: A large retail chain aimed to improve its inventory management and customer experience by implementing SAP Fiori and SAP S/4HANA. The project focused on enhancing real-time inventory tracking and integrating e-commerce capabilities.

Challenges:

- **Real-Time Inventory Tracking:** Implementing real-time inventory tracking across multiple locations.

- **E-Commerce Integration:** Integrating e-commerce platforms with SAP S/4HANA.

- **User Experience:** Enhancing the user experience through SAP Fiori applications.

Approach:

1. **Needs Assessment:**

    o Conducted a thorough needs assessment to identify critical requirements and objectives.

    o Engaged with stakeholders to gather insights and prioritize features.

2. **System Integration:**

    o Developed integration plans to connect e-commerce platforms with SAP S/4HANA.

    o Implemented real-time inventory tracking using IoT devices and SAP Fiori apps.

3. **User Experience Enhancement:**

    o Designed user-friendly SAP Fiori applications to enhance the user experience.

    o Conducted usability testing and gathered feedback to refine the applications.

4. **Training and Support:**

    o Provided comprehensive training for users on the new applications and processes.

    o Established a support team to address user queries and issues post-implementation.

Results:

- Achieved real-time inventory tracking, improving inventory accuracy and reducing stockouts.

- Successfully integrated e-commerce platforms, enhancing the customer experience.

- Improved user satisfaction through intuitive SAP Fiori applications.

Lessons Learned:

- **User-Centric Design:** Designing applications with the end-user in mind enhances adoption and satisfaction.

- **Integration Planning:** Detailed integration planning is crucial for seamless system connectivity.

- **Continuous Feedback:** Gathering and incorporating user feedback ensures the solution meets user needs.

Best Practices:

- Conduct thorough needs assessments to inform project planning and prioritization.

- Focus on user-centric design principles for application development.

- Develop detailed integration plans to ensure seamless connectivity.

- Provide ongoing training and support to facilitate user adoption.

Lessons Learned and Best Practices

Key Lessons Learned

1. **Stakeholder Engagement:**

   - **Importance:** Active stakeholder engagement is crucial for project success.

   - **Best Practice:** Develop a comprehensive stakeholder engagement plan and communicate regularly.

2. **Change Management:**

   - **Importance:** Effective change management is critical to achieving high user adoption.

   - **Best Practice:** Implement robust change management strategies, including training, communication, and support.

3. **Data Management:**

   - **Importance:** Accurate data migration and management are essential for maintaining data integrity.

   - **Best Practice:** Develop a detailed data migration plan, including data cleansing and validation.

4. **Project Governance:**

- o **Importance:** Strong project governance ensures alignment with objectives and effective decision-making.

- o **Best Practice:** Establish a clear governance structure with defined roles and responsibilities.

5. **Risk Management:**

- o **Importance:** Proactive risk management helps mitigate potential challenges and disruptions.

- o **Best Practice:** Conduct regular risk assessments and develop mitigation plans.

Best Practices for SAP Implementation

1. **Comprehensive Planning:**

- o Conduct detailed assessments and planning to identify potential challenges and mitigate risks.

- o Develop clear project plans with defined milestones, deliverables, and timelines.

2. **Effective Communication:**

- o Maintain open and regular communication with stakeholders to ensure alignment and support.

- o Use multiple communication channels to keep stakeholders informed and engaged.

3. **Robust Change Management:**

- o Implement comprehensive training and support programs to facilitate user adoption.

- o Engage change champions to drive change and address resistance.

4. **Data Integrity:**

- o Develop a detailed data migration strategy, including data cleansing and validation.

o Use automated tools to streamline data migration and ensure accuracy.

5. **Continuous Improvement:**

o Gather and incorporate user feedback to continuously improve the solution.

o Conduct post-implementation reviews to identify lessons learned and areas for improvement.

Future Trends in SAP Implementation

1. Cloud Adoption

Overview: The shift to cloud-based SAP solutions is accelerating, offering scalability, flexibility, and cost efficiency.

Key Trends:

- **Cloud-First Strategies:** Organizations adopt cloud-first strategies for new implementations and migrations.
- **Hybrid Cloud Solutions:** Combining on-premises and cloud solutions to meet specific business needs.

Best Practices:

- Evaluate cloud readiness and develop a clear migration strategy.
- Ensure data security and compliance in cloud environments.
- Leverage cloud capabilities for scalability and flexibility.

2. Intelligent Technologies

Overview: Intelligent technologies such as AI, machine learning, and IoT are being integrated into SAP solutions to drive innovation and efficiency.

Key Trends:

- **Predictive Analytics:** Using AI and machine learning for predictive analytics and decision-making.

- **IoT Integration:** Integrating IoT devices with SAP for real-time data and insights.

Best Practices:

- Identify use cases for intelligent technologies to drive business value.

- Develop a roadmap for integrating intelligent technologies with SAP.

- Ensure adequate training and support for users to leverage new capabilities.

3. User Experience Enhancement

Overview: A key focus area is enhancing user experience through intuitive interfaces and personalized experiences.

Key Trends:

- **SAP Fiori:** Adopting SAP Fiori for a modern, user-friendly interface.

- **Personalization:** Providing personalized user experiences based on roles and preferences.

Best Practices:

- Focus on user-centric design principles for application development.

- Conduct usability testing and gather feedback to refine user interfaces.

- Provide ongoing training and support to enhance user experience.

4. Agile Methodologies

Overview: Agile methodologies are increasingly adopted for SAP implementation projects to improve flexibility and responsiveness.

Key Trends:

- **Scrum and Kanban:** Using Scrum and Kanban frameworks for iterative development and continuous improvement.

- **DevOps:** Integrating development and operations to streamline processes and improve collaboration.

Best Practices:

- Adopt agile methodologies to enhance project flexibility and responsiveness.

- Implement continuous integration and delivery practices to improve efficiency.

- Foster a culture of collaboration and continuous improvement.

5. Focus on Sustainability

Overview: Sustainability is becoming a key consideration in SAP implementation projects, with organizations aiming to reduce their environmental impact.

Key Trends:

- **Green IT:** Implementing energy-efficient IT solutions and practices.

- **Sustainable Supply Chain:** Leveraging SAP to enhance supply chain sustainability.

Best Practices:

- Incorporate sustainability goals into the SAP implementation strategy.

- Use SAP tools to monitor and optimize environmental impact.

- Engage stakeholders to support sustainability initiatives.

Conclusion

SAP implementation projects offer significant opportunities for organizations to enhance their operations, improve efficiency, and drive innovation. By learning from real-world case studies and adopting best practices, organizations can navigate the complexities of SAP implementation and achieve their strategic objectives. As the landscape continues to evolve, staying abreast of future trends will be essential for maximizing the value of SAP solutions and maintaining a competitive edge.

P a g e | 379

Chapter 32: Beyond SAP S/4. Where SAP is heading with its roadmap

SAP's evolution has continually adapted to emerging technologies and changing business needs. As organizations look beyond SAP S/4HANA, it's essential to understand the future directions of SAP's roadmap, the integration of artificial intelligence (AI), and the overall future of enterprise resource planning (ERP). This chapter delves into SAP's vision post-S/4HANA, the role of AI in SAP's future, and broader trends in ERP systems.

After S/4: SAP's Future Vision

Overview of SAP S/4HANA

SAP S/4HANA represents a significant advancement in ERP technology, offering an intelligent suite that provides real-time analytics, streamlined processes, and a simplified data model. However, SAP's vision extends beyond S/4HANA, focusing on innovations that drive further digital transformation.

Critical Areas of Focus Post-S/4

1. **Cloud Transformation:**

    o **Objective:** Transitioning more customers to cloud-based solutions to offer scalability, flexibility, and lower total cost of ownership.

    o **Activities:** Enhancing cloud-native functionalities, expanding SAP Business Technology Platform (BTP), and promoting RISE with SAP for a holistic cloud experience.

2. **Integration and interoperability:**

    o **Objective:** Seamlessly integrate SAP applications with third-party systems and other SAP solutions to provide a cohesive ecosystem.

- o **Activities:** Developing APIs, leveraging SAP Integration Suite, and enhancing support for hybrid environments combining on-premise and cloud applications.

3. **Industry-Specific Solutions:**

   - o **Objective:** Delivering tailored solutions that meet the unique requirements of various industries.

   - o **Activities:** Expanding the portfolio of industry-specific solutions, leveraging industry cloud to provide specialized functionalities.

4. **User Experience and Accessibility:**

   - o **Objective:** Improving user experience through modern interfaces and enhanced accessibility.

   - o **Activities:** Expanding the capabilities of SAP Fiori, introducing SAP Conversational AI for intuitive interactions, and developing mobile-first solutions.

Best Practices for Preparing for Post-S/4

1. **Cloud Readiness Assessment:** Evaluate your organization's readiness for cloud adoption and develop a transition strategy.

2. **Integration Planning:** Develop a comprehensive integration plan to ensure seamless interoperability between SAP and third-party systems.

3. **Industry Focus:** Identify industry-specific solutions that align with your business needs and leverage SAP's specialized offerings.

4. **User Experience Enhancement:** Invest in enhancing the user experience through SAP Fiori and other modern interfaces.

AI and SAP: Shaping the Future

Overview of AI in SAP

Artificial intelligence is becoming a core component of SAP's strategy, enhancing automation, decision-making, and user interactions. SAP's AI capabilities are designed to empower businesses with intelligent insights and streamlined processes.

Key AI Innovations in SAP

1. **SAP AI Core and AI Foundation:**

   o **Objective:** Providing a comprehensive platform for developing, deploying, and managing AI applications.

   o **Activities:** Offering tools for machine learning, natural language processing (NLP), and data processing integrated with SAP's core systems.

2. **Intelligent Robotic Process Automation (RPA):**

   o **Objective:** Automating repetitive tasks to improve efficiency and accuracy.

   o **Activities:** Developing RPA bots that integrate with SAP S/4HANA and other SAP applications to automate workflows.

3. **AI-Driven Analytics and Insights:**

   o **Objective:** Enhancing decision-making with predictive and prescriptive analytics.

   o **Activities:** Leveraging AI algorithms to analyze large datasets, predict trends, and provide actionable insights.

4. **Conversational AI and Chatbots:**

   o **Objective:** Improving user interactions through natural language processing and chatbots.

   o **Activities:** Integrating SAP Conversational AI with SAP applications to provide intuitive, conversational user interfaces.

Best Practices for Implementing AI in SAP

1. **Identify Use Cases:** Identify areas where AI can provide the most value, such as process automation, predictive analytics, or customer interactions.

2. **Leverage Existing Tools:** Utilize SAP's AI Core and AI Foundation to develop and deploy AI solutions integrated with your SAP landscape.

3. **Train and Educate Users:** Provide training and support to help users effectively understand and leverage AI capabilities.

4. **Monitor and Optimize:** Monitor AI performance, adjust to optimize outcomes, and address issues.

Future with ERP as a Whole

Overview of ERP Evolution

The ERP landscape is rapidly evolving, driven by technological advancements and changing business requirements. The future of ERP involves greater flexibility, intelligence, and connectivity, enabling businesses to operate more efficiently and adapt to new challenges.

Critical Trends in ERP Evolution

1. **Composable ERP:**

   o **Objective:** Providing modular, flexible ERP systems tailored to specific business needs.

- o **Activities:** Developing modular applications that can be easily integrated and customized, allowing businesses to build an ERP system that fits their unique requirements.

2. **Advanced Analytics and BI:**

   - o **Objective:** Enhancing decision-making with advanced analytics and business intelligence capabilities.

   - o **Activities:** Integrating AI-driven analytics, real-time data processing, and self-service BI tools into ERP systems.

3. **IoT Integration:**

   - o **Objective:** Connecting ERP systems with IoT devices to provide real-time data and insights.

   - o **Activities:** Developing IoT-enabled applications integrating ERP systems to monitor and manage real-time operations.

4. **Enhanced Security and Compliance:**

   - o **Objective:** Ensuring that ERP systems meet the highest security standards and comply with regulatory requirements.

   - o **Activities:** Implementing advanced security measures, such as AI-driven threat detection and blockchain for data integrity, and ensuring compliance with industry regulations.

5. **Sustainability and ESG (Environmental, Social, Governance):**

   - o **Objective:** Integrating sustainability and ESG considerations into ERP systems to support responsible business practices.

   - o **Activities:** Developing tools and features that help businesses monitor and manage their environmental and social impact, such as carbon footprint tracking and supply chain transparency.

Best Practices for Adopting Future ERP Trends

1. **Modular Approach:** Adopt a modular approach to ERP, allowing for greater flexibility and customization.

2. **Invest in Analytics:** Invest in advanced analytics and BI tools to enhance decision-making capabilities.

3. **Embrace IoT:** Leverage IoT integration to gain real-time insights and improve operational efficiency.

4. **Prioritize Security:** Implement advanced security measures and ensure compliance with regulatory requirements.

5. **Focus on Sustainability:** Integrate sustainability and ESG considerations into your ERP strategy to support responsible business practices.

Conclusion

The future of SAP and ERP systems is marked by continuous innovation and the integration of advanced technologies. Beyond SAP S/4HANA, SAP focuses on cloud transformation, integration, industry-specific solutions, and enhanced user experiences. AI is critical in shaping SAP's future, driving automation, analytics, and user interactions. The broader ERP landscape is evolving towards greater flexibility, intelligence, and connectivity, enabling businesses to operate more efficiently and responsibly. By understanding these trends and adopting best practices, organizations can successfully navigate the future of SAP and ERP systems, leveraging these advancements to drive their digital transformation and achieve their strategic goals.

Chapter 33: Program Deliverables

Below is a sample of significant program deliverables that may be produced during SAP Implementation.

DELIVERABLE NAME	DESCRIPTION
PROGRAM IMPLEMENTATION PLAN	The Implementation Plan is a consolidated view of the Detailed Project Plans created and maintained by the Project Workstreams and the Detailed OCM Project Plan created and maintained by the Organization Readiness Tower, including: a) An integrated high-level summary of the detailed work breakdown structures provided by each Tower b) Chronological alignment of the Phases and Stages of each Tower c) Each of the Deliverables, Milestones, and Stage Gates for the entire Project d) Indentation of critical dependencies between the Workstreams e) Other relevant Company initiatives and indication of critical dependencies f) Frequent updates to support visibility to key stakeholders
FUNCTIONAL SPECIFICATIONS DOCUMENT (FSD) TEMPLATE	The Functional Specifications Document (FSD) Template Deliverable defines the format, structure, and descriptions of the required content and level of detail of the Functional Specifications Documents Bundle Deliverable. The template's structure and format should include best practices from the Contractor and reflect Company standard templates.
INTEGRATION AND TECHNICAL SPECIFICATIONS DOCUMENTS (TSD) TEMPLATE	The Integration and Technical Specifications Documents (TSD) Template Deliverable defines the format, structure, and descriptions of the required content and level of detail of the Integration Specification Document Bundles and Technical Specifications Document Bundles Deliverables. The template's structure and format should include best practices from the Contractor and reflect Company standard templates. It also provides a checklist of design features to validate during design review of Program components.
PROCESS DESIGN DOCUMENT (PDD) TEMPLATE	The Process Design Document (PDD) Template Deliverable defines the format, structure, and descriptions of the required content and level of detail of the To-Be Process Design Document. The template's structure and format should include leading practices,

DELIVERABLE NAME	DESCRIPTION
	inputs, and outputs, process flows, roles, steps, FIORI Apps/transactions, change impacts, etc.
REQUIREMENTS TRACEABILITY MATRIX (RTM) TEMPLATE	The Requirements Traceability Matrix (RTM) Template Deliverable outlines the format and structure of the RTM Template. The template should include best practices from the Contractor and reflect the Company standard template. It will be stored and managed in the agreed-upon project tool (e.g., Solution Manager).
CURRENT CAPABILITY AND ANALYTICS CAPABILITY ASSESSMENT	A document that describes how the Company executes each of its In-Scope Business Processes (e.g., financial reporting spreadsheet) and assesses the process against leading practices. Additionally, the document provides a high-level evaluation of current analytical needs and gaps related to In-Scope Business Processes. It prioritizes internal and external resources and sequencing needed to deliver against target capabilities. This Deliverable will also include an inventory/catalog of current analytic capabilities and Reports across all the In-Scope Business Process areas. This document should significantly leverage a company's current enterprise analytics roadmap.
DATA CONVERSION STRATEGY	The Data Conversion Strategy provides a method and approach for conversion based on the type of data and data source. The strategy should address the approach and method for data reconciliation and transformation that needs to be accomplished before or during the migration process. It also defines what data will be converted for each round of testing, the data reconciliation process, and what data will be required for the successful completion of testing. This will also include the number of mock runs/dry runs, control programs, conversion scope decisions, Tools, testing of converted data, and ETL architecture. This Deliverable shall include an accompanying rationale for the conclusions and recommendations made. The contractor will incorporate previous work products related to the data conversion strategy conducted before the start of the Project.
MASTER TEST STRATEGY	The Master Test Strategy ("MTS") describes the elements of testing that are in scope and the key Deliverables required to support the entire testing effort in its entirety and throughout the testing lifecycle. It provides both a high-level strategy and a detailed approach to what will be tested, how the tests will be conducted (e.g., manually vs. automated), who will perform the testing, the timing of each type of test, how defects will be managed, test level exit and exit criteria, testing roles and responsibilities, communication plans, test data requirements and data extraction methods, and test environment requirements. The MTS will include, at a minimum, detailed test plans that cover the following levels of test: unit, string (first-level integration), Assembly (which provides for functional scenarios and scripts, product (full integration), end-to-end, security, and controls (including

DELIVERABLE NAME	DESCRIPTION
	segregation of duties rule sets), data conversion, performance, parallel, disaster recovery, regression, user acceptance testing ("UAT"), and operational readiness testing ("ORT"). The MTS strategy and detailed approach will identify the positive and negative tests that will be run for each data element based on the priority and level of governance classification of each data element. The methodology will describe how and when test data sets will be created and how the data will be validated against the documented business rules for data creation. The MTS will identify which data elements in the developed solution will be tested and which will not. The MTS will be created in alignment with the Company's standard template.
SYSTEM SIZING AND TECH ARCH SIZING WORKSHOPS	System sizing and Tech Arch sizing workshops - Workshop with SAP Max attention, Cloud services, and define sizing & technical settings for all application systems
TECHNICAL ARCHITECTURE STRATEGY DRAFT	Defines the components of the Program (e.g., In-Scope Modules), the technical configuration and interaction of the elements of the Program, and the accompanying rationale for the decisions and recommendations made (including Contractor leading practices where applied) relating to (a) security and controls architecture, (b) reporting and analytics architecture, (c) integration technologies, (d) middleware, and (e) data warehousing technologies. All target solution designs should include a Logical Data Model ("LDM") that covers all data contained in the solution and integrates with any applicable enterprise-level LDM. Each business term/concept/data element identified in the BRD must be mapped to the LDM. All target solution designs must include an architectural model integrating with any applicable enterprise-level LDM. This deliverable will be consistent with the company's overall enterprise architectural framework. By the end of the first month, the team will have the first draft ready for review.
CHANGE STRATGEY & PLAN	The Change Strategy is a macro-level view of the main objectives of the Change Enablement effort for the Program. It highlights the critical reasons for the change and the essential activities of change. The change plan builds upon the change strategy and adds tactical details. It will provide the detailed change activities we'll implement for the program. This document will also include activities on leadership coaching and engagement to enable leaders to manage effectively in the new ways of working.
SECURITY ROLE DESIGN APPROACH DOCUMENT	Security role design approach document

DESCRIPTION

DELIVERABLE NAME

DELIVERABLE NAME	DESCRIPTION
PROJECT MANAGEMENT PLAN 1 - VERSION 1	The Project Management Plan 1 - Plan/Initiate Deliverable is a Project management document created to represent all activities necessary to manage the successful delivery of the Services and maintained throughout the life of the Project, with a focus on activities during the Plan and Initiate Phases of the Project. It is a comprehensive plan for how the Project is organized and how it will be executed, monitored, and controlled. Key areas covered in the Project Management Plan 1 - Plan/Initiate include: • Project organization and team member roles and responsibilities (Contractor(s) and Company Personnel at all levels, inclusive of governance structure and specific Towers and Workstreams) and delineates the primary work activities of each organizational entity in the Project structure, including Company, Contractor, and other third parties. • Clear objectives defined at the start of the Workstream and measurements aligned to the achievement of those objectives • Project resource plans, including engagement percentage for members of the Project team for the Plan and Initiate Phases • Project controls management, including risks, issues, change control, escalation, quality assurance, and Deliverable Acceptance • Project decision matrices, indicating approval and review process for decisions impacting solution during Plan and Initiate Phases •Project approach and scope • Project Tools plan and utilization expectations during the early phases of the Project • Description of how Project status will be monitored, controlled, and communicated • Project document management to ensure version control and appropriately manage warehousing and collection of documentation • Deliverable due date and communication and stakeholder engagement plan for the Plan and Initiate Phases
REQUIREMENTS TRACEABILITY MATRIX ("RTM")	The RTM Deliverable maps the In-Scope Requirements for all In-Scope Business Processes identified and confirmed in the Discovery and Solution Confirmation phases. It is structured to trace In-Scope Requirements from Design and Build activities through future Testing of the requirement in the applicable validation activities. This will also include the non-functional requirements of the solution to satisfy the In-Scope Requirements. The RTM will include requirement dispositions that, where applicable, map requirements to standard systems screens and transactions, manual processes, and RICEFW Objects. This Deliverable will be updated across the phases of the project. At the end of Solution Confirmation, it will include cross-references to related systems and Fit/Gap definition, which determines if requirements can be met via standard configuration or will require custom development, such as a RICEFW Object, with the type of object included. The RTM will be updated during the Design & Build phase to indicate the related module or object specification

DELIVERABLE NAME	DESCRIPTION
	and during Testing Preparation to indicate applicable test scripts in which the requirement will be tested.
SANDBOX ENVIRONMENT	A sandbox environment (e.g., hardware, applications, and Tools) is installed, configured, and operational for the In-Scope Modules (hardware, applications, and software Tools).
TECHNICAL ARCHITECTURE STRATEGY FINAL	Defines the components of the Program (e.g., In-Scope Modules), the technical configuration and interaction of the elements of the Program, and the accompanying rationale for the decisions and recommendations made (including Contractor leading practices where applied) relating to (a) security and controls architecture, (b) reporting and analytics architecture, (c) integration technologies, (d) middleware, and (e) data warehousing technologies. All target solution designs should include a Logical Data Model ("LDM") that covers all data contained in the solution and integrates with any applicable enterprise-level LDM. Each business term/concept/data element identified in the BRD must be mapped to the LDM. All target solution designs must include an architectural model integrating with any applicable enterprise-level LDM. This deliverable will be consistent with the company's overall enterprise architectural framework. The concerned parties should review and approve the document by the second milestone.
STAKEHOLDER ASSESSMENT	Analysis of Stakeholder mapping & alignment of crucial decision and stakeholder management procedures
USER PROFILE STRATEGY	User profiles inventory, User profiles unit test plan, User profiles unit test closure report
PROJECT PROGRAM DEVELOPMENT STANDARDS	Development standards are intended to aid the programming and related maintenance work in the SAP software development area for the Business Transformation Project. They are based on SAP up to and including the release of SAP ECC 6.0.
QUALITY MANAGEMENT PLAN	The Quality Management Plan describes quality assurance (process adherence, Deliverable reviews, reviewers, mitigation strategy, etc.), quality control (testing) procedures, and best practices. It needs to be aligned with existing Company quality management plans and tailored as required to support the implementation.

DELIVERABLE NAME	DESCRIPTION
TO-BE APPLICATION ARCHITECTURE	Defines the Program application architecture for the end-to-end solution, including retained Legacy Applications, including accompanying rationale for the decisions and recommendations made for Program applications (examples: S/4HANA, Boundary System, Workforce, PowerPlan, SuccessFactors, FieldGlass, Ariba) and integrated legacy systems that directly send or receive information from the Program applications whether through an interface or manually. The application architecture shall conform to the Company enterprise roadmap guidelines and existing standards.
TO-BE PROCESS DESIGN AND DOCUMENTATION (ALL) - BUNDLE 1 OF 2	The Process Design and Documentation (each a "PDD" or "BPD") Deliverable includes activities to create the design and provides a detailed description of all the steps required to execute processes down to Level 4 (HPUM work step/activity level). Process documentation at Level 4 (the most detailed of four levels) includes a graphical representation of the relationship between all manual and Program tasks undertaken by a person to meet the business output (each task contains detailed information about the business role, system access, and, as appropriate, functional requirements). The To-Be Process Design and Documentation is a crucial input to Program configuration, application development, security and controls, and the development of end-user training materials. This document also defines the transactions, sequencing, categorization, process procedures, RICEFWs, responsible roles, and control points.
HIGH-LEVEL CONVERSION WORKPLAN	Document showing each Mock's high-level timeline, scope, and data activities for the conversion workstream. It will also provide details of the environment test that will be executed.
DATA RETENTION AND ARCHIVING STRATEGY	A document that provides a strategy for SAP and Non SAP Program components that are in-scope for data archiving and retention and referencing existing Company practices; documents the Tools and processes needed for data retention and archiving; provides leading practices and lessons learned regarding data retention and archiving including information regarding statutory and regulatory retention requirements, data tiering strategy, availability approaches (e.g., hot, warm, cold); and evaluates the impact of decisions on the business case (as associated with legacy application rationalization), and opportunities for updating record retention schedules.
CHANGE MEASUREMENT APPROACH	Defines the scope and objectives of the process to measure change readiness that the Program will adopt. Key areas covered include a description of the objectives, a definition of the population to be surveyed, a description of the measurement methods to be used, and a description of the different roles and responsibilities involved

DELIVERABLE NAME	DESCRIPTION
	in completing the task. This deliverable will include the survey results from the initial baseline TGPS cycle.
CONVERSION ENVIRONMENT	A working conversion environment (e.g., hardware, applications, and Tools) is installed, configured, and operational for the In-Scope Modules (hardware, applications, and software Tools).
USER PROFILE TEST PLAN	User Profile Test Plan
FUNCTIONAL SPECIFICATIONS RELEASE 1	Details the business and regulatory requirements, desired functionality, data requirements, batch jobs, security and controls requirements (IT controls, SOX, SoD, and business process framework), and the test requirements for each development object and component. The Deliverable will include a complete functional description of how each development object and custom change will support the agreed upon business process, including sufficient technical and business detail to support the building of each object and unit test cases subject to approval from the corresponding Company process lead. The documents in this bundle will be consistent with the security and control requirements.
ARCHITECTURE BOARD TERMS OF REFERENCE	The Architecture Board will provide overall Business and Solution/Technical direction to the project, ensure adherence to the Customer's Strategy, Architecture, and Program principles, and enable successful delivery by aligning cross-workstream decisions. The board will meet regularly to review Open Design Questions and endorse/reject critical design decisions. The Architecture Board Terms of Reference will define the board's members, purpose, activities, responsibilities, and meeting frequency. It will also explain the design decisions review process, the guidelines for KDD reviews, and the KDD template.
CHANGE IMPACTS ASSESSMENT	Defines how the changes affect target audiences as they transition from the current to the target state. This assessment describes the high-level changes in organization, people, process, technology, and data and how the users will need to operate differently in each area.

DELIVERABLE NAME	DESCRIPTION
PROJECT MANAGEMENT PLAN 2 - VERSION 2	The Project Management Plan 2 - Delivery Deliverable is a project management document created to represent all activities necessary to manage the successful delivery of the services and maintain them throughout the project's life. It is a comprehensive plan for how the Project is organized and how it will be executed, monitored, and controlled. Key areas covered in the Project Management Plan include: • Project organization and team member roles and responsibilities (Contractor(s) and Company Personnel at all levels, including governance structure and Workstreams) and delineates the primary work activities of each organizational entity in the Project structure, including Company, Contractor, and other third parties. • Clear objectives defined at the start of the Workstream and measurements aligned to the achievement of those objectives • Project resource plans, including engagement percentage for members of the Project team • Project controls management, including risks, issues, change control, escalation, quality assurance, and Deliverable Acceptance • Project decision matrices, indicating approval and review process for decisions impacting solution • Project approach and scope • Project Tools plan and utilization expectations • Description of how Project status will be monitored, controlled, and communicated • Project document management to ensure version control and appropriately manage warehousing and collection of documentation • Management of interfacing systems changes required to support the implementation • Deliverable due dates and communication and stakeholder engagement plan by each Phase and Stage
TO-BE PROCESS DESIGN AND DOCUMENTATION (ALL) BUNDLE 2 OF 2	The Process Design and Documentation (each a "PDD" or "BPD") Deliverable includes activities to create the design and provides a detailed description of all the steps required to execute processes down to Level 4 (HPUM work step/activity level). Process documentation at Level 4 (the most detailed of four levels) includes a graphical representation of the relationship between all manual and Program tasks undertaken by a person to meet the business output (each task contains detailed information about the business role, system access, and, as appropriate, functional requirements). The To-Be Process Design and Documentation is a crucial input to Program configuration, application development, security and controls, and the development of end-user training materials. This document also defines the transactions, sequencing, categorization, process procedures, RICEFWs, responsible roles, and control points.

DELIVERABLE NAME	DESCRIPTION
DEVELOPMENT ENVIRONMENT	A working development environment (e.g., hardware, applications, and Tools) is installed, configured, and operational for the In-Scope Modules (hardware, applications, and software Tools).
REPORTING AND ANALYTICS SOLUTION DESIGN BUNDLE #1 OF 2	The Reporting and Analytics Solution Design provides the functional and technical capabilities necessary to build and implement the analytics solutions that satisfy the Company's business requirements. The design includes the analytics development standards and technical specifications. It includes creating an appropriate data store/structure within the analytics landscape and a solution for populating the data store. This document will include identifying calculations/algorithms in the analytics layer versus reporting layer, semantic layer design (e.g., universe development), data lineage, and the Unit Test Plan and the Unit Test Cases. The contractor will also ensure the deployment of all interfaces for regular ingestion of transactional data into the analytics solution.
DEVELOPMENT OBJECT CODE BUNDLE RELEASE 1	The Development Object Code Bundle Deliverable is executable code that performs to requirements documented in the functional specifications and technical design documented in the technical specification for each development object in the Final Development Object Inventory Deliverable unless such development object was dispositioned to be completed after go-live.
TECHNICAL SPECIFICATIONS BUNDLE RELEASE 1	The Technical Specifications for objects part of Release 1 Deliverable is a document that provides the technical design, batch jobs, security requirements, and implementation details needed to design, build, implement, and unit test each RICEFW object in the RICEFW list (including legacy, middleware, and EDW technical specifications as required to conform to the functional specifications). For each RICEFW object, the specifications should list all new objects, data inputs, outputs, layouts, reusable components, logic flow chart if necessary, and all algorithms, procedures, or functions used.
SIT CLOSURE MEMO - RELEASE 1	SIT Test Results and Closure Memo; with documentation of Entry and Exit Criteria Release 3 Deployment
BASELINE CONFIGURATION	Configuration of the core SAP values and transaction types needed for essential business processes to be carried out within the SAP solution. This base configuration enables the top processes to be further configured and for custom development objects to be built.
SERVICE DELIVERY KNOWLEDGE TRANSFER APPROACH	Documents the critical knowledge transfer ("KT") approach (e.g., operational, functional, technical, security, and controls) for transferring knowledge from the Project team to the Program support resources, including:

DELIVERABLE NAME	DESCRIPTION
	a) methods for conducting KT sessions both before cutover and after the Program live b) potential vital topics such as essential Program items, requirements not satisfied by the Program, warranty item tracking lists c) approach for the handover of Project Deliverables and work product d) templates for the KT materials that will support the KT sessions
QA ENVIRONMENT	A QA Environment is installed, configured, and operational for the In-Scope Modules (hardware, applications, and Tools). This environment also fully configures and appropriately sizes the Product, UAT, and Performance Tests.
SIT TEST STRATEGY DOCUMENT	Test Strategy Document Defining detail cycles, Scope, and Entry-Exit Criteria of the SIT Phase for Release 2
REPORTING AND ANALYTICS SOLUTION DESIGN BUNDLE #2 OF 2	The Reporting and Analytics Solution Design provides the functional and technical capabilities necessary to build and implement the analytics solutions that satisfy the Company's business requirements. The design includes the analytics development standards and technical specifications. It includes creating an appropriate data store/structure within the analytics landscape and a solution for populating the data store. This document will include the identification of calculations/algorithms in the analytics layer versus reporting layer, semantic layer design (e.g., universe development), data lineage, and the Unit Test Plan and the Unit Test Cases. The contractor will also ensure the deployment of all interfaces for regular ingestion of transactional data into the analytics solution.
CONVERSION TECHNICAL SPECIFICATIONS BUNDLE 1	Provides the technical specification for the programs, enabling Program applications to transform and load the required data, including: a) logical source-to-target mappings of existing data elements from Legacy Applications to new Company Software data elements; b) business logic or rules to incorporate within the data conversion process; c) specification for the use of features such as selection criteria, to be field definitions, EMIGALL processing and other similar SAP product types (LSMW, initial, transfer, via KSM, or fixed value), enumerated values and meanings if applicable, and any associated configuration lookup table, identification if transformation rules will be needed or a link to the document specifying the transformation rules; d) critical decisions and rationale for process design; e) definition of optional fields identifying how the field will be populated, documenting the feedback from the functional team and design authority; f) Detailed assumptions made for mapping data elements; and

DELIVERABLE NAME	DESCRIPTION
	g) Detailed transformation and conversion rules for every data element being converted. The delivery of these technical specifications aligns with the beginning of Mock Conversion activities (ex: Mock 0)
COMMUNICATIONS STRATEGY & PLAN WITH PERSONAS	The Communications and Engagement plan provides effective communications interventions with consistent and clear objectives for appropriate people. Interventions are the vehicles for developing stakeholder commitment and include communication methods such as newsletters and webinars. The Communications and Engagement Plan contains the following elements: • Commitment objectives for each persona • Stakeholder engagement guiding principles • Audiences, objectives, owners, interventions • Measurement of effectiveness and commitment • Specific communications and timeline of activities
ENVIRONMENT MANAGEMENT STRATEGY AND PLAN	Provides the description and purpose of production and multiple non-production environments with refresh cycle/priority, a detailed set of processes defined for daily environment management, a change control process (build, configuration changes), and the batch jobs process framework (runbook). Adhering to Company guidelines, the document defines, for new hardware/software, the development, operations, and execution environment scope; includes the guiding principles, framework, roadmap, and methodology to apply during the subsequent steps of realizing the build, test, and production environments. This will include: • Performance/tuning design principles • Archiving component design principles • Technical architecture design principles • EAI/Middleware design principles • Security architecture design principles
FUNCTIONAL SPECIFICATIONS BUNDLE #1 OF 4; INCREMENT 1	Details the business and regulatory requirements, desired functionality, data requirements, batch jobs, security and controls requirements (IT controls, SOX, SoD, and business process framework), and the test requirements for each development object and component. The Deliverable will include a complete functional description of how each development object and custom change will support the agreed upon business process, including sufficient technical and business detail to support the building of each object and unit test cases subject to approval from the corresponding

DELIVERABLE NAME	DESCRIPTION
	Company process lead. The documents in this bundle will be consistent with the security and control requirements.
DEVELOPMENT OBJECT CODE BUNDLE #1 OF 4 (RICEFW/OTHER)	The Development Object Code Bundle Deliverable is executable code that performs according to the requirements documented in the functional specifications. The technical design is noted in the technical specification for each development object in the Initial Development Object Inventory Deliverable unless such development object was dispositioned to be completed after go-live.
INTEGRATION SPECIFICATION BUNDLE #1 OF 3; INCREMENT 1	The Integration Specifications Bundle #1 Deliverable is a document that provides the integration requirements, high-level design, enterprise service use, interface reuse, and security requirements. This Deliverable documents information for each middleware interface object required for developing the Technical Specification, including technical design, batch jobs, security and controls requirements (IT controls, cyber-security, business process framework, and CCM), and implementation details needed to design, build, implement, and unit test each integration. For each integration specification, the specifications should list all new objects, data inputs, data outputs, data mapping, layouts, reusable components, logic flow chart if necessary, and all algorithms, procedures, or functions used. For clarity, this Deliverable excludes specifications for the Development Objects already included in a Functional Specification and Technical Specification Bundle Deliverable. Any integration requiring SAP to connect with another system (internal or external) will include input from the integrating system to confirm a common understanding between the design's source and target.
TECHNICAL SPECIFICATIONS BUNDLE #1 OF 4	The Technical Specifications Bundle #1 Deliverable is a document that provides the technical design, batch jobs, security requirements, and implementation details needed to design, build, implement, and unit test each RICEFW object in the RICEFW list (including legacy, middleware, and EDW technical specifications as required to conform to the functional specifications). For each RICEFW object, the specifications should list all new objects, data inputs, outputs, layouts, reusable components, logic flow chart if necessary, and all algorithms, procedures, or functions used.
REPORTING AND ANALYTICS APPROACH	The Reporting and Analytics Approach defines the high-level development steps, roles, and responsibilities for enabling configurable Reports, BI reports (to be developed as part of RICEFW Objects), self-service reporting, and customer analytics. This includes the approach for correlating historical unconverted data in EDW with converted and new SAP data for Reporting and Analytics, enabling semantic layer, self-service, metadata creation,

DELIVERABLE NAME	DESCRIPTION
	and usage (BG/data dictionary), and additional canned Reports for future use.
SECURITY ROLE DEFINITION AND DESIGN DOCUMENT	A document defining the transaction access and roles required to execute the to-be business process in the Program solution, along with considerations for segregation of duties and job functions relevant to the Customer organization. This design includes business process controls that need to be implemented according to the security and process control requirements included in the process designs.
COMPLIANCE AND CONTROLS DESIGN	The Controls and Compliance Design is a document that is used as input to design the business process, security controls (e.g., privacy, SOD, access, cyber), compliance, and controls (regulatory, operational, financial), where possible within the to-be system environment. In addition, this document will outline the types of controls designed into the Program: • Automated v. manual controls • Preventive v. detective controls • Application controls • IT general controls • Spreadsheet controls • Interface controls
PERFORMANCE TEST APPROACH	The Performance Test Plan Deliverable is a document that includes an approach for performance, volume, stress test, and associated metrics with the production and non-production system infrastructure, including the hardware client and server, application server, system virtualization, web server, OS, network connectivity, storage and backup systems, and database to support the Program. The Deliverable identifies the tester assigned to each script and provides the testing schedule for each cycle. The Deliverable includes documented test scripts and measurement processes for determining whether the test has passed or failed. The Deliverable identifies the tester assigned to each script and provides the testing schedule for each infrastructure and performance test cycle. The Deliverable includes automation of test scripts and documented test scripts for each identified scenario, including data requirements and measurement processes for determining whether the script has passed or failed, identifies industry best practices for approach, and provides a standard template for the creation of test scripts and conditions (positive and negative).
AUTOMATION TEST APPROCH	Automation Test approach document describing the process of selecting the right candidate for automation, selection of regression pack, etc. High-level test automation approach and work plan

DELIVERABLE NAME	DESCRIPTION
FUNCTIONAL SPECIFICATIONS BUNDLE #2 OF 4	Details the business and regulatory requirements, desired functionality, data requirements, batch jobs, security and controls requirements (IT controls, SOX, SoD, and business process framework), and the test requirements for each development object and component. The Deliverable will include a complete functional description of how each development object and custom change will support the agreed upon business process, including sufficient technical and business detail to support the building of each object and unit test cases subject to approval from the corresponding Company process lead. The documents in this bundle will be consistent with the security and control requirements.
INTEGRATION SPECIFICATION BUNDLE #2 OF 3	The Integration Specifications Bundle #2 Deliverable is a document that provides the integration requirements, high-level design, enterprise service use, interface reuse, and security requirements. This deliverable documents information for each middleware interface object required for developing the Technical Specification, including technical design, batch jobs, security and controls requirements (IT controls, cyber-security, business process framework, and CCM), and implementation details needed to design, build, implement, and unit test each integration. For each integration specification, the specifications should list all new objects, data inputs, data outputs, data mapping, layouts, reusable components, logic flow chart if necessary, and all algorithms, procedures, or functions used. For clarity, this Deliverable excludes specifications for the Development Objects already included in a Functional Specification and Technical Specification Bundle Deliverable. Any integration requiring SAP to connect with another system (internal or external) will include input from the integrating system to confirm a common understanding between the design's source and target.
TECHNICAL SPECIFICATIONS BUNDLE #2 OF 4	The Technical Specifications Bundle #2 Deliverable is a document that provides the technical design, batch jobs, security requirements, and implementation details needed to design, build, implement, and unit test each RICEFW object in the RICEFW list (including legacy, middleware, and EDW technical specifications as required to conform to the functional specifications). For each RICEFW object, the specifications should list all new objects, data inputs, outputs, layouts, reusable components, logic flow chart if necessary, and all algorithms, procedures, or functions used.
DEVELOPMENT OBJECT CODE BUNDLE #2 OF 4 (RICEFW/OTHER)	The Development Object Code Bundle Deliverable is executable code that performs according to the requirements documented in the functional specifications. The technical design is noted in the technical specification for each development object in the Initial Development Object Inventory Deliverable unless such development object was dispositioned to be completed after go-live.

DELIVERABLE NAME	DESCRIPTION
CONFIGURATION DESIGN DOCUMENT BUNDLE #1 OF 2	Bundle 1 documents the design for the configuration of each In-Scope Business Process and sub-process to enable the transactions to be executed according to the business requirements and to-be process and sub-process design, including: a) documentation of configurations at the transaction code/form level b) documentation of what will be configured and how to enable in-scope transactions c) documentation of the rationale behind the design decisions d) configuration control values (i.e., values for master data fields that use drop-down lists/validation tables for data entry choices or other drop-down lists within transactions) e) the activities needed to perform configuration, taking into account the configuration design, dependencies, and the overall Project Plan.
REPORTING AND ANALYTICS SOLUTION OBJECT CODE BUNDLE #1 OF 2	The Reporting and Analytics Object Code Bundle Deliverable is executable code confirming requirements documented in the Reporting and Analytics Solutions Design Deliverable for each Reporting and Analytics use case unless such development object was dispositioned to be completed after go-live.
SIT TEST PLAN AND SCENARIOS	The System Integration, Plan Deliverable document, provides the multi-cycle test approach, testing types, test scenario identification by process and technical element, and detailed integration testing plan logistics. Integration testing incorporates the validation of end-to-end business processes and SOD rule sets inclusive of external interfaces if required. The Deliverable identifies the named testers responsible for/assigned to each test cycle and scenario and provides the planned schedule for each integration cycle.
TRAINING ENVIRONMENT	A working training environment (e.g., hardware, applications, and Tools) is installed, configured, and operational for the In-Scope Modules (hardware, applications, and software Tools).
CONVERSION TECHNICAL SPECIFICATIONS BUNDLE 2	Provides the technical specification for the programs, enabling Program applications to transform and load the required data, including: a) logical source-to-target mappings of existing data elements from Legacy Applications to new Company Software data elements; b) business logic or rules to incorporate within the data conversion process; c) specification for the use of features such as selection criteria, to be field definitions, EMIGALL processing and other similar SAP product types (LSMW, initial, transfer, via KSM, or fixed value), enumerated values and meanings if applicable, and any associated configuration lookup table, identification if transformation rules will be needed or a link to the document specifying the transformation rules;

DELIVERABLE NAME	DESCRIPTION
	d) critical decisions and rationale for process design; e) definition of optional fields identifying how the field will be populated, documenting the feedback from the functional team and design authority; f) Detailed assumptions made for mapping data elements; and g) Detailed transformation and conversion rules for every data element being converted. The delivery of these technical specifications aligns with the beginning of Mock Conversion activities (ex: Mock 1 & 2)
INFRASTRUCTURE TECHNICAL DESIGN	Details the solution infrastructure, including (a) infrastructure sizing, related Tools, hardware requirements, and configurations of the infrastructure required to support the application portfolio, supporting architecture, and environment strategy, (b) details regarding Tools needed, installation guides for each In-Scope Module Software system, installation guides for each In-Scope Module Software related third party systems, Tools that will be used to support the execution of the Project, such as those that may be required to support testing or reporting, preparing the infrastructure sizing questionnaire, which will be submitted to Company for procurement and infrastructure setup, and (c) how the production and non-production environments will be sized, and include sizing for on-premise and cloud solutions.
FUNCTIONAL SPECIFICATIONS BUNDLE #3 OF 4 (RICEFW/OTHER)	Details the business and regulatory requirements, desired functionality, data requirements, batch jobs, security and controls requirements (IT controls, SOX, SoD, and business process framework), and the test requirements for each development object and component. The Deliverable will include a complete functional description of how each development object and custom change will support the agreed upon business process, including sufficient technical and business detail to support the building of each object and unit test cases subject to approval from the corresponding Company process lead. The documents in this bundle will be consistent with the security and control requirements.
INTEGRATION SPECIFICATION BUNDLE #3 OF 3 (RICEFW/OTHER)	The Integration Specifications Bundle #3 Deliverable is a document that provides the integration requirements, high-level design, enterprise service use, interface reuse, and security requirements. This deliverable documents information for each middleware interface object required for developing the Technical Specification, including technical design, batch jobs, security and controls requirements (IT controls, cyber-security, business process framework, and CCM), and implementation details needed to design, build, implement, and unit test each integration. For each integration specification, the specifications should list all new objects, data inputs, data outputs, data mapping, layouts, reusable components, logic flow chart if necessary, and all algorithms, procedures, or functions used. For clarity, this Deliverable excludes

DELIVERABLE NAME	DESCRIPTION
	specifications for the Development Objects already included in a Functional Specification and Technical Specification Bundle Deliverable. Any integration requiring SAP to connect with another system (internal or external) will include input from the integrating system to confirm a common understanding between the design's source and target.
TECHNICAL SPECIFICATIONS BUNDLE #3 OF 4 (RICEFW/OTHER)	The Technical Specifications Bundle #3 Deliverable is a document that provides the technical design, batch jobs, security requirements, and implementation details needed to design, build, implement, and unit test each RICEFW object in the RICEFW list (including legacy, middleware, and EDW technical specifications as required to conform to the functional specifications). For each RICEFW object, the specifications should list all new objects, data inputs, outputs, layouts, reusable components, logic flow chart if necessary, and all algorithms, procedures, or functions used.
DEVELOPMENT OBJECT CODE BUNDLE #3 OF 4 (RICEFW/OTHER)	The Development Object Code Bundle Deliverable is executable code that performs to requirements documented in the functional specifications and technical design documented in the technical specification for each development object in the Final Development Object Inventory Deliverable unless such development object was dispositioned to be completed after go-live.
CONFIGURATION DESIGN DOCUMENT BUNDLE #2 OF 2	The final configuration completes the software package configuration according to the Configuration Design and to-be Subprocess Designs. It includes all outstanding configurations to be completed after the Baseline Configuration, all configured items by Software, and detailed descriptions of all configurations to support any to-be business processes.
REPORTING AND ANALYTICS SOLUTION OBJECT CODE BUNDLE #2 OF 2	The Reporting and Analytics Object Code Bundle Deliverable is executable code that confirms the requirements documented in the Reporting and Analytics Solutions Design deliverable for each Reporting and Analytics use case unless such development object was dispositioned to be completed after go-live.
BUILD/UNIT TEST CLOSURE MEMO - RELEASE 2	Summarize the meeting of the Build Phase and all Unit Test Results from Development Bundle #1 through Bundle #3 and Configuration Unit Tests. The document ascertains whether the development objects included in the D/B/V phase, as built, sufficiently meet the Functional Specifications and Technical Specifications and whether the In-Scope Modules were configured to the Functional Design Documents. The document includes the appropriate signoffs to confirm exiting the D/B/V phase.

DELIVERABLE NAME	DESCRIPTION
PRODUCTION SYSTEM ENVIRONMENT	A complete production environment (e.g., hardware, applications, and Tools) is installed, technically configured, and operational for the In-Scope Modules (hardware, applications, and software Tools).
OPERATIONAL READINESS TEST APPROACH (PARALLEL TEST APPROACH)	The Operational Readiness Test Approach defines the types of testing (batch verification, business calibration, business simulation) that the Project will conduct. Provides the general operational (parallel payroll) testing requirements (environments, data sets, interfacing system expectations/needs, test resources, business operations resources, etc.) that will be needed to conduct these tests. Defines the scope and focus areas for the core meter to cash, payments, and billing processes such as bill compare and exception testing, dunning/collections, identifies industry best practices for approach, and provides a standard template for capturing test results of this nature.
SECURITY ACCESS ROLES AND PROCEDURES	The configured Security Access Roles and Procedures are created by building the appropriate security objects for application security roles defined in the security base role design. Roles ('Composite Roles' in SAP) need to represent the functions required to perform a job and need to be void of any SOD conflicts. This deliverable defines the approach for providing user access to the technology solution. It describes how access is managed and provisioned and serves as a guide to handling end-user access requests and authorization issues. The Deliverable will analyze and document requirements for Program job-based roles and identify capabilities necessary to create an appropriate structure for allocating access rights to individuals to adequately support the business's needs (the actual assignment to specific users will occur during the Deploy Phase). This Deliverable should include documentation of role updates, if necessary, in Legacy Applications that integrate with the Program and will include: • Detailed approach to how jobs will map to security and business roles within the Program. • Detailed requirements to support the development of SOD rule sets for assessment of SOD conflicts. • Approach plan for monitoring of SOD conflicts transacted.
INTEGRATION ARCHITECTURE DESIGN	As a follow-up to the Technical Architecture Strategy and To-Be Application Architecture Deliverable from the Plan and Analyze Phase, this Deliverable provides the following: • Middleware platform and integration technologies document • Interface and integration diagram and document requirements • Middleware platform sizing & performance tuning • Integration monitoring & alerting framework **Integration Blue Print**

DELIVERABLE NAME	DESCRIPTION
TECHNICAL ARCHITECTURE DESIGN	Provides additional (i.e., as a follow-up to the Technical Architecture Strategy Deliverable) detailed documents and diagrams describing the technical architecture and the components of the application, highlighting the design principles, and explaining the relationships between them, including: a) Software landscape and list of required technologies b) Security architecture document c) Performance/tuning document d) Archiving component document e) Reporting and analytics architecture document f) Middleware platform and integration technologies document g) Controls technologies document h) Data governance technologies document i) Disaster recovery design and procedures and business continuity document j) Networking document k) Interface and integration diagram and document requirements l) Application availability requirements, including specific availability metrics (e.g., 99.99%, 99.9999%, 99.90%) for the applications and infrastructure m) Disaster recovery RTO and RPO requirements for the applications and infrastructure n) All target solution designs should include a Logical Data Model (LDM) that covers all data in the solution and integrates with any applicable enterprise-level LDM. o) Each business term/concept/data element identified in the BRD must be mapped to the LDM. p) All target solution designs must include an architectural information model integrating with any applicable enterprise-level LDM.
SERVICE DELIVERY KNOWLEDGE TRANSFER PLAN AND SCHEDULE	Documents the critical knowledge transfer ("KT") requirements (e.g., operational, functional, technical, security, and controls), timing, and expected participants for transferring knowledge from the Project team to the Program support resources, including: a) detailed prep and execution plans for conducting KT sessions both before cutover and after the Program goes live b) plans for addressing topics such as critical decisions, requirements not satisfied by the Program, warranty item tracking lists c) plans for explanation and handover of Project Deliverables and work product d) a schedule of KT sessions (e.g., functional, technical, security, and controls)
CRITICAL DESIGN DECISION (KDD)	The KDD documents describe solution decisions that guide the overall solution to be built into the Program applications. KDD documents cover decisions related to Organizational Structures and Master Data, solution alternatives analysis, and recommendations to cover in-scope requirements or resolve a business or technology risk to complete the solution design. KDDs will be created to resolve Open Design Questions during the

DELIVERABLE NAME	DESCRIPTION

Solution Confirmation and Design phases.
The Final Inventory of Key Design Decision documents will be presented at the end of the Design & Build phase.

TRAINING STRATEGY & PLAN

Defines the training and performance support approach for users and the support team. The strategy details the approach using findings from the training needs assessment and documents the following:

A comprehensive approach to deliver training and performance support associated with the implementation of the Program.
Define the detailed requirements for training and performance support.
Determine the delivery strategies that are most appropriate for the scope and type of target audiences.
Define the instructional strategies that are most appropriate given the detailed training objectives.
Define the performance support approach based on needs and current and desired performance support capability.
Define the ongoing training strategy.
Define the training environment and data requirements.
Defines the training timeline for design, development, delivery, and sustainment
Defines the types of training materials that will be produced
Defines the metrics that will be gathered as part of training delivery

PROGRAM APPLICATIONS DISASTER RECOVERY PLAN

It is a document that details how the company will be able to bring the production of S/4HANA and other applications in the program landscape back online in the event of a disaster. This plan enables the S/4HANA, Boundary System MWFM, interfaces, network, and supporting infrastructure.
The Program Disaster Recovery Test Plan Deliverable for the Program is a document that provides the testing approach, types of testing, and test scenario identification for disaster recovery testing and plan logistics. The Deliverable includes documented test scripts for each identified scenario, including data requirements and measurement processes for determining whether the script has passed or failed, identifies industry best practices for approach, and provides a standard template for creating test scripts and conditions (positive and negative).

CUTOVER PLAN

The initial draft of the cutover plan, which defines the detailed steps required to convert from a legacy application to a Program including (a) the required activities, (b) any internal Project or other Company dependencies, (c) the parties/resources responsible for the cutover activities (all internal and external stakeholders), (d) required blackout periods, (e) an hourly schedule for the activities, (f) initial post-go-live activities for testing, validation, and known "day 2" needs, and (g) the additional elements from the previous

DELIVERABLE NAME	DESCRIPTION
	Cutover Plan Deliverables. The plan will be updated based on the Trial Cutover Results.
STABILIZATION SUPPORT PLAN	The plan for the Project team members to support business and IT users of the system during its life and afterlife as part of stabilization. This includes support numbers, command center plans, floor walkers, and coordination with the Customer help desk and support staff.
BATCH JOBS SCHEDULE	The Batch Jobs Schedule Deliverable will provide a completed schedule, timing, frequency, owners, processes, and runbooks for all batch jobs that must be created as part of the Project for the program's production operations.
SUPPORT MODEL STRATEGY	A document that covers the support strategy, resources, skills, and types of roles needed to support the Customer Program solution following the Stabilization of the First Release with considerations for the future. This will include role descriptions, a proposed resource plan, proposed SLAs, and an approach for mobilizing the support organization across Customers and other parties leading up to the stabilization period.
TRAINING DATA RELEASE 1	The Training Environment is populated with validated Training Data to enable all trainers participating in training to perform all their required training.
FINAL GO/NO-GO CRITERIA	The final list of criteria defined by Project leadership and key Project stakeholders, including recommendations from the Contractor, identifies whether the Program is ready for production and whether the organization is prepared to accept and operate the new Program.
DEPLOYMENT STRATEGY	A document that outlines the overall strategy for deployment and cutover of Program applications and retired systems in Release 2. This document also outlines critical business and IT activities to be completed in preparation for and during the go-live cutover time frame.
DISASTER RECOVERY ENVIRONMENT	A disaster recovery environment (e.g., hardware, applications, and Tools) is installed, configured, and operational for the In-Scope Modules (hardware, applications, and software Tools).
GO-LIVE READINESS CHECKLIST	Used to determine if the Project is ready to go live from a technical and overall business perspective and to evaluate the readiness of each business and technical area going live with the new Program. The checklist should:

DELIVERABLE NAME	DESCRIPTION
	a) address all components of the Project Plan b) provide mitigation and escalation plans if areas are at risk of not being ready for go-live c) includes the business continuity plan, as well as a checklist of Acceptance Criteria for Operational Readiness Review and Production Readiness Review d) be a "checklist of checklists" by including by reference the other checklists to be completed as part of the deployment (e.g., Production Security Configurations Checklist, Quality Management Review Checklist)
PERFORMANCE TEST RESULTS	The Performance Test Results Deliverable is a document that includes detailed output and executive summary of the performance and stress tests, performance-tuning recommendations, and graphs and charts that illustrate the performance of these and other tested tiers: database, middleware, application, connectivity and performance of hosted components, applications, web, and batch. It also includes a detailed report of the infrastructure tests, performance-tuning recommendations, Program errors, and graphs and charts illustrating the performance of the tested Program environment and architecture and required infrastructure changes before going live. It also includes data on service level compliance, data throughput at performance volumes, transaction throughput at anticipated data volumes, Program monitoring and performance, Program maintenance activities, and security, along with descriptions of criteria needed to perform Program performance analysis and data relating to service level adherence.
SIT CLOSURE MEMO - RELEASE 2	SIT Test Results and Closure Memo, with documentation of Entry and Exit Criteria For Release 2 Deployment
FINAL CUTOVER PLAN	Defines the detailed steps required to convert from a legacy application to a Program including (a) the required activities, (b) any internal Project or other Company dependencies, (c) the parties/resources responsible for the cutover activities, (all internal and external stakeholders), (d) required blackout periods, (e) an hourly schedule for the activities, (f) initial post-go-live activities for testing, validation, and known "day 2" needs, and (g) the additional elements from the previous Cutover Plan Deliverables. The plan will be updated based on the Trial Cutover Results.
TRAINING DATA RELEASE 2	The Training Environment is populated with validated Training Data to enable all trainers participating in training to perform all their required training.

DELIVERABLE NAME	DESCRIPTION
FUNCTIONAL SPECIFICATIONS BUNDLE #4 OF 4 (RICEFW/OTHER)	Details the business and regulatory requirements, desired functionality, data requirements, batch jobs, security and controls requirements (IT controls, SOX, SoD, and business process framework), and the test requirements for each development object and component. The Deliverable will include a complete functional description of how each development object and custom change will support the agreed upon business process, including sufficient technical and business detail to support the building of each object and unit test cases subject to approval from the corresponding Company process lead. The documents in this bundle will be consistent with the security and control requirements.
DRESS REHEARSAL RESULTS SUMMARY	A document that summarizes the results of dress rehearsals, including evaluation of the ability to execute against the cutover plan, lessons learned, and critical decisions made during each dress rehearsal
FINAL CONTROLS PACKAGE	The Final Controls Package Company deliverable will include the finalized and approved controls strategy, controls Project plan, including end-user control procedures, and updates to the Controls, Risk, and Compliance Assessment Deliverables.
FINAL DATA MIGRATION TO IN-SCOPE SOFTWARE SUMMARY REPORT	This document will include a comprehensive reconciliation report between Legacy Applications and Software for all data objects, a summary of all data conversion issues and exceptions and the causes of the exceptions, and a detailed summary for all objects with exceptions and the complete count of objects that failed conversion.
LIVE PRODUCTION SYSTEM	The production Program environment has been configured and tested and is ready for production operations to commence. It includes the definition of the associated processes needed to manage it.
OPERATIONAL READINESS REVIEW	The Operational Readiness Review Deliverable is an executive-level presentation confirming that the organization has met its go-live criteria, that the required training is complete, that users are certified as required, that the support organizations and super users are in place, that the change readiness assessment indicates the Company is ready to go-live, and that users have the required credentials to access the new environments.
PRODUCTION READINESS REVIEW	The Production Readiness Review Deliverable is an executive-level presentation confirming that the Program go-live criteria have been met, testing is complete, all issues are resolved, the environment is prepared, the cutover is in place, and the final conversion plan is in place and validated. This Deliverable is also used to determine whether the Project is ready to go live from a technical and overall

DELIVERABLE NAME	DESCRIPTION
	business perspective, along with a mitigation and escalation plan if areas are at risk of being unprepared for go-live.
DEVELOPMENT OBJECT CODE BUNDLE #4 OF 4 (RICEFW/OTHER)	The Development Object Code Bundle Deliverable is executable code that performs to requirements documented in the functional specifications and technical design documented in the technical specification for each development object in the Final Development Object Inventory Deliverable unless such development object was dispositioned to be completed after go-live.
TECHNICAL SPECIFICATIONS BUNDLE #4 OF 4	The Technical Specifications Bundle #4 Deliverable is a document that provides the technical design, batch jobs, security requirements, and implementation details needed to design, build, implement, and unit test each RICEFW object in the RICEFW list (including legacy, middleware, and EDW technical specifications as required to conform to the functional specifications). For each RICEFW object, the specifications should list all new objects, data inputs, outputs, layouts, reusable components, logic flow chart if necessary, and all algorithms, procedures, or functions used.
FINAL REQUIREMENTS TRACEABILITY MATRIX	The Final RTM will include the updates from the Design and build phase to indicate the related module or object specification and from Testing to indicate the applicable test scripts in which the requirement will be tested and the outcome of test execution. In cases in which the test result was not successful, a decision will be made about a workaround and proposed fixing plan. Additional requirements or requirements cancellation will also be presented in the Final RTM with Change Order ID reference.
SERVICE DELIVERY KNOWLEDGE TRANSFER REPORT	Summarizes the outcome of activities to prepare the Program application maintenance provider (including the Stabilization Contractor to assume responsibility for the application scope), as well as any outstanding knowledge transfer tasks.
FINAL DEVELOPMENT OBJECT INVENTORY	The Final Development Object Inventory will include a final list of Development Objects (e.g., reports, interfaces, including identification of legacy and middleware objects as part of the overall integrations, conversions, enhancements, forms, and workflows) and end-to-end integrations, including the Bundle # (i.e., associated with each of the "Bundle" Deliverables), name, object type, and complexity.
POST GO-LIVE SUPPORT RESULTS	This report summarizes the outcome of post-go-live support, including customer support, data integrity, Program availability, stability, open items, and workarounds. It also verifies that the Program has met the required stabilization metrics/criteria to transition to post-project service delivery. This Deliverable will be

DELIVERABLE NAME	DESCRIPTION
	updated and delivered to the Company at an agreed-upon schedule.
PROJECT CLOSURE REPORT	The Project Closure Report is a document used in the close project task of the Project management discipline to provide a brief Project summary and capture feedback from the Project team regarding lessons learned, best practices, and process improvement suggestions. The Project Closure report will include stage gate sign-off documentation. The Project Closure Report also has sections to document and address any outstanding items, decisions for the Project, and activities required to secure all personally identifiable information. The report will summarize Project tasks and timelines, an inventory of all Deliverables and current approval status, information regarding any outstanding commercial items, and confirmation that the Project has been delivered according to the specified scope.

Dave Karpinsky, PhD, MBA, PMP, is a globally recognized consultant, executive leader, and professional author whose work bridges business transformation, strategy, and personal development. With over three decades of experience advising Fortune 500 companies, government agencies, and high-growth startups where he traveled to more than 60 countries, Dave brings a rare blend of practical insight, operational excellence, and visionary thinking to every project — and every page.

His career spans top-tier consulting firms including McKinsey & Company, Accenture, SAP, Cognizant, BearingPoint, Ernst & Young, Infosys, and IBM. He has led multi-million-dollar strategic and technology initiatives for global leaders such as Capital One, Coca-Cola, Costco, DHS/TSA, Google, HP, Janus Henderson, John Deere, Lockheed Martin, McLaren, Merck, Nike, PetSmart, QuidelOrtho, and ViaSat, as well as large-scale public sector programs for the US Government, States of Alaska, Arizona, California, Florida, and Georgia.

As the author of numerous books on project turnaround, leadership, SAP implementation, and personal mastery, Dave is known for translating complex challenges into actionable strategies that deliver measurable impact. His writing combines analytical precision with compelling storytelling — whether he's decoding enterprise system failures or exploring the psychological dynamics of decision-making and influence.

Dave holds advanced degrees in business, technology and psychology, along with a portfolio of elite professional certifications. He is a sought-after speaker, strategist, and transformation advisor who empowers individuals and organizations to break through barriers and unlock lasting success.

Outside of his professional pursuits, Dave is an avid traveler and photographer, with a passion for astrophotography and a curated collection of high-performance and exotic cars. His global perspective, intellectual curiosity, and relentless drive to improve systems and people continue to inspire readers and clients alike.

To my constant joy and loyal hearts — you make life lighter

"Governance without accountability is noise. In SAP S/4, strong leadership turns plans into performance."
— *Dave Karpinsky*